Marketing and Distribution

10

Editorial Advisory Board

The Career Information Center includes:

- Agribusiness, Environment, and Natural Resources / 1
- Communications and the Arts / 2
- Computers, Business, and Office / 3
- Construction / 4
- Consumer, Homemaking, and Personal Services / 5
- Engineering, Science, Technology, and Social Science / 6
- Health / 7
- Hospitality and Recreation / 8
- Manufacturing / 9
- Marketing and Distribution / 10
- Public and Community Services / 11
- Transportation / 12
- Employment Trends and Master Index / 13

Marketing and Distribution

Career Information Center

Ninth Edition

MACMILLAN REFERENCE USA
An imprint of Thomson Gale, a part of The Thomson Corporation

Detroit • New York • San Francisco • New Haven, Conn. • Waterville, Maine • London

Career Information Center, Ninth Edition

Paula Kepos, Series Editor

Project Editor
Mary Rose Bonk

Editorial
Jennifer Greve

Imaging
Lezlie Light, Daniel Newell, Christine O'Bryan

Permissions
Kelly A. Quin, Tim Sisler, Andrew Specht

Manufacturing
Rhonda Dover

For permission to use material from this product, submit your request via Web at http://www.gale-edit.com/permissions, or you may download our Permissions Request form and submit your request by fax or mail to:

Permissions
Thomson Gale
27500 Drake Rd.
Farmington Hills, MI 48331-3535
Permissions Hotline:
248-699-8006 or 800-877-4253 ext. 8006
Fax: 248-699-8074 or 800-762-4058

Since this page cannot legibly accommodate all copyright notices, the acknowledgments constitute an extension of the copyright notice.

While every effort has been made to ensure the reliability of the information presented in this publication, Thomson Gale does not guarantee the accuracy of the data contained herein. Thomson Gale accepts no payment for listing; and inclusion in the publication of any organization, agency, institution, publication, service, or individual does not imply endorsement of the editors or publisher. Errors brought to the attention of the publisher and verified to the satisfaction of the publisher will be corrected in future editions.

ISBN 0-02-866047-1 (set)
ISBN 0-02-866048-X (v.1)
ISBN 0-02-866049-8 (v.2)
ISBN 0-02-866050-1 (v.3)
ISBN 0-02-866051-X (v.4)
ISBN 0-02-866052-8 (v.5)
ISBN 0-02-866053-6 (v.6)
ISBN 0-02-866054-4 (v.7)
ISBN 0-02-866055-2 (v.8)
ISBN 0-02-866056-0 (v.9)
ISBN 0-02-866057-9 (v.10)
ISBN 0-02-866058-7 (v.11)
ISBN 0-02-866059-5 (v.12)
ISBN 0-02-866060-9 (v.13)
ISSN 1082-703X

This title is also available as an e-book.
ISBN 0-02-866099-4
Contact your Thomson Gale representative for ordering information.

Printed in the United States of America
10 9 8 7 6 5 4 3 2 1

Contents

Job Summary Chart

Job	Salary	Education/ Training	Employment Outlook	Page
Job Profiles—No Specialized Training				
Auto Parts Counter Worker	Median—$15.16 per hour	High school plus training	Poor	29
Auto Sales Worker	Median—$18.61 per hour	High school plus training	Very good	31
Cashier	Median—$7.81 per hour	Training	Fair	34
Comparison Shopper	Average—$24,643 per year	High school plus training	Fair	36
Direct Sales Worker	Average—$12.92 per hour	Training	Poor	37
Receiving, Shipping, and Traffic Clerk	Median—$24,400 per year	High school plus training	Poor	40
⭐ Rental Clerk	Median—$8.79 per hour	Training	Very good	42
⭐ Retail Store Sales Worker	Median—$8.98 per hour	Training	Good	44
Retail Store Sales Worker Supervisor	Median—$32,720 per year	Training	Fair	46
⭐ Sales Demonstrator and Product Promoter	Median—$9.95 per hour	High school plus training	Good	47
Stock Clerk	Median—$9.66 per hour	Training	Poor	49
Supermarket Worker	Median—$7.90 to $15.08 per hour	Training	Fair	51
Telemarketer	Average—$23,520 per year	Training	Poor	54
Vending Machine Servicer and Repairer	Median—$26,333 per year	Training	Fair	56
Warehouse Worker	Varies—see profile	Training	Good	57
Job Profiles—Some Specialized Training/Experience				
Auctioneer	Average—$46,062 per year	Varies—see profile	Varies—see profile	60
Food Broker	Median—$45,400 to $46,829 per year	Varies—see profile	Good	62
Insurance Agent and Broker	Median—$41,720 per year	High school plus training; license	Fair	64
⭐ Manufacturers' Sales Worker	Median—$45,400 to $58,580 per year	College plus training	Good	66
Real Estate Sales Agent and Broker	Median—$35,670 to $58,720 per year	High school plus training; license	Good	69
Retail Butcher	Median—$27,030 per year	Training	Good	71
Small Business Owner	Varies—see profile	Varies—see profile	Good	72
Title Examiner	Average—$39,420 per year	High school plus training	Fair	75
⭐ Wholesale Sales Worker	Median—$45,400 to $58,580 per year	Varies—see profile	Good	77

⭐ High-growth job

Job	Salary	Education/Training	Employment Outlook	Page
Job Profiles—Advanced Training/Experience				
Advertising Account Executive	Median—$40,300 per year	College	Good	80
☆ **Advertising Manager**	Median—$63,610 to $107,030 per year	College or advanced degree	Very good	82
☆ **Distribution Manager**	Average—$73,050 per year	College or advanced degree plus training	Good	84
☆ **E-Commerce Marketing Manager**	Median—$84,246 per year	College or advanced degree	Very good	85
Import and Export Worker	Varies—see profile	Varies—see profile	Good	87
Marketing Director	Median—$138,470 per year	Advanced degree plus training	Very good	89
☆ **Marketing Research Worker**	Varies—see profile	College	Very good	91
Media Buyer	Median—$56,279 per year	College plus training	Very good	94
Product Manager	Median—$95,900 per year, including bonuses	College or advanced degree plus training	Very good	95
Purchasing Agent	Median—$47,680 per year	College or advanced degree	Fair	97
Real Estate Appraiser	Median—$43,390 per year	2- or 4-year college plus training; license	Very good	99
Retail Buyer	Median—$42,230 per year	College plus training	Fair	101
☆ **Sales Engineer**	Median—$70,620 per year	College plus training	Good	104
☆ **Sales Manager**	Median—$84,220 per year	College plus training	Very good	105
Sports Management Professional	Varies—see profile	Varies—see profile	Good	107
☆ **Store Manager**	Median—$48,880 to $57,512 per year	Varies—see profile	Good	109
Trade Show Manager	Median—$58,748 per year	Varies—see profile	Very good	111

☆ **High-growth job**

Foreword

The ninth edition of the *Career Information Center* mirrors the ongoing changes in the job market caused by new technological and economic developments. These developments continue to change what Americans do in the workplace and how they do it. People have a critical need for up-to-date information to help them make career decisions.

The *Career Information Center* is an individualized resource for people of all ages and at all stages of career development. It has been recognized as an excellent reference for librarians, counselors, educators, and other providers of job information. It is ideally suited for use in libraries, career resource centers, and guidance offices, as well as in adult education centers and other facilities where people seek information about job opportunities, careers, and their own potential in the workforce.

This ninth edition updates many of the features that made the earlier editions so useful.

- A Job Summary Chart, a quick reference guide, appears in the front section of each volume to help readers get the basic facts and compare the jobs described in the volume. High-growth jobs are highlighted and identified with a star.

- Each volume of the *Career Information Center* begins with an overview of the job market in that field. These "Looking Into..." sections have been completely revised and updated. They also include new graphs, charts, and boxes providing information such as industry snapshots and the fastest-growing and top-dollar jobs in the field. The "Global View" feature tells how the new global economy is affecting jobs in the field.

- Each volume has a section called "Getting Into...," which contains useful information on entering the particular field. It offers self-evaluation tips and decision-making help, and it relates possible job choices to individual interests, abilities, and work characteristics. There is also practical information on job hunting, using the Internet and classified ads, preparing resumes, and handling interviews. "Getting Into..." also includes a section on employee rights.

- Each volume has a listing of all job profiles in the series and the volumes in which they appear, making access to profiles in other volumes easy.

- *Career Information Center* contains 694 job profiles. Each profile describes work characteristics, education and training requirements, getting the job, advancement and employment outlook, working conditions, and earnings and benefits.

- Job summaries, provided for each job profile, highlight the education or training required, salary range, and employment outlook.

- Volume 13 has been revised to reflect career concerns of the new century and employment trends through the year 2014. This volume includes updated articles on benefits, employment law, health in the workplace, job search strategies, job training, job opportunities at home, and identifying opportunities for retraining.

- More than 530 photographs provide a visual glimpse of life on the job. Photos have been selected to give the reader a sense of what it feels like to be in a specific field or job.

- Updated bibliographies in each volume include recommended readings and Web sites in specific job areas. Additional titles for the vocational counselor are included in Volume 13.

- Each volume also contains a comprehensive directory of accredited occupational education and vocational training facilities listed by occupational area and grouped by state. Directory materials are generated from the IPEDS (Integrated Postsecondary Education Data System) database of the U.S. Department of Education.

The *Career Information Center* recognizes the importance not only of job selection, but also of job holding, coping, and applying life skills. No other career information publication deals with work attitudes so comprehensively.

Using the Career Information Center

The *Career Information Center* is designed to meet the needs of many people—students, people just entering or reentering the job market, those dissatisfied with present jobs, those without jobs—anyone of any age who is not sure what to do for a living. The *Career Information Center* is for people who want help in making career choices. It combines the comprehensiveness of an encyclopedia with the format and readability of a magazine. Many professionals, including counselors, librarians, and teachers, will find it a useful guidance and reference tool.

The *Career Information Center* is organized by occupational interest area rather than in alphabetical order. Jobs that have something in common are grouped together. In that way people who do not know exactly what job they want can read about a number of related jobs. The *Career Information Center* classifies jobs that have something in common into clusters. The classification system is adapted from the cluster organization used by the U.S. Department of Labor. Each of the first twelve volumes of the *Career Information Center* explores one of twelve occupational clusters.

To use the *Career Information Center*, first select the volume that treats the occupational area that interests you most. Because there are many ways to group occupations, you may not find a particular job in the volume in which you look for it. In that case, check the central listing of all the profiles, which is located in the front of Volumes 1 through 12. This listing provides the names of all profiles and the volume number in which they appear. Volume 13 also includes a comprehensive index of all the jobs covered in the first twelve volumes.

After selecting a volume or volumes, investigate the sections that you feel would be most helpful. It isn't necessary to read these volumes from cover to cover. They are arranged so that you can go directly to the specific information you want. Here is a description of the sections included in each volume.

- **Job Summary Chart**—This chart presents in tabular form the basic data from all profiles in the volume: salary, education and training, employment outlook, and the page on which you can find the job profile. Jobs with a high growth potential are highlighted and starred.

- **Looking Into...**—This overview of the occupational cluster describes the opportunities, characteristics, and trends in that particular field.

- **Getting Into...**—This how-to guide can help you decide what jobs may be most satisfying to you

and what strategies you can use to get the right job. You will learn, for example, how to write an effective resume, how to complete an application form, what to expect in an interview, how to use networking, and what to do if someone has discriminated against you.

- **Job Summary**—These summaries, located at the beginning of each profile, highlight the most important facts about the job: education and training, salary, and employment outlook.

Education and Training indicates whether the job requires no education, high school, college, advanced degree, vocational/technical school, license, or training.

Salary provides median or average salaries that may vary significantly from region to region.

Employment Outlook is based on several factors, including the Bureau of Labor Statistics' projections through the year 2014. The ratings are defined as follows: *poor* means there is a projected employment decrease of any amount; *fair* means there is a projected employment increase of 0 to 8 percent; *good* means there is a projected employment increase of 9 to 17 percent; *very good* means there is a projected employment increase of 18 to 26 percent; and *excellent* means there is a projected employment increase of 27 percent or more. The outlook is then determined by looking at the ratings and other employment factors. For example, a job with excellent projected employment growth in which many more people are entering the field than there are jobs available will have an outlook that is good rather than excellent.

For all categories, the phrase *Varies—see profile* means the reader must consult the profile for the information, which is too extensive to include in the Job Summary.

- **Job Profiles**—The job profiles are divided into three categories based on the level of training required to get the job. Each profile explores the following topics: description of the job being profiled, the education and training requirements, ways to get the job, advancement possibilities and employment outlook, the working conditions, the earnings and benefits, and places to go for more information.

Job Profiles—No Specialized Training includes jobs that require no education or previous work experience beyond high school.

Job Profiles—Some Specialized Training/Experience includes jobs that require one, two, or three years of vocational training or college, or work experience beyond high school.

Job Profiles—Advanced Training/Experience includes jobs that require a bachelor's degree or advanced degree from a college or university and/or equivalent work experience in that field.

- **Resources—General Career Information** includes a selected bibliography of the most recent books and Web sites on general career information, including how-to books on such topics as resume writing and preparing for tests. In addition, there is a special guide to readings for the career counselor in Volume 13.

- **Resources**—Each volume also contains a bibliography of books and Web sites for specific fields covered in that volume.

- **Directory of Institutions Offering Career Training**—This listing, organized first by career area, then by state, includes the schools that offer occupational training beyond high school. For jobs requiring a bachelor's degree or an advanced degree, check a library for college catalogs and appropriate directories.

- **Index**—This index, which is located at the end of each volume, lists every job mentioned in that volume. It serves not only to cross-reference all the jobs in the volume but also to show related jobs in the field. For example, under the entry OCEANOG-

RAPHER, you will find chemical oceanographer, marine biologist, and marine geophysicist.

- **Volume 13, Employment Trends and Master Index**—This volume includes several features that will help both the job seeker and the career counselor. A useful guide provides the *DOT (Dictionary of Occupational Titles)* number of most of the job profiles in the *Career Information Center*. There is also a special section on career information for Canada. The updated and revised "Employment Trends" section contains articles on health in the workplace; search strategies for finding your first job; employment trends for women, minorities, immigrants, older workers, and the physically challenged; employment demographics; benefit programs; training; employment opportunities at home; employment law; and identifying opportunities for retraining. The articles provide job seekers and career professionals with an overview of current employment issues, career opportunities, and outlooks. Finally, there is a master index to all the jobs included in all 13 volumes.

The *Career Information Center* is exactly what it says it is—a center of the most useful and pertinent information you need to explore and choose from the wide range of job and career possibilities. The *Career Information Center* provides you with a solid foundation of information for getting a satisfying job or rewarding career.

Comprehensive Job Profile List

The following list includes job profiles and corresponding volume numbers.

Accountant, Management, 3
Accountant, Public, 3
Actor, 2
Actuary, 3
Acupuncturist, 7
Administrative Assistant, 3
Admitting Interviewer, 7
Adult Education Worker, 11
Advertising Account Executive, 10
Advertising Copywriter, 2
Advertising Manager, 10
Aerospace Engineer, 6
Aerospace Engineering and Operations
    Technician, 6
Aerospace Industry, 9
Agricultural Engineer, 1
Agricultural Inspector, 1
Agricultural Technician, 1
Agronomist, 1
AIDS Counselor, 7
Air Pollution Control Technician, 1
Air Traffic Controller, 12
Air-Conditioning Engineer, 6
Air-Conditioning, Heating, and
    Refrigeration Mechanic and
    Installer, 4
Aircraft Dispatcher, 12
Aircraft Mechanic, 12
Airline Baggage and Freight Handler, 12
Airline Flight Attendant, 12
Airline Reservations Agent, 12
Airline Ticket Agent, 12
Airplane Pilot, 12
Airport Manager, 12
Airport Utility Worker, 12
Alternative Fuels Vehicle Technician, 6
Aluminum and Copper Industries, 9
Ambulance Driver, 7
Amusement and Recreation Attendant, 8
Anatomist, 6
Anesthesiologist, 7
Animal Caretaker, 8
Animal Scientist, 1
Animal Trainer, 1
Announcer, 2
Anthropologist, 6
Apparel Industry, 9
Apparel Workers, 9
Appliance Service Worker, 5
Appraiser, 5
Architect, 4
Architectural Drafter, 4
Architectural Model Maker, 4
Armed Services Career, 11
Art Director, 2
Artificial Intelligence Specialist, 6
Artist, 2
Assembler and Fabricator, 9

Astronomer, 6
Athletic Coach, 8
Athletic Trainer, 8
Auctioneer, 10
Audiologist, 7
Auditor, 3
Auto Body Repairer, 12
Auto Parts Counter Worker, 10
Auto Sales Worker, 10
Automobile Driving Instructor, 12
Automotive Exhaust Emissions
    Technician, 12
Automotive Industry, 9
Automotive Mechanic, 12
Avionics Technician, 12

Baker, 1
Bank Clerk, 3
Bank Officer and Manager, 3
Bank Teller, 3
Barber and Hairstylist, 5
Bartender, 8
Bicycle Mechanic, 12
Billing Clerk, 3
Biochemist, 6
Biological Technician, 6
Biologist, 6
Biomedical Engineer, 6
Biomedical Equipment Technician, 7
Boilermaker, 9
Bookbinder, 2
Bookkeeper, 3
Border Patrol Agent, 11
Botanist, 6
Bricklayer, 4
Bridge and Lock Tender, 12
Broadcast News Analyst, 2
Broadcast Technician, 2
Brokerage Clerk, 3
Building Custodian, 11
Building Inspector, 4
Bulldozer, Grader, or Paving Machine
    Operator, 4
Business Family and Consumer
    Scientist, 5
Business Machine Operator, 3

Cable Television and
    Telecommunications Technician, 6
Cable Television Engineer, 6
Cafeteria Attendant, 8
Camera Operator, 2
Candy Manufacturing Worker, 1
Car Rental or Leasing Agent, 12
Car Wash Worker, 12
Cardiac Monitor Technician, 7
Cardiac Perfusionist, 7
Cardiology Technologist, 7

Carpenter, 4
Cartographer, 1
Cartoonist and Animator, 2
Cashier, 10
Caterer, 8
Ceiling Tile Installer, 4
Cement Mason, 4
Ceramic Engineer, 6
Ceramics Industry, 9
Chauffeur, 5
Cheese Industry Worker, 1
Chemical Engineer, 6
Chemical Technician, 6
Chemist, 6
Child Care Worker, Private, 5
Chiropractor, 7
Choreographer, 2
City Manager, 11
Civil Engineer, 4
Civil Engineering Technician, 4
Claims Adjuster, 3
Claims Examiner, 3
Clinical Laboratory Technician, 7
Clinical Laboratory Technologist, 7
College Student Personnel Worker, 11
College/University Administrator, 3
Companion, 5
Comparison Shopper, 10
Compensation and Benefits Analyst, 3
Composer, 2
Computer and Information Systems
    Manager, 3
Computer and Office Machine
    Repairer, 3
Computer Consultant, 3
Computer Control Operator, 9
Computer Control Programmer, 9
Computer Database Administrator, 3
Computer Network Technician, 3
Computer Operator, 3
Computer Programmer, 3
Computer Security Specialist, 3
Computer Software Documentation
    Writer, 3
Computer Software Engineer, 3
Computer Support Specialist, 3
Computer Systems Analyst, 3
Conservation Scientist, 1
Construction Electrician, 4
Construction Equipment Dealer, 4
Construction Equipment Mechanic, 4
Construction Laborer, 4
Construction Millwright, 4
Construction Supervisor, 4
Consumer Advocate, 5
Consumer Credit Counselor, 5
Controller, 3
Cook and Chef, 8

Looking Into Marketing and Distribution

Say that a manufacturer of cellular phones has just developed a new phone that can be used anywhere in the world. The company is eager to showcase its innovative product, and the best way to do that is to develop a plan—a marketing plan.

MARKETING A PRODUCT

A marketing plan is a step-by-step blueprint for introducing, advertising, selling, and delivering a product, a service, or even an idea. To develop such a plan, the cell phone company will need to conduct market research and gather information on what types of people are likely to buy its phones. Once the ideal customer is defined, the manufacturer can develop packaging and an advertising campaign that will appeal directly to that target audience.

Next, the company will decide on a price that is competitive with the prices of other cell phones. Finally, the company will have to decide where to sell its new product—in retail stores, through catalogs, or on the Internet at the company's Web site—and how to get it to their customers quickly. All of these steps are part of marketing and distribution work.

A Marketing Revolution

Marketing has changed radically since it was first introduced at the beginning of the twentieth century. The latest innovation, interactive marketing, has sparked an electronic (e) revolution that includes e-products, e-retailing (also called e-tailing), e-advertising, e-research, and even e-delivery in the form of downloadable news, books, and music. Consumers shop from home using the Internet to compare products, prices, and ratings, and then they

Marketing involves the transfer of goods from producers to consumers. This field includes all the people who work in retail sales, advertising, and distribution. (© Dex Images, Inc./Corbis.)

Global View: Marketing and Distribution

Almost all companies depend on advertising and marketing to reach potential customers and convince them to buy the firm's products. Twenty-first century companies are expanding their markets to include foreign countries. The need to communicate with people in different cultures and different languages has changed the way advertisers and marketers approach their work.

Perhaps the most basic challenge is using the right words to convey a sales message to a foreign audience. Many English words and phrases do not translate well into foreign languages, so a catchy slogan in the United States may be puzzling to consumers in other countries. Even the use of certain numbers or types of artwork can be problematic. For example, some Japanese people associate the numbers four and nine with death. Advertisers are working more with local writers to make sure that their messages are translated in an appropriate and positive way. Foreign firms are doing the same, hiring American writers to help them with their advertising campaigns in the United States.

As more companies branch out into foreign markets, they are finding a need to adjust their strategies for reaching customers. Direct mail marketing, for example, is a big business in the United States. However, in some countries delivery of direct mail pieces may take several weeks. In addition, foreign postal laws can make it difficult to distribute mass mailings overseas. Another significant change is the growing resistance to U.S. brands in overseas markets. A soft drink manufacturer who once marketed the same product to all of its customers around the world may need to diversify by selling other products specifically developed to appeal to local tastes.

The shape of the industry itself is also changing in response to the global market. The need to establish an international presence is hitting small advertising agencies especially hard. Large advertising firms are now buying out small agencies that once promoted themselves as alternatives to large firms.

Perhaps the most revolutionary change in marketing and distribution involves the Internet and e-commerce. Companies can quickly and easily reach any consumer who has a computer and an Internet connection—whether that consumer is across town or on the other side of the world. Advertising through Web sites and e-mail saves time and money by reducing the need for such expenses as foreign postage and long-distance phone calls. The Internet virtually eliminates the borders between countries and even continents, allowing for a truly global marketplace. As with other forms of advertising, however, Web advertising must take into account the unique needs and expectations of a global audience.

purchase those products online. In 2005 e-commerce revenues totaled $86 billion, up from $67.2 billion the previous year, according to the *Monthly Retail Trade Survey* produced by the U.S. Census Bureau. While e-commerce sales represented only 2.2 percent of all retail sales in 2005, analysts with Jupiter-Research predicted that by the year 2008 this number could jump to 5 percent.

Marketing is a dynamic discipline, one that must adapt quickly to new technologies, new products, and new consumer tastes. This volume explores the history of marketing and distribution, how they have changed over time, and how they are likely to evolve in the future.

Marketing through the Ages

The history of marketing is the history of commerce. People have been exchanging goods and services for thousands of years. As early as 3000 B.C. the Phoenicians developed trade and distribution routes as they sailed the seas in search of spices, precious metals, and rare textiles.

Archaeologists have found evidence of marketplaces in the ruins of ancient civilizations around the world. As trade spread across borders, marketplaces along trade routes became centers of economic and cultural exchange. Along the Silk Road, the legendary 4,000-mile trade route that stretched from eastern China to the Mediterranean Sea, hundreds of these marketplaces facilitated the exchange of goods and ideas.

When European colonists landed in North America, they settled along the Atlantic Coast. Routes of commerce were difficult to establish because roads were undeveloped and many rivers were as yet unexplored. By the early 1800s, however, roads and canals linked many towns together, allowing products to be shipped to distant markets.

Advances in technology aided the spread of commerce. The railroads offered a fast, reliable way to transport freight across vast distances. The invention of lithography (printing from a metal plate) in Germany toward the end of the 1700s made the printing of posters easy and inexpensive, and they soon became a popular medium for advertising.

The late 1800s saw the emergence of product "brands," such as Coca-Cola and Procter & Gamble, which were marketed nationwide. Another boost to commerce was the introduction of installment-plan purchasing, which allowed consumers to pay for products over a specified period of time rather than all at once.

In 1900 Milton Hershey had the idea of mass-producing small bars of individually wrapped chocolate. Because they were mass produced, Hershey's chocolate bars could be shipped in bulk around the country and sold for just five cents apiece. Soon other manufacturers were following Hershey's lead by producing large quantities of their products, shipping nationwide, and selling inexpensively.

Advertising, which was developed originally to introduce consumers to products, began to take on other functions. It was used to create brand identities, to point out product benefits, and to create a sense of "need" among consumers. The advent of radio and television gave advertisers new arenas for product promotion. By the end of the twentieth century Internet sites were sporting interactive ads, some of which were incredibly sophisticated. A few car manufacturers, for instance, created ads where users could sit in the driver's seat of a virtual, new sports car without ever setting foot in a dealer's showroom. The Internet has provided companies with the capability to take online surveys of their customers to see exactly what interests them most.

Marketing Today

Early in the twenty-first century marketing became more customer focused. Merchandisers competing for consumer dollars got to know their customers as thoroughly as possible and tailored their products and services to specific consumer tastes.

Market Research Data To discover what consumers want and don't want or like and dislike, producers turn to market research.

Market research is just what the name implies—discovering and making sense of marketplace trends and consumer demands. Some producers conduct their own research. Others hire independent firms to carry out the research. These firms gather, organize, and interpret customer information. After analyzing the data, market researchers can create profiles of typical consumers, predict buying patterns, and assist producers in creating products that have been "pre-approved" by consumers. For instance, researchers may determine that a particular type of shampoo is appealing to suburban women between the ages of twenty-five and thirty-four. Armed with this information the shampoo manufacturer can focus on advertising the product during television shows that this group is likely to watch. The manufacturer may also choose to have the product distributed in more suburban locations than urban or rural ones.

Another form of marketing research involves the collection of customer lists, which give the names and addresses of actual consumers who are likely to be interested in a given product. These names and addresses are gathered from a variety of sources, including telephone surveys, supermarket checkout counters, and credit card applications. Virtually any demographic information that customers send

New Jobs Projected in Sales, Marketing, and Distribution, 2004–2014*

OCCUPATION	NEW JOBS	PERCENT INCREASE
Retail Sales Workers	937,000	11.1
Cashiers	113,000	3.2
Sales Supervisors	74,000	3.4
Real Estate Brokers and Sales Agents	60,000	13.0
Insurance Agents	26,000	6.6

*Projected

SOURCE: Bureau of Labor Statistics, *Monthly Labor Review*, November 2005.

Industry Snapshots

MARKETING

Marketing, the process of introducing, advertising, and selling products, services, and ideas to consumers, will continue to be a critical industry in the global marketplace. Web-based marketing is expanding the industry's reach and fundamentally changing the way producers sell and consumers buy. According to employment outlook projections from the U.S. Bureau of Labor Statistics, employment in marketing is expected to grow faster than the average for all occupations from 2004 to 2014, especially in light of more global competition.

PACKAGING

The packaging industry has bounced back from lackluster performance during the 1980s. New packaging designs and manufacturing technologies mean steady revenue growth for this industry. Increased automation, however, will continue to eliminate some packaging industry jobs. Positions for receiving, shipping, and traffic clerks are expected to decline. The U.S. Bureau of Labor Statistics predicts that employment in this field will grow slower than the average for all occupations from 2004 to 2014.

RETAILING

The U.S. Bureau of Labor Statistics reported that retail salespersons filled about 4.1 million positions in 2004. Retailers have watched their business landscape change dramatically with the introduction of e-tailing—buying and selling online— as a marketing strategy. Retail employment is expected to grow about as fast as the average for all occupations from 2004 to 2014, according to employment projections by the Bureau of Labor Statistics.

ADVERTISING AND PUBLIC RELATIONS

Advertising has continued to evolve as a critical component of selling strategies. With the arrival of e-commerce and cable television advertising channels, this industry is developing imaginative approaches to targeting, swaying, and selling new products to consumers. The U.S. Bureau of Labor Statistics projected that advertising and public relations employment would grow faster than the average for all occupations from 2004 to 2014. The competition for these jobs, however, will be intense.

WHOLESALING AND DISTRIBUTION

The performance of the nation's wholesalers and distributors depends on evolving practices in manufacturing and retailing. New approaches, such as just-in-time inventory delivery, will define the future of these two vital industries. Employment in wholesale and distribution is expected to increase about as fast as the average for all occupations between 2004 and 2014, according to U.S. Bureau of Labor Statistics projections.

to a company—even a filled-out warranty card—can be added to a list and shared with other companies or marketing firms; in fact, it is customary for companies to sell such lists to each other. Customer lists give companies a way to market directly to a target audience. Some stores offer listed customers "loyalty cards," which provide repeat customers with discounts on future purchases. Other companies use the lists to design custom catalogs, which are then sent to specific customers.

Databases of this type have been around for a number of years. However, new computer software makes data compilation and analysis simpler and more cost effective than ever before. One system—called PRIZM (Potential Rating Index by Zip Market) New Evolution—is a database created by Claritas, Inc. It divides U.S. Census Bureau data into zip codes and categorizes purchasing data by income, ethnicity, level of education, and other criteria. The database then compiles lists of groups, attaching catchy titles to each, and sells the lists to companies that are interested in reaching a specific set of consumers. For instance, a company that wants to target upper-middle-class consumers who live in the suburbs might use the PRIZM list titled "Movers and Shakers," whereas a company looking for urban eighteen- to thirty-year-olds might use the list called "Young Didgerati."

Database marketing can prove extremely lucrative for modern manufacturers and retailers. Take the case of Milton's, a small discount clothing chain. With the help of a commercial marketing database service, Milton's developed a database from credit card receipts and used the information to design and implement a direct mail campaign targeted at likely consumers. The result was a $100,000 increase in sales.

The Internet has made the collection of consumer information much easier. Many Web sites employ small software applications called "cookies" that track where a user goes when visiting a particular site. These are called Internet leads. Such information can enable webmasters to design more effective sites, eliminating those pages that are rarely visited and expanding and polishing those that generate the most traffic. Other sites, such as news sites or reference sites, may ask users to rate how appealing or useful certain information is. If, for example, users consistently give positive ratings to entertainment news and negative ratings to stories about nature or finance, the site will likely increase its coverage of the entertainment industry while downplaying stories about endangered animals or the bond market. All of this information can be quite helpful to companies trying to market their goods and services effectively via the Internet.

Push Marketing When online e-tailor Amazon.com began selling books and CDs from its Web site in the mid-1990s, its customers soon noticed that the site was paying special attention to them. Say, for example, an individual purchased a Vietnamese cookbook: the next time that individual visited the site he or she would be greeted by name and offered a selection of similar cookbooks that might be of interest. If the customer bought a number of jazz CDs, the site might recommend additional jazz titles, books about jazz and jazz artists, travel guides to cities famous for their jazz clubs, and so on.

This is called "push marketing." Simply put, push marketing uses known information about individuals as a consumer to push specific advertising messages on them. While one person is offered information about jazz, another checking out the same site at the same time might be seeing ads touting motorcycles, soccer, or whatever he or she has shown interest in on earlier trips to the site.

Demographic Trends

Market research provides manufacturers and retailers with information not only on consumer buying habits but also on how the demographics of our society are changing. This information helps them target emerging consumer groups and tailor their products to meet the needs of those groups.

Marketing researchers have found that today's consumers are different from their predecessors. According to the U.S. Census Bureau's *Current Population Survey*, the number of households consisting of married couples fell from nearly 61 percent in 1980 to about 52 percent in 2003. In contrast, the number of people living alone continued to rise. The number of American teenagers has leveled off, while the number of men age twenty to forty-four has been decreasing slowly and will continue to do so throughout the first half of this century. Perhaps most notable in terms of marketing is the fact that the eldest of America's baby boomers—those people born from 1946 to 1964—are hitting retirement age.

These demographic changes affect the buying patterns and needs of consumers and influence the way in which manufacturers choose to market their goods. For instance, the growing number of people living alone has led many food manufacturers to package their products in single-serving sizes. The number of U.S. teenagers with money to spend has encouraged manufacturers to develop a greater variety of electronic products, including video game platforms, cell phones, and MP3 players. Successful middle-aged baby boomers are likely to have extra income, which will energize the market for goods such as furniture. As more specific market data become available, manufacturers will be able to finely tune their marketing strategies and distribution methods.

PACKAGING

Once a manufacturer determines who its customers are likely to be, it sets about making its product both appealing and accessible to them. This process starts with the packaging. Today's packaging incorporates elaborate graphic images, photos, and other illustrations that stand out from the competition.

Technology is constantly changing the way goods are packaged and sometimes solves age-old problems. For example, toothpaste was traditionally packaged in squeezable screw-capped tubes. However, some customers complained that the tubes were difficult to squeeze; others found that they were left with wasted toothpaste at the bottom of the tubes; and still others were frustrated over continually misplacing the tiny screw-on caps. Toothpaste companies responded to these problems by offering consumers a softer tube with a permanently attached flip-top cap and a "pump" package in addition to a conventional tube. Another example is soap products. Pump bottles have replaced bar soaps for the kitchen and countertop. Marketers appeal to children with brightly colored liquid soaps, character-laden labels, and an inviting, foamy consistency.

The U.S. government also plays an important role in the packaging of goods. In response to overflowing landfills and other environmental concerns, the government has enacted a number of regulations aimed at ensuring the use of "eco-friendly" packaging practices. As a result many manufacturers now use packaging materials that are recyclable

Manufacturers use information on consumer buying habits to tailor their products to meet the needs of specific consumer groups. Then they package the products and advertise them to appeal to people in those groups. (© Piotr Redlinski/Corbis.)

or biodegradable. The amount of materials needed to package an item has decreased as well. For example, when compact discs first arrived on the market, they were sold in packaging that was much larger than the CDs themselves; today music CDs are packaged in a small plastic case covered only in cellophane. Manufacturers will continue to develop lighter plastics, fibrous glass, and recyclable composite materials. In addition, technological advances in food packaging will provide manufacturers with new designs that increase the shelf life of their products.

The Flexible Packaging Web site noted that as of 2005 the packaging industry was estimated to be a 420-billion-dollar global industry, with the United States accounting for about $124 billion, or 29 percent of it.

ADVERTISING AND PUBLIC RELATIONS

Advertising is critical to an effective marketing strategy and has become omnipresent throughout the world. Piccadilly Circus in London, the Ginza district of Tokyo, Times Square in Manhattan—each is awash in flashing neon, jumbo video screens, and electronic billboards. Advertising also enters Americans' lives via television, radio, newspapers, magazines, and the Internet. The goal of advertising is convincing consumers to Buy This Product or to Use This Service.

The U.S. advertising industry was the largest in the world in 2006. According to the American Association of Advertising Agencies, the United States is home to more than thirteen thousand ad agencies. Some are big companies with offices in cities throughout the world; others are small shops employing as few as ten or fifteen professionals. Competition for clients is fierce and the financial stakes are high. The success or failure of a product or service may well rest on its ad campaign.

Today's ad agencies perform a variety of marketing tasks. Creating print and electronic advertisements is only one part of the business. Agencies often put together complete marketing strategies for their clients. If a soft drink manufacturer is developing a new flavor, its ad agency may play an important role in all aspects of the process: conducting consumer taste tests, developing a product image, designing logos and packaging, creating advertisements, buying advertising time and space, and deciding where and how the product will be sold. Such an integrated approach not only keeps the product's image and message consistent, it also frees the manufacturer to concentrate on what it does best—developing and manufacturing soft drinks.

Many large corporations hire advertising agencies to promote themselves and their employees. These agencies send out press releases to various local media in an attempt to create a community-minded image for a specific company. For example, a local real estate office may team up with a nonprofit organization to raise money through fundraisers, raffles, or dances.

Television and Radio Advertising

Television and radio advertisements offer manufacturers the chance to familiarize millions of consumers with their products. Advertisers use actors, sports figures, and other celebrities to sell everything from sneakers and soft drinks to trucks and brokerage firm services. These commercials are carefully scripted and often use state-of-the-art film and editing techniques.

Manufacturers buy airtime during specific programs, often using available demographic data regarding a show's audience to determine which time

spots to buy. Although television commercials have proven extremely effective, they come at a very high price. A thirty-second television commercial can cost hundreds of thousands of dollars. "Event" programming, such as the Super Bowl, can generate many millions of dollars in advertising revenue. Often this is money well spent. For instance, CareerBuilder.com aired Super Bowl ads about a man who worked in an office full of monkeys. The ads caught the nation's attention and remained popular long after their first appearance, leading to a surge of new visitors to the CareerBuilder Web site.

Despite the success of television commercials, some industry observers believe that this type of advertising will become less and less influential. At a time when viewers are offered more than one hundred channels (with more on the way) and remote controls provide an easy exit, television commercials face a big challenge in retaining consumers' interest.

Print Media Advertising

Retail stores and other local businesses do much of their advertising through print media, which include newspapers, magazines, the Yellow Pages, and supermarket fliers. Advertising is serious business for our country's daily newspapers. In 2003 advertis-

Daily newspapers derive more than 75 percent of their total income from selling space to advertisers. Most newspaper advertisers are retail stores and other local businesses. (© Martha Tabor/ Working Images Photographs. Reproduced by permission.)

ing accounted for more than 77 percent of their total receipts, according to the U.S. Census Bureau's 2006 *Statistical Abstracts of the United States*. In recent years, however, other types of media have started to eat away at the newspaper industry's market share. In 2004 daily newspaper circulation was 54.6 million, down from previous years because of digital cable, the Internet, and mass mailers.

Sports, fashion, and computer magazines are some of the most popular advertising vehicles in the nation. The U.S. Census Bureau reported that magazine advertising expenditures rose from $3.1 billion in 1980 to $12.1 billion in 2004. Newspapers and magazines now have Web sites that include classifieds ads. The Internet has provided another outlet for the publishing media to attract advertising.

Online Advertising The newest channel for advertising—the Internet—arrived as the twentieth century came to a close. It did not take long for ad agencies and their clients to realize that at any given moment tens of millions of people around the world were sitting in front of computer screens. Soon this captive audience was bombarded with electronic banner ads running across the tops and down the sides of Internet pages and pop-up ads springing up in front of them. These ads were unique because they were interactive—they could be linked to other information the consumer might want to know about a product or service. Through a series of mouse clicks, a small banner ad or larger pop-up ad could provide a potential customer with pages of information, including product comparisons, selling pitches, and special offers. The information might be presented in print, audio, or video formats or some combination of the three. However, many programs also became available that allowed users to "turn off" banner ads and block pop-up ads.

Promotions

Three-fourths of today's marketing budget goes not to advertising but to promotions. Manufacturers promote their products by sponsoring major events such as figure skating competitions and jazz concerts. Across the country sports arenas are being renamed for corporate sponsors who pay to have their names attached to the arenas. Most of the new ballparks—from San Francisco's AT&T Park to Philadelphia's Citizens Bank Park—are named for corporate sponsors.

Some manufacturers sponsor promotions with more charitable goals. For example, Colgate-Palmolive helped to create the Starlight Starbright Children's Foundation to fulfill the wishes of terminally ill children. Newspaper inserts alerted people to the foundation. When consumers used the coupons in the insert, a percentage of the money was donated to Starlight.

Many companies use a marketing method called product sampling to introduce their new items to the public. Taste tests at restaurants and bars are a good example of product sampling. This method gives business owners and managers of food establishments the opportunity to decide firsthand which products to market to their clientele. Point-of-purchase advertising is another promotional technique, and it is the most immediate form of advertising available to a manufacturer or retailer. It includes any advertising that occurs where the product is sold, such as photos of mouthwatering burgers and fries at fast food restaurants.

Pricing

Product pricing is another function of a manufacturer's marketing department. Pricing is based on a number of factors, the first of which is the cost to manufacture the item. This figure includes labor costs, the price of the materials from which the product is made, and the cost of packaging the product. Money spent on advertising and promoting the product must also be recouped through sales, thus adding to the price of the product. The manufacturer must settle on a price that allows for profit yet stays competitive with other brands of the same or similar products. But the product does not go directly to the customer. It must first make a journey through distributors and then take up valuable space on a store's shelves. These steps add to the item's cost.

SELLING THE PRODUCT

Wholesalers and Distributors

Once a manufacturer has made potential customers aware of its product, the next step is to make that product available. Most consumer products follow a path from producer to consumer—a path maintained by wholesalers and distributors. National, regional, or local wholesalers buy goods in large quantities from manufacturers, then sell the goods to retailers and large institutions.

The actual movement of goods from factory to warehouse to retailer is done by workers in the transportation industry, with help from stock clerks, shipping and receiving clerks, and warehouse workers. In recent years the movement from producer to consumer has been made far more efficient through the use of "just-in-time" inventory systems. By ordering goods so that they arrive just in time to sell or ship to retailers, wholesalers and

Top-Dollar Jobs in Marketing and Distribution

These are the high-paying jobs described in this volume. The figures represent typical salaries or earnings for experienced workers.

$80,000–$140,000	• E-Commerce Marketing Manager
	• Marketing Director
	• Product Manager
	• Sales Manager

$60,000–$80,000	• Advertising Manager
	• Distribution Manager
	• Sales Engineer

$40,000–$60,000	• Advertising Account Executive
	• Auctioneer
	• Food Broker
	• Insurance Agent and Broker
	• Manufacturers' Sales Worker
	• Media Buyer
	• Purchasing Agent
	• Real Estate Appraiser
	• Retail Buyer
	• Store Manager
	• Trade Show Manager
	• Wholesale Sales Worker

large retail stores can keep their costly inventories smaller.

Just as it has affected nearly every other aspect of marketing, the Internet is also becoming its own distribution channel. Traditionally, after a book has been written it must be set in type, printed, bound, shipped to a wholesaler's warehouse, inventoried, shipped out to bookstores, and possibly even shipped from the bookstore to a customer. The Internet enables publishers to skip most of these steps and their associated costs. Once the book is set in type, it can be offered in a downloadable format at a publisher's site. Customers select which books they want, pay for them, and then download them to their printers. No more binding, packing, shipping, warehousing, or doing inventory. For publishers and book buyers, this process is nothing short of a distribution revolution.

Retailing

Retail stores are one of the country's most significant sources of jobs. In the 2006 edition of *Statistical Abstracts of the United States*, the U.S. Census Bureau reported that retail jobs accounted for one out of every seven non-farm jobs in the private sector in 2004. Retail outlets sell merchandise—everything from cereal to socks—for personal use. Supermarkets, department stores, discount stores, convenience stores, and restaurants are some of the many types of retail stores.

Retail stores also provide manufacturers with a powerful way to get their products into the hands of

Warehouse workers, such as this forklift operator, are involved in the movement of goods from factory to warehouse to retailer. (© Martha Tabor/Working Images Photographs. Reproduced by permission.)

consumers. According to the Census Bureau's *Monthly Retail Trade Survey*, retail sales exceeded $3.7 trillion in 2005.

An increasingly competitive climate has caused many of today's retailers to rethink their sales strategies. Many are streamlining their operations and cutting staff and inventory to decrease overhead expenses. At the same time they are adding new services. Some superstores have expanded their services to include hair salons, portrait studios, vision centers, nail salons, and restaurants. Superstore customers can find groceries, clothes, shoes, housewares, and even auto and garden supplies all under one roof. The convenience offered by superstores has made them increasingly popular among busy Americans.

A variety of retailers offer consumers a comfortable environment in which to browse, relax, and engage in various types of activities. For example, some national bookstore chains have opened coffee areas, couches for reading, and recreational areas for children. To maintain their competitive edge, these stores focus on keeping prices low, limiting expenses, and maintaining a fresh supply of stock. One way that retailers achieve this is through a technique called Quick Response.

Quick Response was developed in 1986 by Roger Milliken, president and CEO of Milliken and Company. Quick Response is a business strategy that minimizes the time required for a product to be manufactured, distributed, and sold. This system has revolutionized the way in which products are moved from manufacturer to customer. Using the Quick Response system a salesperson scans a bar code attached to the packaging of each product brought to the checkout counter. This bar code contains identifying information about the product. The information is sent electronically to a computer system at the store's distributor. The distributor's computer automatically schedules a replacement to be delivered to the store and passes this information on to the manufacturer. The manufacturer then creates a replacement product to be delivered to the distributor. Quick Response has succeeded in helping many retailers operate in a more cost-effective manner.

Direct Sales

Not all producers market their goods to retailers through distributors. Many companies are turning instead to the lucrative mail-order catalog business. In 2003 alone U.S. mail-order sales exceeded $90 billion, according to the U.S. Census Bureau's *Statistical Abstracts of the United States*. Marketers such as L.L. Bean, Neiman Marcus, and a large number of computer hardware and software vendors have revolutionized the way Americans purchase products. The industry uses customer lists provided by marketing researchers to target new customers and solicit business.

Home shopping television networks provide manufacturers with another way to market their products directly to consumers. These twenty-four-hour-a-day cable channels, which include QVC (an acronym for Quality, Value, and Convenience) and HSN (the Home Shopping Network), enable viewers to order products by phone. QVC, one of the biggest home shopping networks, claimed it reached 85 million households in 2006 and sold merchandise to more than 190,000 customers a day. In some cases the prices charged by cable channel retailers are comparable to or even cheaper than those in conventional retail outlets.

Some manufacturers go directly to consumers via the Internet. Internet stores may be electronic branches of traditional retail outlets or stores created specifically for the Web. E-tail stores have several advantages over traditional retailers—no parking problems, no crowds, no annoying store music, and purchases delivered right to the consumer's door. Wedding, baby, and bridal registries are often listed online, allowing guests one-stop shopping.

These shoppers may opt to have their gifts wrapped and shipped directly to the recipient, which is especially convenient for guests who are traveling or cannot attend a special occasion.

Business-to-Business Marketing

Business-to-business marketing is the process by which businesses sell goods or services to other businesses. This type of marketing is an increasingly important factor in the modern economy. Many large manufacturers purchase raw materials (such as metals or chemicals), finished components (such as computer chips, electronic circuitry, or auto parts), or service operations (such as payroll, customer service, or accounting) from other businesses. Investment firms, insurance companies, and health care providers often seek out businesses with better returns on investments and lower group rates. Business-to-business marketing can be very competitive and lucrative. It is the responsibility of the business providing those goods or services to build and maintain a long-term relationship with its various business clients.

The first step in business-to-business marketing is making prospective customers aware of a business's goods or services. Because those goods or ser-

Retail stores are a major source of employment in the United States as well as an effective way for manufacturers to get their products to consumers. (Photograph by Kelly A. Quin. Thomson Gale. Reproduced by permission.)

vices are generally expensive purchases involving long-term contracts, the decision-making process can take a long time. Salespeople must be ready to answer any questions potential customers may have and be able to describe clearly the differences between their company's goods or services and those offered by the competition. In addition, business-to-business marketers must maintain good relationships with their customers after the purchase is made. Many economists feel that positive interactions with existing customers is a key to the success of a business selling to other businesses.

Business-to-business marketing on the Internet, known as B2B, took off in the late 1990s. Producers and customers found the Internet a great environment in which to establish long-term contacts between businesses. For sellers and buyers alike, the Internet is a fast, reliable international marketplace of a type that was never before possible.

SERVICES MARKETING

A major shift in the U.S. economy has taken place over the past few decades. Once dominated by the production of goods, the economy is now dominated by the production of services. As a result the marketing and distribution of services have developed into a major new industry.

The "service industry" centers on large-scale operations in which major corporations sell consumers credit cards, telecommunications devices, cable television access, utilities, and the like. The industry also includes the services of trained professionals such as health care providers, insurance brokers, real estate salespeople, lawyers, accountants, and stockbrokers. Other "services" marketed to families and individuals include the arts (music, theater, dance), education (colleges and continuing education programs), and physical fitness (health clubs and personal training). Just about every facet of American culture has adopted marketing strategies to serve its own purposes.

The process of marketing services begins with the hiring of professionals to design effective marketing strategies; however, these strategies focus on the quality of the *services* provided rather than on the quality of the *goods* produced. Services are marketed through a combination of traditional print and broadcast advertising, direct mail advertising, telemarketing, and e-tailing.

Diverse service marketers often bundle their offerings. For instance, credit card companies, long distance telephone companies, and airlines may pool their offerings to allow consumers to earn "frequent flier miles" for signing on with a certain credit card or telephone service. Such partnerships allow consumers to gain additional benefits as they use a company's services. Bundling is expected to remain an important strategy for acquiring and maintaining service customers. As the services sector continues to grow in size and the various campaigns to market those services grow ever more complex, the demand for skilled services-marketing personnel will also grow.

Some marketing techniques have been scrutinized and even banned by federal regulations. In October 2003 the U.S. government created the Do-Not-Call list. Americans could add their names and telephone numbers to the list by visiting a Web site (www.donotcall.gov). Once people posted their numbers on the list, telemarketers were forbidden to solicit them for five years. Exemptions included charitable and political organizations. In addition, the CAN-Spam Act, which was passed by Congress in 2003, required spammers (senders of unwanted junk e-mails) to provide recipients an easy way to opt out of future spam.

THE FUTURE OF MARKETING AND DISTRIBUTION

Occupations in the fields of marketing and distribution are being radically transformed by the information revolution propelling the early twenty-first century. Although industry experts can predict trends with a good degree of accuracy, technological innovations will continue to transform our world in ways that are difficult to forecast. In the 1980s few people could have predicted how rapidly computers would make it into the home. Only 15 million American households had personal computers in 1990. By 2004, however, 69 million American homes had at least one personal computer, according to the U.S. Census Bureau's *Statistical Abstracts of the United States*. Of these more than half had access to the Internet.

No matter how our world changes, technology will continue to play a role in our lives. Because of this, manufacturers, marketing firms, and distributors will most likely seek employees who have attained a relatively high level of education and who possess technical knowledge and skills.

Good jobs do not magically appear. Anyone who has been in the job market knows that landing the right job takes planning, preparation, perseverance, and patience. This is true whether you are looking for your first job, reentering the job market, trying to get a new job, or planning a mid-career change. This essay is designed to guide you through the process of finding a job, from helping you define your career objectives to suggesting ways to prepare yourself for interviews. Use the advice and checklists below to help identify the kind of work that fits your personality, skills, and interests. Then learn how to locate job openings that match your criteria. Finally, use these tips to help you create a resume and prepare for the interview that helps you land the job that's right for you.

PLANNING YOUR CAREER

What are your unique skills? What kind of workplace appeals to you? What do you find most rewarding in your daily life? Answering these questions can help you identify a career path that will enrich your life, financially and otherwise. Most people enjoy doing a job well. There is an inner satisfaction that comes from taking on a challenge and accomplishing something worthwhile. Whether you are just starting out in the working world or you are at the midpoint of a career, it is worth taking some time to consider whether or not you are in the right kind of work—or looking for the right kind of job. If you are unhappy or dissatisfied in your daily work and are just trying to do enough to get by, you may not be in the right job or the right field. The following ideas can help you match your skills and interests with the kind of work you will find most rewarding.

Evaluate Yourself

Before you make any career decisions, think about subjects or topics that interest you and tasks you do well. This can help you pinpoint the kind of work you would be happy doing. One way to go about this is to compile a self-inventory chart. Such a chart will be helpful as you decide which jobs you want to consider. Including details about your work history and educational background will also make the chart useful to you as you compile your resume, write cover letters, complete job application forms, and prepare for job interviews.

Begin your self-inventory chart by listing all the jobs you have ever had, including summer employment, part-time jobs, volunteer work, and any freelance or short-term assignments you have done. Include the dates of employment, the names and addresses of supervisors, and the amount of money you earned. Then compile a similar list of your hobbies and other activities, including any special experiences you have had, such as travel. Next, do the same for your educational history, listing schools attended, major courses of study, grades, special honors or awards, courses you particularly enjoyed, and extracurricular activities.

At this point, you may see a career pattern emerging: perhaps your list is already suggesting a direction for your career search. If the picture still lacks detail or focus, expand your self-inventory chart by compiling a list of standard workplace aptitudes, and rate yourself *above average*, *average*, or *below average* for each one. Some skill categories to include in your list are administrative, analytic, athletic, clerical, language, leadership, managerial, manual, mathematical, mechanical, sales, and verbal abilities. Also rate your willingness to accept responsibility and your ability to get along with people. In combination with your educational background, work history, and list of personal interests, this information should help you understand why some kinds of work appeal to you and others do not.

Evaluate Workplace Characteristics

Another tool to help you find a rewarding job is the "Work Characteristics Checklist" below. Some of these characteristics will be attractive to you. Some will not. Perhaps you will discover that having a workplace with flexible hours, for example, is more important to you than being able to work outdoors. Or maybe you will find that these are both very significant issues in your quality of life.

This checklist can be useful as a guide as you compile your own list of what is important to you in a job or workplace. Do not expect a job to meet all your requirements, however. Focusing on the job characteristics that are most important to you will

Work Characteristics Checklist

Do you want a job in which you can

- work outdoors?
- be physically active?
- work with your hands?
- be challenged mentally?
- work with machines?
- work independently?
- work on a team?
- follow clear instructions?
- earn a lot of money?
- have a chance for rapid advancement?
- have good benefits?
- travel in your work?
- work close to home?
- work regular hours?
- have a flexible schedule?
- have a variety of tasks?
- have supervisory responsibilities?
- express your own ideas?
- be a decision maker?

help you identify the type of work you would find most rewarding. It will also be helpful when it is time to decide whether or not to apply for jobs you discover during the search process.

Evaluate Career Options

Now that you've evaluated your personal skills, aptitudes, interests, and experience, and you've identified the kinds of workplace characteristics that are important to you, do you feel confident that you know what kinds of jobs you'd be good at? If not, you may wish to consult an experienced career counselor or take advantage of online resources that can help you find a good career field match.

Most high schools, vocational schools, and colleges provide vocational testing and career counseling guidance for students and alumni. Some local offices of the state employment services affiliated with the federal employment service offer free counseling. Commercial career centers also offer guidance services.

There are many tools available to test your interests and aptitudes for the purpose of career counseling. The personal profile that emerges from a skills inventory can be matched with potential career fields to show you what kinds of jobs might be good matches for your interests. These assessment tools will also show you what kind of training is necessary to qualify for jobs in these career fields. You may find programs like this online that you can try for yourself. For a more comprehensive approach, you may prefer to look into aptitude tests that are administered and interpreted by a career counselor.

Most major cities have professional career consultants and career counseling firms. You should make sure to check their reputations before paying for their services. A list of counseling services in your area is available from the American Counseling Association in Alexandria, Virginia (http://www.counseling.org).

You can also search the Internet for many services that career counselors provide. Some sites have online counselors who can help you with a variety of tasks, such as obtaining information on jobs, careers, and training. They may be able to provide information on available services, including housing assistance, day care facilities, and transportation. A list of career planning resources, including Web sites, is available at the end of this volume.

EVALUATE SPECIFIC JOBS

After you have considered what you do well and what you enjoy doing, and identified some career options that provide a good match with your interests and abilities, you're ready to focus on the specific types of jobs that may be available to you. First, make a note of all the jobs in this volume that interest you. Then examine the education and training required for these jobs. Decide whether you qualify or would be able to gain the qualifications.

If possible, talk with people who have the kinds of jobs you are considering. Firsthand information can be invaluable. Also look through the appropriate trade and professional journals listed at the end of this essay and check the section at the end of the volume called "Resources" for books and Web sites that contain more detailed information about the jobs. In addition, counselors usually are helpful. For more detailed information, you can contact the trade and professional associations listed at the end of each occupational profile.

Once you have found out all you can about a particular type of job, compare the features of the job with your work characteristics checklist. See how many characteristics of the job match your work preferences. By completing these steps for all the jobs that appeal to you, you should be able to come up with a list of jobs that match your interests and abilities.

FINDING JOB OPPORTUNITIES

Once you've decided what kind of job suits you, the next step is to look for available positions. Obviously, the more openings you can find, the better your chance of landing a job. People usually apply

Job Finder's Checklist

The following list of job-hunting tips may seem obvious, but getting all the bits and pieces in order beforehand helps when you're looking for a job.

Resume Find out whether you will need a resume. If so, bring your resume up to date or prepare a new one. Assemble a supply of neatly printed copies and have an electronic version ready to e-mail to prospective employers.

References Line up your references. Ask permission of the people whose names you would like to use. Write down their addresses, phone numbers, and job titles.

Contacts Put the word out to everyone you know that you are looking for a job.

Job market Find out where the jobs are. Make a list of possible employers in your field of interest.

Research Do a little homework ahead of time—it can make a big difference in the long run. Find out as much as you can about a job, the field, and the company before you apply. A knowledgeable job applicant makes a good impression.

Organization Keep a file on your job-hunting campaign with names and dates of employers contacted, ads answered, results, and follow-up.

Appearance Make sure that the clothes you plan to wear to an interview are neat and clean. You may need to dress more formally than you would on the job, particularly if you are visiting a personnel office or meeting with a manager. Keep in mind that people will form an opinion of you based on their first impressions.

---

for many job openings before they find the right employment match.

There are many ways to find out about or apply for job openings. Some of these job-hunting techniques are explained on the pages that follow, along with information about how to follow up on job leads.

Applying in Person

For some jobs, especially part-time or entry-level jobs, you may be able to find employment by visiting the company or companies for which you would like to work. This works best when a company is expanding or jobs are plentiful for other reasons, or when a "help wanted" sign is posted at the company. Applying in person can sharpen your interviewing techniques and give you a chance to see a variety of workplaces. This direct approach is best for hourly labor or service jobs; when applying for other types of work, it is not the method to use unless you are directed to do so. Applicants for professional or supervisory jobs should always send a letter and resume to the company.

Phone and Letter Campaigns

To conduct a phone campaign, use the business listings of your telephone directory to build a list of companies for which you might like to work. Call their personnel departments and find out whether they have any openings. This technique is not useful

in all situations, and it has its drawbacks: you may not be able to make a strong impression by phone, and you will not have a written record of your contacts.

Letter writing campaigns can be very effective if the letters are well thought out and carefully prepared. Your letters should always be typed. Handwritten letters and photocopied letters convey a lack of interest or motivation.

You may be able to compile a good list of company addresses in your field of interest by reading the trade and professional publications listed at the end of this essay. Many of the periodicals publish directories or directory issues. Other sources you can use to compile lists of companies are the trade unions and professional organizations listed at the end of each job profile in this volume. The reference librarian at your local library can also help you find appropriate directories.

You can also e-mail letters to human resource departments of many companies. Be sure to follow all the same guidelines as you would for traditional letter correspondence.

Whether they are paper or electronic, your letters should be addressed to the personnel or human resources department of the organization. If possible, send the letter to a specific person. If you don't know who the correct person is, try to find the name of the personnel director through the directories in the library. You can also call on the phone and say, "I'm writing to ask about employment at your company. To whom should I address my letter?" If you can't find a name, use a standard salutation. It's a good idea to enclose a resume (described later in this essay) with the letter to give the employer a brief description of your educational and work experience.

Keep a list of all the people you write to, along with the date each letter was mailed, or keep a photocopy of each letter. Then you can follow up by writing a brief note or calling people who do not reply within about three weeks.

Job Databases Online

The World Wide Web can be an excellent resource for job hunters. The Internet currently has thousands of career-related sites where you can read about job openings or post your resume in a database for a possible match with available jobs. Some sites, such as The Monster Board (http://www. monster.com), help you build a resume and post it online as well as allow you to search through a massive database of help-wanted listings. Others employ a search engine to find jobs that match your background, then post your resume online for employers. The Web site called CareerBuilder (http://www. careerbuilder.com) uses an interactive personal search program that lets you select job criteria such as location, title, and salary; you are then notified by e-mail when a matching position is posted in the database.

Many companies post job openings in their human resource Web pages. You can usually access these lists by visiting the Web site of a company and clicking on a link called "jobs," "careers," or "employment opportunities." If you find a job that interests you during your online search, whether it's posted at a company's own Web site or on a general listing of jobs, follow the directions given for applying for the position. Some online ads will provide the contact information you need to send your resume and cover letter directly to the employer, either by e-mail or by traditional mail, but other ads direct job hunters to apply directly through a link at the job description.

Many career-related Web sites can be found on the Internet. This hypothetical site (for illustration purposes only) allows job-seekers to search for a position by location and job category.

Job hunters can often find job listings through the Web sites of the professional associations in their career fields. State government Web sites may also provide links to job listings—or to nongovernment sites that list available jobs.

Help-Wanted Ads

Many people find out about job openings by reading the "help-wanted" sections of newspapers, trade journals, and professional magazines. Employers and employment agencies often, though not always, use these classified ad sections to publicize available jobs.

Classified ads use unique terms to convey basic information. You will find some common abbreviations in the chart in this essay titled "Reading the Classifieds." You can usually decode the abbreviations by using common sense, but if something puzzles you, call the newspaper and ask for a translation. Classified ads usually list the qualifications that are required for a particular job and explain how to contact the employer.

As you find openings that interest you, answer each ad using the method requested. Record the date of your contact, and if you don't hear from the employer within two or three weeks, place another call or send a polite note asking whether the job is still open. Don't forget to include your phone number and address in your initial contact.

Some help-wanted ads are "blind ads." These ads give contact information for replying but provide no name, phone number, or address that would identify the company. Employers and employment agencies may place these ads to avoid having to reply to all of the job applicants or being contacted directly by job-seekers.

Situation-Wanted Ads

Another way to get the attention of potential employers is with a situation-wanted ad. You can place one of these in the classified section of your local newspaper or of a trade journal in your field of interest. Many personnel offices and employment agencies scan these columns when they're looking for new employees. The situation-wanted ad is usually most effective for people who have advanced education, training, or experience, or who are in fields where their unique skills are in great demand.

A situation-wanted ad should be brief, clear, and to the point. Its main purpose is to interest the employer enough so you are contacted for an interview. It should tell exactly what kind of job you

Reading the Classifieds

HELP WANTED	CLASSIFIED ABBREVIATIONS	SITUATION WANTED

AUTO PARTS
Counter Help F/T—exp. pfd. gd. bnfts. Apply in person. 72 Broad 2:30-7.

AUTO SALES
Foreign car exp. and proven track record a must. New and used, 5 days. Salary & commission & profit sharing. Call Jack Angeli 000-0000 or resume to 44 South 18th Street.

BUYER   F/P
Major Sun Belt Distributor. Exp. in hard goods & cookware. Ask for Jane Bailey. Simpson Agency. Michigan Ave. 000-0000 ext 402.

EXPORT MANAGER
INTERNATIONAL FREIGHT FORWARDER seeks aggressive, highly motivated self-starter w/heavy export bkgd to assume full responsibility for internal operations. Sal to 00K. Full knowl. of air & ocean shipping nec.
Resume to A. Frankfurt.
Box 7906A Star.

INVENTORY CONTROL CLERK
Exp. w/mens sportswear pfd. Piece goods inventory, stock inventory & misc. Downtown location. 000-0000.

MRKT. RSCH., top pkg. mfr. 2-4 yrs. consumer goods. Computer skills a plus. Immed. Personnel Mgr., Under Wraps, Inc. Box 27, Hillside Station.

P/T CASHIER—no exp. req. Pleasant personality, neat appearance. No evening work req. Apply in person. Flowers by Dominique. South Harrison at Central Ave.

SALES TRAINEE
Career oppty. for insurance sales agt. trnees. Some col. pfd. Sal. & comm. first yr. Mgt. potential 3-5 yrs. Mr. Lin, Hills Life, 000-0000. An Equal Opportunity Employer.

Shipping/Receiving Clerk—looking for motivated, f/t or p/t help in all areas of shipping. Call for appt. 000-0000. Ask for Mr. Smith.

---

admin.	administrative, administration
agt.	agent
bkgd.	background
co.	company
col.	college
comm.	commission
exp.	experience
ext.	phone extension
fee neg.	fee negotiable (fee can be worked out with employer)
figs.	figures
f/p., f/pd.	fee paid (agency fee paid by employer)
f/t	full time
gd. bnfts.	good benefits
grad.	graduate
K	thousand
knowl.	knowledge
M	thousand
mfg.	manufacturing
mfr.	manufacturer
mgr.	manager
mgt., mngmt.	management
misc.	miscellaneous
mrkt.	market
nec.	necessary
oppty.	opportunity
perm.	permanent
pfd.	preferred
pkg.	package
p/t	part time
rsch.	research
sal.	salary
temp.	temporary
trnee.	trainee
typ.	typist, typing
w/	with

ADVERTISING AGENCY ADMINISTRATOR
Take charge, manage internal operation. Strong media buying, traffic, finance bkgd. (000) 000-0000.

BORN SALESMAN
College Grad—Marketing/Mgt. Looking for promising career. Competitive grades, self-starting personality, four summers sales experience door-to-door and wholesale. Matthew Gordon, 24 Elm Street, or call (000) 000-0000.

EXPERIENCED SALES REP
Paper, corrugated cartons—office forms. Seeks to represent major lines in metropolitan area. Expert in setting up customer inventory control systems. (000) 000-0000.

IMPORT/EXPORT MGR.—Solid all-around exp. Knowl. French, German, Italian. Z473 Chronicle.

PURCHASING. Many years experience varied industries. Adaptable any position including control, systems, etc. F753 Tribune.

RETAIL MANAGER
Experienced professional will manage, motivate & sell for your company on a daily/weekly basis when illness, vacation, or resignation leaves you without key personnel. Cost-conscious, profit-oriented service. All inquiries in confidence. 000-0000.

SALES—Hard worker w/3 yrs. exp. in electronics seeks f/t position. Call Brian at 000-0000.

WE DO WINDOWS
Highly creative, exp. partners handle all aspects of retail display. Point-of-purchase, window dressing, conception through design and construction. No job too small. Satisfied customers throughout Tri-City area. Call 000-0000.

want, why you qualify, and whether you are available for full-time or part-time work. Use the same abbreviations that employers use in classified ads.

If you are already employed and do not want it known that you are looking for a new position, you can run a blind ad. A blind ad protects your privacy by listing a box number at the publication to which all replies can be sent. They are then forwarded to you. You do not need to give your name, address, or phone number in the ad.

Networking

A very important source of information about job openings is networking. This means talking with friends and acquaintances about your area of interest. If any of them have friends or relatives in the field, ask if they would be willing to speak with you. There's nothing wrong with telling anyone who will

listen that you are looking for a job—family, friends, counselors, and former employers. This will multiply your sources of information many times over.

You can use the Internet to make contacts, too. You can meet people with similar interests in news groups, which are organized by topic. Then you can correspond individually via e-mail. Many fields have professional organizations that maintain Web sites. These can help you keep current on news affecting your field, including employment opportunities.

Sometimes a contact knows about a job vacancy before it is advertised. You may have an advantage, then, when you get in touch with the employer. Don't, however, use the contact's name without permission. Don't assume that a contact will go out on a limb by recommending you, either. Once you have received the inside information, rely on your own ability to get the job.

Placement Services

Most vocational schools, high schools, and colleges have a placement or career service that maintains a list of job openings and schedules visits from companies. If you are a student or recent graduate, you should check there for job leads. Many employers look first in technical or trade schools and colleges for qualified applicants for certain jobs. Recruiters often visit colleges to look for people to fill technical and scientific positions. These recruiters usually represent large companies. Visit your placement office regularly to check the job listings, and watch for scheduled visits by company recruiters.

State Employment Services

Another source of information about job openings is the local office of the state employment service. Many employers automatically list job openings at the local office. Whether you're looking for a job in private industry or with the state, these offices, which are affiliated with the federal employment service, are worth visiting, online or in person, if there are offices locally.

State employment service offices are public agencies that do not charge for their services. They can direct you to special programs run by the government in conjunction with private industry. These programs, such as the Work Incentive Program for families on welfare, are designed to meet special needs. Some, but not all, of these offices offer vocational aptitude and interest tests and can refer interested people to vocational training centers. The state employment service can be a valuable first stop in your search for work, especially if there are special circumstances in your background. For ex-

Notes on Networking

Let people know you're looking. Tell friends, acquaintances, teachers, business associates, former employers—anyone who might know of job openings in your field.

Read newspapers and professional and trade journals. Look for news of developments in your field and for names of people and companies you might contact.

Use the World Wide Web. Make contacts through news groups, or find information on Web sites for professional organizations in your field.

Join professional or trade associations. Contacts you make at meetings could provide valuable job leads. Association newsletters generally carry useful information about people and developments in the field.

Attend classes or seminars. You will meet other people in your field at job-training classes and professional development seminars.

Participate in local support groups. You can gain information about people and places to contact through support groups such as those listed by *The Riley Guide*, available online at http://www.rileyguide.com/support.html, as well as through alumni associations.

Be on the lookout. Always be prepared to make the most of any opportunity that comes along. Talk with anyone who can provide useful information about your field.

ample, if you did not finish high school, if you have had any difficulties with the law, or if you are living in a difficult home environment, your state employment service office is equipped to help you.

Private Employment Agencies

State employment services, though free, are usually very busy. If you are looking for more personal service and want a qualified employment counselor to help you find a job, you might want to approach a private employment agency.

Private employment agencies will help you get a job if they think they can place you. Most of them get paid only if they're successful in finding you a job, so you need to show them that you are a good prospect. These agencies will help you prepare a resume if you need one, and they will contact employers they think might be interested in you.

Private employment agencies are in the business of bringing together people who are looking for jobs and companies that are looking for workers. For some positions, usually mid- and higher-level jobs, the employment agency's fee is paid by the employer. In such cases, the job seeker pays no fee. In other cases, you may be required to pay the fee, which is usually a percentage of your annual salary. Paying a fee can be a worthwhile investment if it leads to a rewarding career.

Some agencies may also ask for a small registration fee whether or not you get a job through them. Some agencies may demand that you pay even if you find one of the jobs they are trying to fill through your other contacts. Be sure to read and understand the fine print of any contract you're expected to sign, and ask for a copy to take home. Since the quality of these agencies varies, check to see if an agency is a certified member of a state or national association.

Some employment agencies, called staffing services, operate in a different way. They are usually paid by employers to screen and refer good candidates for job openings. They earn money when they refer a candidate who is hired by the employer. The employee pays no fee. Staffing firms, however, only spend time on candidates they think they may be able to place.

Private employment agencies are usually helping many people at one time. They may not have the time to contact you every time they find a job opening. Therefore, you may need to phone them at reasonable intervals after you have registered.

Civil Service

In your search for work, don't forget that the civil service—federal, state, and local—may have many jobs in your field. You may contact the state employment office or apply directly to the appropriate state or federal agency. The armed services also train and employ civilians in many fields. Don't neglect these avenues for finding jobs. Civil service positions usually require you to take a civil service examination. Books are available to help you prepare for these exams, and your local civil service office can also provide information.

Unions

In certain fields, unions can be useful sources of information. If you are a member of a union in your field of interest, you may be able to find out about jobs in the union periodical or through people at the union local. If you do not belong to a union, you may contact a union in the field you are interested in for information about available employment services. You will find addresses for some unions in the job profiles in this book.

Temporary Employment

A good way to get a feel for the job market—what's available and what certain jobs are like—is to work in a temporary job. There are both private and state agencies that can help place people in short-term jobs. Some jobs are seasonal, and extra workers may be needed in the summer or at another busy time.

Temporary employment can increase your job skills, your knowledge of a particular field, and your chances of hearing of permanent positions. In today's tight labor market, many companies are using the services of temporary workers in increasing numbers. In fact, temporary agencies may sign multimillion-dollar contracts to provide businesses with a range of temporary workers. In some cases, temporary workers are in such demand that they may receive benefits, bonuses, and the same hourly wages as equivalent permanent employees. Some temporary agencies are even joining with companies to create long-term career paths for their temporary workers.

MARKETING YOURSELF

An employer's first impression of you is likely to be based on the way you present yourself on print. Whether it is in an application form or on a resume, you will want to make a good impression so that employers will be interested in giving you a personal interview. A potential employer is likely to equate a neat, well-written presentation with good work habits, and a sloppy, poorly written one with bad work habits.

DO YOU KNOW YOUR RIGHTS?

JOB DISCRIMINATION—WHAT IT IS

Federal and State Law

An employer cannot discriminate against you for any reason other than your ability to do the job. By federal law, an employer cannot discriminate against you because of your race, color, religion, sex, or national origin. The law applies to decisions about hiring, promotion, working conditions, and firing. The law specifically protects workers who are over the age of forty from discrimination on the basis of age.

The law also protects workers with disabilities. Employers must make their workplaces accessible to individuals with disabilities—for example, by making them accessible to wheelchairs or by hiring readers or interpreters for blind or deaf employees.

Federal law offers additional protection to employees who work for the federal government or for employers who contract with the federal government. State law can also provide protection, for example by prohibiting discrimination on the basis of marital status, arrest record, political affiliations, or sexual orientation.

Affirmative Action

Affirmative action programs are set up by businesses that want to make a special effort to hire women and members of minority groups. Federal employers and many businesses that have contracts with the federal government are required by law to set up affirmative action programs. Employers with a history of discriminatory practices may also be required to establish affirmative action programs.

Discrimination against Job Applicants

A job application form or interviewer may ask for information that can be used to discriminate against you illegally. The law prohibits such questions. If you are asked such questions and are turned down for the job, you may be a victim of discrimination. However, under federal law, employers must require you to prove that you are an American citizen or that you have a valid work permit.

Discrimination on the Job

Discrimination on the job is illegal. Being denied a promotion for which you are qualified or being paid less than coworkers are paid for the same job may be forms of illegal discrimination.

Sexual, racial, and religious harassment are forms of discrimination and are prohibited in the workplace. On-the-job harassment includes sexual, racial, or religious jokes or comments. Sexual harassment includes not only requests or demands for sexual favors but also verbal or physical conduct of a sexual nature.

JOB DISCRIMINATION—WHAT YOU CAN DO

Contact Federal or State Commissions

If you believe that your employer practices discrimination, you can complain to the state civil rights commission or the federal Equal Employment Opportunity Commission (EEOC). If, after investigating your complaint, the commission finds that there has been discrimination, it will take action against the employer. You may be entitled to the job or promotion you were denied or to reinstatement if you were fired. You may also receive back pay or other financial compensation.

Contact a Private Organization

There are many private organizations that can help you fight job discrimination. For example, the American Civil Liberties Union (ACLU) works to protect all people from infringement on their civil rights. The National Association for the Advancement of Colored People (NAACP), National Organization

Writing an Effective Resume

When you write to a company to follow up a lead or to ask about job openings, you should send information about yourself. The accepted way of doing this is to send a resume with a cover letter.

The work resume is derived from the French word résumer, meaning "to summarize." A resume does just that—it briefly outlines your education, work experience, and special abilities and skills. A resume may also be called a curriculum vitae, a personal profile, or a personal data sheet. This summary acts as your introduction by mail or e-mail, as your calling card if you apply in person, and as a convenient reference for you to use when filling out an application form or when being interviewed.

A resume is a useful tool in applying for almost any job, even if you use it only to keep a record of where you have worked, for whom, and the dates of employment. A resume is required if you are being considered for professional or executive jobs. Prepare it carefully. It's well worth the effort.

for Women (NOW), and Native American Rights Fund may negotiate with your employer, sue on your behalf, or start a class action suit—a lawsuit brought on behalf of all individuals in your situation.

WHAT TO DO IF YOU LOSE YOUR JOB

Being Fired and Being Laid Off

In most cases, an employer can fire you only if there is good cause, such as your inability to do the job, violation of safety rules, dishonesty, or chronic absenteeism.

Firing an employee because of that employee's race, color, religion, sex, national origin, or age (if the employee is over forty) is illegal. Firing an employee for joining a union or for reporting an employer's violation (called whistle-blowing) is also prohibited. If you believe you have been wrongfully discharged, you should contact the EEOC or the state civil rights commission.

At times, employers may need to let a number of employees go to reduce costs. This reduction in staff is called a layoff. Laying off an employee has nothing to do with the employee's job performance. Federal law requires employers who lay off large numbers of employees to give these employees at least two months' notice of the cutback.

Unemployment Compensation

Unemployment insurance is a state-run fund that provides payments to people who lose their jobs through no fault of their own. Not everyone is entitled to unemployment compensation. Those who quit their jobs or who worked only a few months before losing their jobs may not be eligible.

The amount of money you receive depends on how much you earned at your last job. You may receive unemployment payments for only a limited period of time and only so long as you can prove that you are actively looking for a new position.

Each claim for unemployment compensation is investigated before the state makes any payments. If the state unemployment agency decides to deny you compensation, you may ask the agency for instructions on how to appeal that decision.

OTHER PROTECTIONS FOR EMPLOYEES

Honesty and Drug Testing

Many employers ask job applicants or employees to submit to lie detector tests or drug tests. Lie detector tests are permitted in the hiring of people for high security positions, such as police officers. Some states prohibit or restrict the testing of applicants or employees for drug use. Aptitude and personality tests are generally permitted.

Other Federal Laws

The Fair Labor Standards Act prescribes certain minimum wages and rules about working hours and overtime payments. Workers' compensation laws provide payment for injuries that occur in the workplace and wages lost as a result of those injuries.

The Occupational Safety and Health Act sets minimum requirements for workplace safety. Any employee who discovers a workplace hazard should report it to the Occupational Safety and Health Administration (OSHA). The administration will investigate the claim and may require the employer to correct the problem or pay a fine.

Rights Guaranteed by Contract

Not every employee has a written contract. If you do, however, that contract may grant you additional rights, such as the right to severance pay in the event you are laid off. In addition, employees who are members of a union may have certain rights guaranteed through their union contract.

Before you sign any contract, make sure you understand every part of it. Read it thoroughly and ask the employer questions. Checking the details of a contract before signing it may prevent misunderstanding later.

The goal of a resume is to capture the interest of potential employers so they will call you for a personal interview. Since employers are busy people, the resume should be as brief and as neat as possible. You should, however, include as much relevant information about yourself as you can. This is usually presented under at least two headings: "Education" and "Experience." The latter is sometimes called "Employment History." Some people add a third section titled "Related Skills," "Professional Qualifications," or "Related Qualifications."

If you prepare a self-inventory such as the one described earlier, it will be a useful tool in preparing a resume. Go through your inventory, and select the items that show your ability to do the job or jobs in which you are interested. Plan to highlight these items on your resume. Select only those facts that point out your relevant skills and experience.

Once you have chosen the special points to include, prepare the resume. At the top, put your name, address, and phone number. After that, de-

LORRAINE FLORIO
APARTMENT 3C
RAVEN'S LANDING
EDISON, NJ 12345
(609) 123-5678
LFLORIO@EMAIL.COM

OBJECTIVE: Position in retail sales.

SALES EXPERIENCE:

1999 to 2004   ***Sales Worker***, Housewares Department, Powell's Department Store, Edison, NJ.

Assisted customers with purchases. Operated cash register; accepted payment by cash, check, or credit card. Maintained stock records. Arranged gift wrap and shipping for gift purchases. Organized displays of sale items. Acted as manager during absence of department head.

1998 to 1999   ***Part Time Sales Worker***, Soft Step Shoe Shop, Edison, NJ.

Assisted customers with purchases. Assisted with annual inventory.

1996 to 1998   ***Part Time Sales Assistant***, The Fashion Shop, Plainsboro, NJ.

EDUCATION: ***Diploma***, Sands County
General business program

REFERENCES: Available upon request.

- State your name, address, telephone number, and email first.
- State job objective or general career goal in a few words.
- List education and work experience in reverse chronological order, with most recent item first.

RAJIV CHAUDRY

12-20 Walnut Street
Pittsburgh, PA 12345
(215) 123-4567
rjchaudry@email.com

OBJECTIVE: Position as marketing manager with manufacturing firm.

EDUCATION:

2001 to 2004   Courses in marketing, sales, advertising techniques, market research.
Wharton School of Business, Philadelphia, PA.

1997   ***Bachelor of Science***
Major in Economics, University of Virginia, Charlottesville, VA.

EXPERIENCE:

2000 to 2004   ***Account Executive***
Diaz and Romero Agency, Philadelphia, PA.
Worked closely with clients on target market and product identity. Developed yearly advertising plans, including schedules and budgets. Coordinated work of art department and copywriters. Hired as account representative; promoted in 1996.

1999 to 2006   ***Copywriter***
Media Associates, Philadelphia, PA.
Planned and composed copy for direct-mail, newspaper, magazine, and radio advertising. Responsible for a variety of clients and products. Worked with management, artists, and production.

1997 to 1999   ***Market Researcher***
Gunther Opinion Corporation, Arlington, VA.
Conducted interviews, coded and tabulated data, prepared reports based on findings. Received commendation for contribution to major consumer research program.

REFERENCES: Available upon request.

- List your work experience first if it is more important than your educational background.
- Keep descriptions of your education and work experience brief.
- List special skills and qualifications if they are relevant to the job.

cide which items will be most relevant to the employer you plan to contact.

State Your Objective Some employment counselors advise that you state a job objective or describe briefly the type of position for which you are applying. The job objective usually follows your name and address. Don't be too specific if you plan to use the same resume a number of times. It's better to give a general career goal. Then, in a cover letter, you can be more specific about the position in which you are interested.

Describe What You've Done Every interested employer will check your educational background and employment history carefully. It is best to present these sections in order of importance. For instance, if you've held many relevant jobs, you should list your work experience first, followed by your educational background. On the other hand, if you are just out of school with little or no work experience, it's probably best to list your educational background first and then, under employment history, to mention any part-time and summer jobs you've held or volunteer work you've done.

Under educational background, list the schools you have attended in reverse chronological order, starting with your most recent training and ending with the least recent. Employers want to know at a glance your highest qualifications. For each educational experience, include years attended, name and location of the school, and degree or certificate earned, if any. If you have advanced degrees (college and beyond), it isn't necessary to include high school and elementary school education. Don't forget to highlight any special courses you took or awards you won, if they are relevant to the kind of job you are seeking.

Chronological and Functional Resumes Information about your employment history can be presented in two ways. The most common format is the chronological resume. In a chronological resume, you summarize your work experience year by year. Begin with your current or most recent employment and then work backward. For each job, list the name and location of the company for which you worked, the years you were employed, and the position or positions you held. The order in which you present these facts will depend on what you are trying to emphasize. If you want to call attention to the type or level of job you held, for example, you should put the job title first. Regardless of the order you choose, be consistent. Summer employment or part-time work should be identified as such. If you held a job for less than a year, specify months in the dates of employment.

It is important to include a brief description of the responsibilities you had in each job. This often reveals more about your abilities than the job title. Remember, too, that you do not have to mention the names of former supervisors or how much you earned. You can discuss these points during the interview or explain them on an application form.

The functional resume, on the other hand, emphasizes what you can do rather than what you have done. It is useful for people who have large gaps in their work history or who have relevant skills that would not be properly highlighted in a chronological listing of jobs. The functional resume concentrates on qualifications—such as familiarity with particular equipment, organizational skills, or managerial experience. Specific jobs may be mentioned, but they are not the primary focus of this type of resume.

Explain Special Skills You may wish to include a third section called "Related Skills," "Professional Qualifications," or "Related Qualifications." This is useful if there are points you want to highlight that do not apply directly to educational background or work experience. Be sure these points are relevant to the kind of work you are seeking. This section is most effective if you can mention any special recognition, awards, or other evidence of excellence. It is also useful to mention if you are willing to relocate or can work unusual hours.

Have References Available Employers may also want to know whom they can contact to find out more about you. At the start of your job search, you should ask three or four people if you may use them as references. If you haven't seen these people for a while, you may want to send them a copy of your resume and let them know what kind of position you're seeking. Your references should be the kind of people your potential employer will respect, and they should be able to comment favorably on your abilities, personality, and work habits. You should indicate whether these people are personal references or former work supervisors. Avoid using any relatives. You can list the names and addresses of your references at the end of your resume or in a cover letter. Or, you can simply write, "References available upon request." Just be sure you have their names, addresses, and phone numbers ready if you are asked.

Present Yourself Concisely Tips for making your resume concise include using phrases instead of sentences and omitting unnecessary words. When appropriate, start a phrase with a verb, such as "maintained" or "coordinated." There is no need to say "I"—that is obvious and repetitive.

LORRAINE FLORIO

APARTMENT 3C
RAVEN'S LANDING
EDISON, NJ 12345
(609) 123-5678
LFLORIO@EMAIL.COM

June 20, 2005

Mr. Robert Richards
Richards Furniture Gallery
55 Brooke Street
Hightstown, NJ 12355

Dear Mr. Richards:

I read in the *Town Record* that a new branch of your store is scheduled to open next month in Spring Valley Mall. I am writing to inquire whether you will be hiring any sales workers to staff the new store.

I have sales experience in housewares, shoes, and women's clothing. Powell's Department Store, my most recent place of employment, was also located in Spring Valley Mall. I am familiar with the schedule of the mall, its busy periods, and the seasonal sales and promotional events.

I would like to work in furniture sales since I am interested in home decorating. I particularly enjoyed housewares sales, where I helped customers coordinate appliances, china, and kitchen decor.

I enclose my resume and would be pleased to meet
skills.

Sincerely yours,

Lorraine Florio

Lorraine Florio

Enclosure

RAJIV CHAUDRY

12-20 Walnut Street
Pittsburgh, PA 12345
(215) 123-4567
rjchaudry@email.com

November 2, 2005

Ms. Doreen Jacobi
Director of Personnel
Goldman Brothers Incorporated
67 East Market Street
Pittsburgh, PA 12345

Dear Ms. Jacobi:

Lionel Bachman, controller at Goldman Brothers, mentioned that your marketing manager for the textile and apparel division resigned recently. I am looking for a position as marketing manager and would like to apply for the job.

I have worked in advertising and market research. My clients have included apparel manufacturers specializing in women's clothing as well as companies in other industries. I am familiar with all print and broadcast media, including some of the innovative work being done in catalog sales and designer promotions.

I recently left the Diaz and Romero Agency to move back to the Pittsburgh area. I enclose my resume and am available for an interview at your convenience.

Very truly yours,

Rajiv Chaudry

Rajiv Chaudry

Enclosure

Present Yourself Well Employment counselors often recommend that resumes be no longer than one page because employers won't take the time to read a second page. If you've held many positions related to your occupation, go on to the second page, but don't include beginning or irrelevant jobs. If you have a lot of work experience, limit the education section to just the essentials.

You should also concentrate on the appearance of your resume. A traditional resume should be printed on a good grade of 8½" x 11" white paper. Consult a resume preparation guide for specific information about the best ways to format a resume that will be processed by e-mail or other electronic means. If you don't have access to a computer and printer, you can pay someone to type your resume, but it is up to you to read it carefully and ensure that it is error-free. Be sure that it is neatly typed with adequate margins. The data should be spaced and indented so that each item stands out. This enables a busy executive or personnel director to see at a glance the facts of greatest interest.

These suggestions for writing a resume are not hard-and-fast rules. Resumes may be adapted to special situations. For example, people with a variety of work experience often prepare several versions of their resumes and use the experience that's most relevant when applying for a particular job.

If this is your first resume, show it to someone else, perhaps a guidance counselor, for constructive advice. Make sure there are no spelling or punctuation mistakes anywhere on the page. No matter what, be truthful while emphasizing your assets. You can do that by showing the abilities, skills, and specific interests that qualify you for a particular job. Don't mention any weaknesses or deficiencies in your training. Do mention job-related aptitudes that showed up in previous employment or in school. Don't make things up; everything that's in your resume can, and often will, be checked.

Writing Cover Letters

Whenever you send your resume to a prospective employer, whether it's on paper or in e-mail form, you should send a cover letter with it. This is true whether you are writing to apply for a specific job or just to find out if there are any openings.

A good cover letter should be neat, brief, and well written, with no more than three or four short paragraphs. Since you may use your resume for a variety of job openings, your cover letter should be very specific. Your goal is to get the person who reads it to think that you are an ideal candidate for a particular job. If at all possible, send the letter to a specific person—either the personnel director or the person for whom you would be working. If necessary, call the company and ask to whom you should address the letter.

Start your letter by explaining why you are writing. Say that you are inquiring about possible job openings at the company, that you are responding to an advertisement in a particular publication, or that someone recommended that you should write. (Use the person's name if you have received permission to do so.) Let your letter lead into your resume. Use it to call attention to your qualifications. Add information that shows why you are well suited for that specific job.

Completing the Application Form

Many employers ask job applicants to fill out an application form. This form usually duplicates much of the information on your resume, but it may ask some additional questions. Give complete answers to all questions except those that are discriminatory. If a question doesn't apply to you, put a dash next to it.

You may be given the application form when you arrive for an interview, or it may be sent to your home. When filling it out, print neatly in ink. Follow the instructions carefully. For instance, if the form asks you to put down your last name first, do so.

The most important sections of an application form are the education and work histories. As in your resume, many applications request that you write these in reverse chronological order, with the most recent experience first. Unlike your resume, however, the application form may request information about your earnings on previous jobs. It may also ask what rate of pay you are seeking on the job you are applying for.

Be prepared to answer these and other topics not addressed on your resume. Look at the sample application form, and make note of the kinds of questions that you are likely to be asked—for example, your Social Security number, the names of previous supervisors, your salary, and your reason for leaving. If necessary, carry notes on such topics with you to an interview. You have a responsibility to tell prospective employers what they need to know to make an informed decision.

Neatness Counts Think before you write on an application form so you avoid crossing things out. An employer's opinion of you may be influenced just by the general appearance of your application form. A neat, detailed form may indicate an orderly mind and the ability to think clearly, follow instructions, and organize information.

Know Your Rights Under federal and some state laws, an employer cannot demand that you answer

1. Always print neatly in blue or black ink. When completing an application at home, type it, if possible.

2. Read the application carefully *before* you start to fill it out. Follow instructions precisely. Use standard abbreviations.

3. If you aren't applying for a specific job, indicate the kind of work you're willing to do.

4. You don't have to commit to a specific rate of pay. Write "open" or "negotiable" if you are uncertain.

5. Traffic violations and so on do not belong here. Nor do offenses for which you were charged but not convicted.

6. If a question doesn't apply to you, write "NA" (for not applicable) or put a dash through the space.

7. Take notes along to remind you of school names, addresses, and dates.

8. If you're short on "real" employment, mention jobs such as babysitting, lawn mowing, or any occasional work.

9. Your references should be people who can be objective about you, such as former employers, teachers, and community leaders.

10. Under the heading "Reason for Leaving," a simple answer will do. Avoid saying "better pay"—even if it's so.

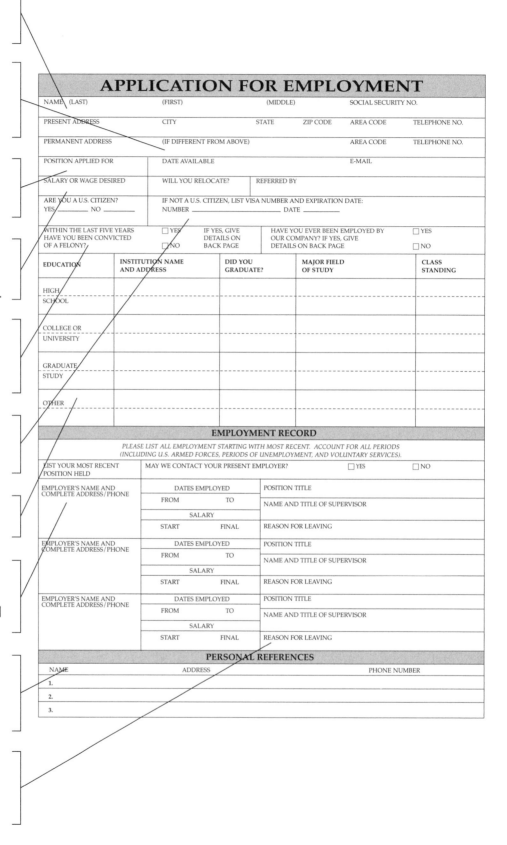

APPLICATION FOR EMPLOYMENT

NAME (LAST) | (FIRST) | (MIDDLE) | SOCIAL SECURITY NO.

PRESENT ADDRESS | CITY | STATE | ZIP CODE | AREA CODE | TELEPHONE NO.

PERMANENT ADDRESS | (IF DIFFERENT FROM ABOVE) | AREA CODE | TELEPHONE NO.

POSITION APPLIED FOR | DATE AVAILABLE | E-MAIL

SALARY OR WAGE DESIRED | WILL YOU RELOCATE? | REFERRED BY

ARE YOU A U.S. CITIZEN? YES ____ NO ____ | IF NOT A U.S. CITIZEN, LIST VISA NUMBER AND EXPIRATION DATE: NUMBER ____ DATE ____

WITHIN THE LAST FIVE YEARS HAVE YOU BEEN CONVICTED OF A FELONY? ☐ YES ☐ NO | IF YES, GIVE DETAILS ON BACK PAGE | HAVE YOU EVER BEEN EMPLOYED BY OUR COMPANY? IF YES, GIVE DETAILS ON BACK PAGE ☐ YES ☐ NO

EDUCATION	INSTITUTION NAME AND ADDRESS	DID YOU GRADUATE?	MAJOR FIELD OF STUDY	CLASS STANDING
HIGH SCHOOL				
COLLEGE OR UNIVERSITY				
GRADUATE STUDY				
OTHER				

EMPLOYMENT RECORD

PLEASE LIST ALL EMPLOYMENT STARTING WITH MOST RECENT. ACCOUNT FOR ALL PERIODS (INCLUDING U.S. ARMED FORCES, PERIODS OF UNEMPLOYMENT, AND VOLUNTARY SERVICES).

LIST YOUR MOST RECENT POSITION HELD | MAY WE CONTACT YOUR PRESENT EMPLOYER? ☐ YES ☐ NO

EMPLOYER'S NAME AND COMPLETE ADDRESS/PHONE	DATES EMPLOYED	POSITION TITLE
	FROM TO	NAME AND TITLE OF SUPERVISOR
	SALARY	
	START FINAL	REASON FOR LEAVING
EMPLOYER'S NAME AND COMPLETE ADDRESS/PHONE	DATES EMPLOYED	POSITION TITLE
	FROM TO	NAME AND TITLE OF SUPERVISOR
	SALARY	
	START FINAL	REASON FOR LEAVING
EMPLOYER'S NAME AND COMPLETE ADDRESS/PHONE	DATES EMPLOYED	POSITION TITLE
	FROM TO	NAME AND TITLE OF SUPERVISOR
	SALARY	
	START FINAL	REASON FOR LEAVING

PERSONAL REFERENCES

NAME	ADDRESS	PHONE NUMBER
1.		
2.		
3.		

any questions about race, color, creed, national origin, ancestry, sex, marital status, age (with certain exceptions), number of dependents, property, car ownership (unless needed for the job), or arrest record. Refer to the information on job discrimination in this essay for more information about your rights.

PRESENTING YOURSELF IN AN INTERVIEW

If your qualifications, as presented in your resume, cover letter, and application, are a strong match for the requirements of the job, you may be invited to a job interview. On the basis of this meeting, the prospective employer will decide whether or not to hire you, and you will decide whether or not you want the job.

Prepare in Advance

Before an interview, there are a number of things you can do to prepare. Begin by giving thought to why you want the job and what you have to offer. Then review your resume and any lists you made when you were evaluating yourself so that you can keep your qualifications firmly in mind.

Learn as much as you can about the organization. Check with friends who work there, read company brochures, search the Internet, or devise other information-gathering strategies. Showing that you know something about the company and what it does will indicate your interest and demonstrate that you are a well-informed job candidate.

Try to anticipate some of the questions an interviewer may ask and think about how you would answer. For example, you may be asked: Will you work overtime when necessary? Are you ready to go to night school to improve some of your skills? Preparing answers in advance will make the process easier for you. It is also wise to prepare any questions you may have about the company or the position for which you are applying. The more information you have, the better you can evaluate both the company and the job.

Employers may want you to demonstrate specific skills for some jobs. An applicant for a job in a lumber mill or a mine, for example, might be required to demonstrate mechanical ability. Prospective technicians might be expected to demonstrate mathematical skills.

On the appointed day, dress neatly and in a style appropriate for the job you're seeking. When in doubt, it's safer to dress on the conservative side, wearing a shirt and tie rather than a turtleneck or wearing a dress or blouse and skirt rather than pants and a T-shirt. Be on time. Find out in advance exactly where the company is located and how to get there. Allow extra time in case you get lost, get caught in a traffic jam, can't find a parking spot, or encounter another type of delay.

Maintain a Balance

When your appointment begins, remember that a good interview is largely a matter of balance. Don't undersell yourself by sitting back silently, but don't oversell yourself by talking nonstop about how wonderful you are. Answer all questions directly and simply, and let the interviewer take the lead.

Instead of saying, "I'm reliable and hardworking," give the interviewer an example. Allow the interviewer to draw conclusions from your example.

It's natural to be nervous before and during a job interview. However, you need to try to relax and be yourself. You may even enjoy the conversation. Your chances of being hired and being happy if you get the job are better if the employer likes you as you are.

Avoid discussing money until the employer brings it up or until you are offered the job. Employers usually know in advance what they are willing to pay. If you are the one to begin a discussion about the salary you want, you may set an amount that's either too low or too high.

Be prepared to ask questions, but don't force them on your interviewer. Part of the purpose of the interview is for you to evaluate the company while you are being evaluated. For instance, you might want to ask about the company's training programs and its policy on promotions.

Don't stay too long. Most business people have busy schedules. It is likely that the interviewer will let you know when it's time for the interview to end.

Don't expect a definite answer at the first interview. Employers usually thank you for coming and say that you will be notified shortly. Most employers want to interview all the applicants before they make a hiring decision. If the position is offered at the time of the interview, you can ask for a little time to think about it. If the interviewer tells you that you are not suitable for the job, try to be polite. Say, "I'm sorry, but thank you for taking the time to meet with me." After all, the company may have the right job for you next week.

Follow Up after the Interview

If the job sounds interesting and you would like to be considered for it, say so as you leave. Follow up after the interview by writing a brief thank-you note to the employer. Express your continued interest in the position and thank the interviewer for taking the time to meet with you.

It's a good idea to make some notes and evaluations of the interview while it is still fresh in your mind. Write down the important facts about the job—the duties, salary, promotion prospects, and so on, which will help you make a decision should you be offered the job. Also evaluate your own performance in the interview. List the things you wish you had said and things you wish you had not said, which will help you prepare for future interviews.

Finally, don't hesitate to contact your interviewer if you haven't heard from the company after a week or two (unless you were told it would be longer). Write a brief note or make a phone call in which you ask when a decision might be reached. Making such an effort will show the employer that you are genuinely interested in the job. Your call will remind the interviewer about you and could work to your advantage.

TAKE CHARGE

Job hunting is primarily a matter of organizing a well-planned campaign. Scan the classified ads, search through online job banks, watch for trends in local industry that might be reported in the news, and check with people you know in the field. Take the initiative. Send out carefully crafted resumes and letters. Respond to ads. Finally, in an interview, state your qualifications and experience in a straightforward and confident manner.

TRADE AND PROFESSIONAL JOURNALS

The following is a list of some of the major journals in the fields of marketing and distribution. These journals can keep you up to date with what is happening in your field of interest and can lead you to jobs through their classified advertising sections.

Marketing and Advertising

Advertising Age, 711 Third Avenue, New York, NY 10017-4036.
  http://www.adage.com
Adweek, 770 Broadway, New York, NY 10003.
  http://www.adweek.com
Business Week, 1221 Avenue of the Americas, 43rd Floor, New York, NY 10020.
  http://www.businessweek.com
Direct, Prism Business Media, 249 W. 17th Street, New York, NY 10011.
  http://www.directmag.com
Direct Marketing, 224 Seventh Street, Garden City, NY 11530.
  http://www.directmarketingmag.com
Fortune Magazine, Time & Life Building, Rockefeller Center, New York, NY 10020-1393.
  http://money.cnn.com/magazines/fortune
Journal of Marketing, American Marketing Association, 311 South Wacker Drive, Suite 5800, Chicago, IL 60606.
  http://www.marketingjournals.org/jm
Management Accounting Research, 360 Park Avenue South, New York, NY 10010.
Marketing News, American Marketing Association, 311 South Wacker Drive, Suite 5800, Chicago, IL 60606.

Retail and Wholesaling

DSN Retailing Today, 425 Park Avenue, New York, NY 10022.
  http://www.dsnretailingtoday.com
Journal of Retailing and Consumer Services, Reed Business, 360 Park Avenue South, New York, NY 10010.
Progressive Grocer, 770 Broadway, New York, NY 10003.
  http://www.progressivegrocer.com
Training and Development, 1640 King Street, P.O. Box 1443, Alexandria, VA 22313-2043.
  http://www.astd.org/astd/publications/td_magazine
Vending Times, 1375 Broadway, 6th Floor, New York, NY 10018.
  http://www.vendingtimes.com/ME2/Default.asp
Women's Wear Daily, Fairchild Publications, 750 Third Avenue, 5th Floor, New York, NY 10017.
  http://www.wwd.com

Auto Parts Counter Worker

Definition and Nature of the Work

Auto parts counter workers, also known as auto parts salespersons, sell parts for motor vehicles. They deal in spare parts, replacement parts, accessories, and other equipment for cars, trucks, and other vehicles. In addition to selling directly to the public, auto parts salespersons take orders over the telephone and by e-mail.

Many auto parts counter workers work for dealerships. Dealerships are companies that sell and service vehicles made by one or two manufacturers. The counter workers they employ sell parts only for the makes of cars and trucks sold by the dealer. While these counter workers sometimes sell parts to private customers, they spend most of their time supplying parts to mechanics who service and repair vehicles within the dealership.

Some auto parts counter workers work for wholesale dealers who buy parts at cost from manufacturers and sell them to individual customers or other businesses. Counter workers employed by wholesale dealers sell parts for many different makes of automobiles and trucks. Their customers include independent repair shops, service stations, self-employed mechanics, and people who do their own car repairs. Counter workers also work for retail automobile parts stores. In large trucking companies and bus lines, counter workers supply parts to mechanics who keep the fleets in good repair.

In addition to selling parts, counter workers order parts and store them in the stockroom. They must be able to find parts when customers ask for them. Auto

Education and Training
High school and on-the-job training

Salary
Median—$15.16 per hour

Employment Outlook
Poor

An auto parts counter worker at a dealership sells parts to customers and supplies parts to the mechanics in the dealership who service and repair vehicles. (© Martha Tabor/ Working Images Photographs. Reproduced by permission.)

parts counter workers are generally familiar with the appearance and purpose of thousands of parts. They use catalogs and price lists to identify parts their customers need. This information is likely to be stored in a computer or on the Internet. If the parts are not in stock, counter workers may order them or suggest substitutes. To make sure a substitute part will fit, they use measuring devices such as micrometers and calipers. When customers bring in defective parts, counter workers may have to repair them. In some wholesale stores they are responsible for repairing or rebuilding parts.

Counter workers also keep catalogs and price lists up to date. They use computer tracking to take inventory and order more parts when they are needed. Auto parts counter workers unpack and store incoming shipments and perform sales transactions as well.

Many dealers and some independent garages employ service writers, also known as service advisers. They are experienced counter workers or former auto mechanics. When customers bring in vehicles to be repaired, service writers obtain written permission from them to service their vehicles and write estimates of the cost of repairs. To write estimates, they may have to diagnose the problem first. Service writers may also perform customer service work such as settling complaints from dissatisfied customers.

Education and Training Requirements

Auto parts counter workers are trained on the job. Employers prefer to hire high school graduates. Because counter workers deal with prices and sales, they must understand mathematics and be able to write clearly. High school or vocational school courses in business math, bookkeeping, and automobile technology are useful. Practical experience relating to cars or trucks is a great advantage. In addition, counter workers must be tactful and courteous when dealing with customers.

Getting the Job

Individuals interested in becoming auto parts counter workers should apply directly to automobile and truck dealers and to retail and wholesale parts stores. The state employment service may list job openings. Career sites on the Internet and classified ads in local newspapers often advertise openings.

Advancement Possibilities and Employment Outlook

Auto parts counter workers may advance to become parts department managers or service writers. Some become outside sales workers for large parts wholesalers or distributors. They call on automobile repair shops, service stations, and other businesses that service motor vehicles. Some even open their own stores.

According to the U.S. Bureau of Labor Statistics, the number of jobs for auto parts counter workers is expected to decline through the year 2014. As automobile dealerships and wholesalers continue to consolidate, many auto parts counter worker jobs will be eliminated. In addition, the Internet allows an increasing number of customers to order parts online directly from the manufacturer, bypassing the need to visit auto parts stores. Growth in the field of auto parts counter worker is related to increases in the number of motor vehicles on the road and to the introduction each year of new mechanical features in those vehicles. Other job openings are expected to occur each year to replace workers who retire or transfer to other occupations.

Working Conditions

Auto parts counter workers can expect to work in stockrooms that are usually well lighted, orderly, and ventilated. Good eyesight is helpful for reading closely printed lists in catalogs and on computer screens. Counter workers stand for most of the day and may have to carry heavy parts. They generally work forty hours a week, including some weekend and evening hours. Many counter workers belong to labor unions.

Earnings and Benefits

Auto parts counter workers employed in dealerships made a median hourly wage of $15.16 in 2004, according to the Bureau of Labor Statistics. Some parts stores pay counter workers a commission based on sales. Benefits may include paid holidays and vacations, life and health insurance, and retirement plans.

Where to Go for More Information

Automotive Aftermarket Industry
   Association
7101 Wisconsin Ave., Ste. 1300
Bethesda, MD 20814-3415
(301) 654-6664
http://www.aftermarket.org/

International Brotherhood of Teamsters
25 Louisiana Ave. NW
Washington, DC 20001
(202) 624-6800
http://www.teamster.org/

Sheet Metal Workers International
   Association
1750 New York Ave. NW
Washington, DC 20006
(202) 783-5880
http://www.smwia.org/

Auto Sales Worker

Definition and Nature of the Work

Auto sales workers sell new and used automobiles. Some work in used car lots, where they sell vehicles made by many manufacturers. Many work for car dealerships—companies that sell cars made by certain manufacturers. The manager of a dealership, sometimes called the dealer, may work alone or employ one or more sales workers. Sales workers in dealerships typically sell new cars of only one or two makes, along with a variety of used cars.

Dealership sales workers approach and assist potential new customers who come to look at cars in the showroom. Other times they get repeat business from former customers. Some drivers trade in their cars for new models every few years. Sales workers keep lists of their customers and contact them regularly to see if they are ready to make a new purchase.

To sell cars to customers, sales workers find out how much their clients are willing to spend, as well as the size, model, and features they want in a vehicle. Sales workers discuss the cars in the showroom, see which ones interest their customers the most, and then emphasize the features they think will make the car attractive to a particular buyer.

Because vehicles are such a major investment, most car buyers must finance their purchases. Some borrow the full amount of the cost of the car from a bank or other lending institution. The lending institution pays the dealer in full and the customers make monthly payments to the lender until the loan is paid off. Other customers arrange financing through a dealership or a car maker. Auto sales workers must know the details of financing to help their customers make arrangements for loans.

Education and Training
High school and on-the-job training

Salary
Median—$18.61 per hour

Employment Outlook
Very good

Auto sales workers explain the features of cars to customers and arrange for financing through the dealership. (© Don Mason/Corbis.)

Sales workers must be able to figure the trade-in allowance that can be given on an old car against the price of a new car. When the customer has chosen a car, the sales worker adds up the total sales price (including special accessories and equipment, sales tax, and the license and registration fee), and subtracts rebates, other discounts, and the trade-in allowance. Often the salesperson must negotiate with the customer over the final price of the car. A sales contract is then prepared for the customer's signature. The same method is used in selling used cars.

Individuals and companies that use their cars for business often lease them rather than buy them. In these cases the sales worker prepares the necessary leasing documents.

In large dealerships with many employees, sales workers are supervised by sales managers. Sales managers meet with sales workers to keep them up to date on new features and new models of vehicles. Sales meetings can provide a forum for praising top sales workers, giving suggestions on sales methods, and screening films sent to the dealers by the auto manufacturers.

Education and Training Requirements

Auto sales workers are generally required to have a high school education. Courses in business, English, and public speaking are useful. A basic knowledge of math is important because computing various credit and cost terms is part of the job. Often some college or work experience is an asset because it helps build self-confidence. Employers generally prefer to hire sales workers who know a good deal about cars and automobile technology. In addition, auto sales workers should have an interest in and enjoy working with people.

Beginning auto sales workers receive training on the job. Some automobile manufacturers may require newly hired individuals to undergo a training program that lasts several months. Large dealerships may provide several days of classroom training for newly hired workers. Beginners also learn by observing experienced sales workers.

Automobile manufacturers provide training manuals and other materials that sales workers can study and incorporate into their sales presentations. Sales managers may hold periodic meetings that help train new sales workers. Manufacturers sometimes hold special training programs for sales managers before the introduction of new sales campaigns.

Getting the Job

Anyone interested in becoming an auto sales worker should apply directly to dealerships and used car businesses in the area. Job openings for sales workers are often listed in newspaper want ads and on Internet job sites.

Advancement Possibilities and Employment Outlook

Many successful auto sales workers prefer to remain in selling jobs. They advance by increasing their sales volume. Those who enjoy administrative work may want to become sales managers. They may be promoted to the job of sales manager in the dealership for which they work, or they may go to another dealership that has an opening. Some become auto dealers. Many car manufacturers offer training courses in dealership management.

According to the U.S. Bureau of Labor Statistics, 269,000 people were employed as auto sales workers in 2004. Employment of auto sales workers was expected to increase faster than the average for all occupations between 2004 and 2014. Though some people are turning to the Internet to buy their cars, many others prefer to talk to a salesperson and test drive automobiles before making a purchase.

Working Conditions

The showrooms of automobile dealers are almost always bright and pleasant. Hours are usually irregular because most people shop for cars in the evenings or on weekends or holidays. A fifty-hour workweek is not unusual. Sales workers know that the more time they spend on the job, the more sales and commissions they will make. In addition to working with customers, sales workers are responsible for handling paperwork. They must also keep abreast of new developments in car design and engineering by reading literature provided by the manufacturer.

Earnings and Benefits

Generally, auto sales workers work on commission. This means they earn a percentage of the sale price of each car they sell. Sometimes they receive a small base salary in addition to commissions. Altogether, auto sales workers earned a median income of $18.61 per hour in 2004, according to the Bureau of Labor Statistics. Some very experienced sales workers earn much more.

Nearly all automobile dealers offer paid vacations as well as insurance and retirement plans for their full-time employees. In addition, sales workers may receive automobiles for personal use at no cost or at low cost.

Where to Go for More Information

American Automotive Leasing Association
675 N. Washington St., Ste. 410
Alexandria, VA 22314
(703) 548-0777
http://www.aalafleet.com/

National Automobile Dealers Association
8400 Westpark Dr.
McLean, VA 22102
(703) 821-7000
http://www.nada.org/

National Independent Automobile Dealers
  Association
2521 Brown Blvd.
Arlington, TX 76006
(817) 640-3838
http://www.niada.com/

Cashier

Education and Training
On-the-job training

Salary
Median—$7.81 per hour

Employment Outlook
Fair

Cashiers' duties vary depending on the type of business. In food service, cashiers ring up food items, replenish inventory, and assist customers. *(Photograph by Kelly A. Quin. Thomson Gale. Reproduced by permission.)*

Definition and Nature of the Work

Cashiers handle customers' payments in retail stores, restaurants, theaters, and offices. Their exact duties depend on the business that employs them. Usually cashiers scan or type the price of items into a computer that calculates a total. They then collect payment for goods and services, make change, and hand out receipts. Cashiers may also issue cash refunds and credit slips to customers or cash checks for customers and employees. At the end of their shift, they must balance the amount of money they have taken in with the total sales recorded. They do this to make sure they have not made any mistakes. If the balance does not match up on a regular basis, a cashier can lose his or her job.

Some cashiers have additional duties, including paying for company supplies and equipment, preparing paychecks or pay envelopes, making out sales tax reports, or readying cash and checks for bank deposit. Many cashiers work flexible hours.

Cashiers who work in theaters also operate ticket dispensing machines and may give out information on the telephone. Those who work in restaurants sell candy, cigarettes, and other small items. They also may be required to know the prices of the various items on the menu. Some restaurant cashiers take care of telephone reservations, take-out orders, and hosting duties.

Most cash registers function like computer terminals. They report information about sales to a central computer or company computer network so that the store does not have to keep inventory. In most large operations and grocery stores cashiers pass merchandise price tags across a scanner. The scanner reads a bar code on the tags and records the price and item description onto a computer system. In small retail operations the cashier sometimes must enter a coded description of each item sold as well as its price into the cash register.

Cashiers who work in grocery stores and supermarkets must check coupons and food stamps to make sure they are valid. They may have to weigh and price produce and bag customers' purchases. In slack periods they sometimes help restock shelves and mark prices on items or shelves.

Cashiers in department, variety, and specialty stores may have to remove security devices from clothing. They tell customers whether purchases can be returned and, if so, under what conditions. They sometimes arrange to ship items to customers or other recipients. Some cashiers gift wrap merchandise and wrap packages for shipment.

Cashiers who work in offices often perform a variety of duties. They may act as receptionists, operate the switchboard, or provide office support such as word processing.

Education and Training Requirements

Employers prefer applicants who have a high school education and who understand basic mathematics. Some vocational high schools offer cashier courses, but most workers are trained on the job in the use of electronic or computerized registers and other aspects of the position.

Getting the Job

Newspaper want ads and Internet job sites generally list jobs for cashiers. Individuals interested in becoming cashiers can also apply directly to restaurants, theaters, amusement parks, retail stores, hospitals, hotels, and business firms.

Advancement Possibilities and Employment Outlook

Cashiers who work for large retail stores may become department managers or store managers. Those who work in offices may move into more responsible positions.

According to the U.S. Bureau of Labor Statistics, cashiers held 3.5 million jobs in 2004. Employment of full-time cashiers was expected to grow more slowly than the average for all occupations between 2004 and 2014. As more Americans buy products online, the need for cashiers will likely continue to diminish. Many retail operations, particularly grocery stores, are also installing self-service checkout systems that eliminate cashier jobs. Openings will occur as workers retire or leave their jobs. Opportunities for part-time work, however, remain good.

Working Conditions

Nearly 50 percent of cashiers work part time because restaurants and stores need more workers during rush hours than at other times. Full-time cashiers may work split shifts. Holiday, weekend, and night work may be required. Cashiers employed by large retail firms usually work a forty-hour week and are restricted from taking time off around the holidays as most stores are busiest at these times.

Cashiers need to have good finger dexterity and a knowledge of math. Many cashiers spend their working day standing in small, confined spaces that allow little physical movement. Cashier booths are often near doorways, which may subject cashiers to drafts and frequent temperature changes. Some cashiers work outdoors. Even when customers are impatient and demanding, cashiers must remain pleasant and courteous. Some cashiers belong to unions.

Earnings and Benefits

According to the Bureau of Labor Statistics, the median hourly income for cashiers in 2004 was $7.81. The top-paid 10 percent made more than $11.30 per hour. Benefits vary according to the employer. Large companies generally offer paid vacations and health insurance. Many stores offer their employees discounts on merchandise. Restaurants and cafeterias often provide free or discounted meals for their workers while they are at work. Some employers offer stock option and education reimbursement plans.

Where to Go for More Information

Hotel Employees and Restaurant Employees
International Union
275 Seventh Ave.
New York, NY 10001-6708
(212) 265-7000
http://www.unitehere.org/

National Retail Federation
325 Seventh St. NW, Ste. 1100
Washington, DC 20004
(800) 573-4692
http://www.nrf.com/

United Food and Commercial Workers
International Union
1775 K St. NW
Washington, DC 20006
(202) 223-3111
http://www.ufcw.org/

Comparison Shopper

Definition and Nature of the Work

Comparison shoppers work for retail department, specialty, and variety stores. They visit competitors' stores and Web sites to compare the prices, type, and quality of merchandise found there to the merchandise sold in their own store. Comparison shoppers make detailed written and oral reports to the management of their own store. The management then uses this information to set prices, merchandising procedures, and buying policies.

Comparison shoppers usually specialize in one particular type of merchandise such as furniture or children's clothing. When visiting competitors' stores, they act as customers, taking note of merchandise that seems to be selling well and examining sale items to see if they match advertising claims. Comparison shoppers write down the price, style, and identification numbers of the merchandise and may purchase new or unusual items so that closer study can be made of them. At times these shoppers return or complain about the merchandise sold at competitors' stores to test the effectiveness of their customer service departments.

Comparison shoppers also perform functions that do not involve shopping. They study merchandise displays and sales techniques in other stores and compare them with those of their own store. They frequently visit the sales floors and stockrooms of their own store to keep themselves up to date on merchandise stocked and sold. In addition, comparison shoppers are responsible for checking advertising copy for their store to make sure it is accurate and meets the legal requirements regarding descriptions of price reductions, fabric fiber content, and origin of merchandise.

Education and Training Requirements

Many employers hire high school graduates, but some employers give preference to applicants who have a college background. Workers generally receive on-the-job training. Students can prepare themselves for a career as a comparison shopper by taking courses in English, business, and marketing. In some cases sales workers are promoted to the position of comparison shopper, so taking a summer or part-time selling job may be helpful.

Successful comparison shoppers should be able to express themselves effectively in speech and writing. They also need to have good clerical abilities and a basic understanding of computers and the Internet. Most comparison shoppers are expected to be neat in appearance.

Getting the Job

Job openings for comparison shoppers are sometimes advertised in newspaper want ads and on career sites on the Internet. Interested individuals can apply directly to department and other retail

Comparison shoppers visit competitors' stores to compare the prices, type, and quality of products found there to the products sold in their own stores. (© Tom and Dee Ann McCarthy/Corbis.)

stores that employ comparison shoppers. School placement offices may be helpful in finding such a job.

Advancement Possibilities and Employment Outlook

Comparison shoppers can advance to other positions in retailing such as buyer, merchandising manager, or service manager. In many cases further education is required for advancement.

Because the field is attractive to many people, there are generally more applicants than job openings. Competition for jobs is expected to continue since the Internet has curtailed much of the need for comparison shoppers. Most medium and large retail operations list their prices and merchandise descriptions on the Web for managers and market researchers to see, eliminating the need to send someone out into the field to obtain the information.

Working Conditions

Comparison shoppers usually work forty hours a week. Although they generally have a desk in a pleasant office, they spend much of their time in the field. Comparison shoppers travel to competitors' stores on foot, by bus, by train, or by car and do a lot of standing and walking during the workday. They constantly reach for and handle objects and carry packages that may weigh up to twenty pounds.

Earnings and Benefits

Earnings for comparison shoppers vary greatly, depending on experience, location, and store size. According to Salary Expert.com, comparison shoppers made an average salary of $24,643 per year in 2006. Employers generally provide benefits such as paid holidays and vacations, health insurance, and retirement plans. Many stores also give their employees a discount on merchandise purchased at the store.

Where to Go for More Information

American Collegiate Retailing Association
Department of Consumer Affairs
Auburn University
308 Spidle Hall
Auburn, AL 36849
(334) 844-6458
http://www.acraretail.org/

American Marketing Association
311 S. Wacker Dr., Ste. 5800
Chicago, IL 60606
(800) 262-1150
http://www.marketingpower.com/

National Retail Federation
Liberty Place
325 Seventh St. NW, Ste. 1100
Washington, DC 20004-2608
(800) 673-4692
http://www.nrf.com/

Direct Sales Worker

Definition and Nature of the Work

Direct sales workers work for manufacturers of consumer goods. Through these sales workers, companies sell directly to consumers rather than to retail stores. At one time almost all direct sales workers went from door to door selling their goods. They arrived without phoning beforehand. Most of them worked throughout the day, calling on homemakers and selling everything from cleaning agents to household appliances and encyclopedias. Most of these sales workers were men. Now most direct sales workers are women.

Because most women and men of the twenty-first century work outside the home during the day, modern door-to-door sales workers do much of their work in the evenings and on weekends. They often call ahead to make appointments or have other people called canvassers make appointments for them. Door-to-

Education and Training
On-the-job training

Salary
Average—$12.92 per hour

Employment Outlook
Poor

Before visiting customers' homes to sell consumer goods, most direct sales workers call ahead to make appointments. (© Rob Lewine/Corbis.)

door sales workers are assigned areas by their companies; they are not permitted to work outside these areas.

Many companies are adopting the party-plan method of direct selling. These companies set up temporary booths in shopping malls, display some of their products, and try to persuade people to host parties for their sales workers. A host or hostess invites friends and acquaintances to an evening party that begins with a presentation by the direct sales worker. The sales worker then takes orders from the guests. The evening ends with refreshments and socializing. The host or hostess pays for the refreshments but receives free products (depending on the volume of sales during the evening) for throwing the party. Party-plan sales workers are not confined to one area. They may give presentations wherever they can find individuals to host parties for them. Crystal, china, flatware, cosmetics, and luggage are often sold this way.

Sales workers who engage in direct selling in the workplace are permanent employees of other companies who are permitted to sell products at work. They act as direct sales workers during the lunch hour and just before or after the regular working day, selling only to their colleagues. Employers often allow these sales workers to set up a small booth in the lunchroom or employee lounge where they can display new items, offer samples, and distribute catalogs and order forms. These sales workers rarely give demonstrations or presentations. The types of goods displayed are often personal care items, cosmetics, fragrances, or jewelry. The sales workers distribute order forms, which are completed and returned to their desks with the necessary payments. Items usually arrive in a truck that makes a scheduled delivery once each week.

Direct sales workers must be friendly, eager to give good service, and able to explain the advantages of their products to potential customers. Some must give demonstrations; cosmetics sales workers, for instance, often show customers how to apply makeup. Direct sales workers work alone and need plenty of initiative, good organizational skills, and proficiency in handling cash, checks, and credit card payments.

Education and Training Requirements

Most employers prefer to hire applicants with a high school education. A neat appearance, a pleasant and enthusiastic personality, and a willingness to work hard are the most important requirements for the position. Direct sales workers must have neat handwriting and be able to speak clearly. Self-confidence and poise are assets in direct sales jobs.

Most companies give their sales workers some initial training. During this period the sales workers become familiar with the products and learn selling techniques. Many companies send beginners out with an experienced worker at first. Party-plan sales workers typically watch their managers run several parties before going out on their own. Managers may attend their sales workers' first parties and then offer feedback and advice on sales techniques.

Getting the Job

To find jobs in direct sales candidates should choose a product that really interests them and then approach the manufacturer either by phone or via the Internet. Interested individuals can also obtain the names and addresses of many direct sales companies from the Direct Selling Association. Some direct sales jobs are listed in newspaper want ads and with career sites on the Internet.

Advancement Possibilities and Employment Outlook

Depending on the product there are plenty of opportunities to earn a substantial first or second income through direct selling. Those who are successful can enlist others to work for them. They can become field representatives or managers in their direct selling companies or move into positions in retailing, merchandising, or marketing. A college degree is helpful, but not essential to become an executive. Very successful demonstrators may go into business for themselves or work for cable television marketing programs.

According to the Bureau of Labor Statistics, door-to-door salespeople and other direct sales workers held 239,000 jobs in 2004. Employment of direct sales workers was expected to decline between 2004 and 2014. The Internet and at-home shopping channels now allow manufacturers to reach potential buyers directly. As a result the need for direct salespeople is dwindling. Jobs are still available, however, as there is a high turnover rate in this field.

Working Conditions

Direct sales workers are not closely supervised. They work on their own under contract to a company. Those who sell to individual families usually have to work long hours in the evenings and on weekends. In rural areas where houses are spread far apart, direct sales workers may have to drive long distances. Only the self-motivated are successful.

Earnings and Benefits

Nearly all direct sales workers work under contract and are paid on a straight commission basis. The size of the commission varies with the amount and type of items sold. The commission on necessary items is much lower than that on luxury items. Commissions commonly range from 10 to 40 percent but are often higher on expensive items. According to a Bureau of Labor Statistics survey, door-to-door salespeople and other direct sales workers earned an average hourly wage of $12.92 in 2004. Full-time direct sales workers must supply their own benefits such as health insurance.

Where to Go for More Information

Direct Selling Association
1667 K St. NW, Ste. 1100
Washington, DC 20006
(202) 347-8866
http://www.dsa.org/

Receiving, Shipping, and Traffic Clerk

Definition and Nature of the Work

Receiving, shipping, and traffic clerks help keep the flow of merchandise moving from one company to another. They pack and unpack merchandise and perform clerical tasks. They also keep records of incoming and outgoing merchandise. Receiving, shipping, and traffic clerks work for manufacturers that receive products from suppliers and ship finished goods to customers. They also work for wholesale and retail distributors. In some large firms the jobs of shipping clerk, receiving clerk, and traffic clerk are distinct and performed by different people. In many smaller firms, however, all three jobs are performed by the same person.

Shipping clerks are in charge of all items that are shipped from the company. They carefully check the merchandise that is taken from the stockroom against each customer's order to see that it is filled correctly. If some items are not available, they notify the customer. They may be responsible for sending the goods at a later date. After the order has been checked, the merchandise is specially packed for shipping. All shipments must be weighed and the cost of postal or freight rates recorded. Shipping clerks prepare mailing labels, shipping documents, and invoices. When the merchandise is ready for shipment, shipping clerks move it to loading docks—sometimes with the help of a forklift. They may direct other workers to load the shipment on trucks for delivery to customers.

Receiving clerks work at the other end of this process, but their tasks are very similar to those of shipping clerks. They receive and check the goods that are sent to their firm, comparing the original order form, bill, or invoice with the merchandise to see that the order has been filled correctly. If a shipment has been lost or damaged in transit, they notify the transportation firm to make the necessary adjustment for this loss. Receiving clerks are usually responsible for moving the shipment to the stockroom, warehouse, or appropriate department. Like shipping clerks, receiving clerks keep careful records that company offi-

Shipping clerks handle all items that are shipped from a company. Receiving clerks handle all incoming shipments. *(Photograph by Kelly A. Quin. Thomson Gale. Reproduced by permission.)*

cials use to determine the profit and loss of their firms. Much of the information needed for these records is on bar codes attached to the products or packages. The clerks read these codes with handheld scanners, and the information in the scanners is fed into a computer to update the company's computerized inventory-control systems.

Traffic clerks maintain shipping records. They track and record the destination, weight, and charges on incoming and outgoing freight. They verify any rate changes by comparing what is being shipped to prices on rate charts or computer databases. In addition, they may keep a record of claims for damaged goods or for overcharges on shipping.

Education and Training Requirements

Most employers prefer applicants who have a high school education. Some employers also require good typing ability and a basic knowledge of computers. Shipping and receiving clerks may need physical strength to handle heavy or bulky packages. Traffic clerks must be good at basic math. Clerks are trained on the job. At first they may do routine tasks under the guidance of a supervisor. These tasks may include studying the tracking software, labeling packages, learning postal and freight rates, and practicing safe procedures for packing or unpacking merchandise. With the growing use of computers, the jobs of traffic, shipping, and receiving clerks have become machine oriented.

Getting the Job

Students interested in becoming receiving, shipping, or traffic clerks should visit their school placement office. They should check newspaper want ads and career sites on the Internet as well. Prospective clerks can also apply directly to companies for which they would like to work. Private or state employment offices may be helpful.

Advancement Possibilities and Employment Outlook

With training and experience, receiving, shipping, and traffic clerks may be given a range of duties and responsibilities. Some become heads of their department. However, higher-level jobs such as purchasing agent require further education.

According to the U.S. Bureau of Labor Statistics, 751,000 people were employed as receiving, shipping, and traffic clerks in 2004. Employment of receiving, shipping, and traffic clerks was expected to increase slower than the average for all occupations between 2004 and 2014. Openings are likely to occur as experienced workers retire or leave their jobs, but some jobs will be eliminated as automated package-handling equipment and computerized record-keeping systems come into use. New jobs may be created if the amount of merchandise shipped from the United States increases.

Working Conditions

Receiving, shipping, and traffic clerks do physically strenuous work, some of which may be done outdoors on loading platforms. Sometimes their work is done in large, often drafty and cold warehouses. Receiving, shipping, and traffic clerks have a forty-hour workweek. Overtime is often required when shipments are late and materials are required for production lines. Overtime may mean working nights, weekends, or holidays. Many receiving, shipping, and traffic clerks belong to labor unions.

Earnings and Benefits

Clerks' wages vary with experience and employer. Receiving, shipping, and traffic clerks earned a median annual wage of $24,400 in 2004, according to the Bureau of Labor Statistics. The highest-paid 10 percent made in excess of $37,610. Benefits often include paid sick leave, health insurance, and retirement plans.

Rental Clerk

Education and Training
High school diploma preferred; on-the-job and classroom training

Salary
Median—$8.79 per hour

Employment Outlook
Very good

Definition and Nature of the Work

When an individual or business needs an item but does not want to buy it, rental and leasing businesses offer an excellent and increasingly popular alternative. Rental clerks help customers get what they need through rental and leasing businesses. Rental clerks man the front desk and answer customers' questions about product availability, specifications, and cost. They also take customer orders, retrieve merchandise for customers, ring up orders on cash registers, and accept payment. In addition, they may be required to restock returned merchandise and keep an inventory of the items available for rent.

Rental and leasing businesses rent or lease a huge range of items, including skis, cars, computers, furniture, musical instruments, tools, DVDs, medical equipment, construction machinery, and party supplies. Rental clerks may be required to perform duties specific to a particular rental or leasing operation. For instance, rental clerks at ski rental shops may sharpen and wax skis for customers and help them try on ski boots. Rental clerks working at car leasing establishments may spend a good part of their day picking up people who need rental cars. Rental clerks at movie rental stores may give recommendations to customers on which movies to rent.

Education and Training Requirements

No formal education is required for rental clerks, but companies prefer to hire people with a high school diploma. Rental clerk workers usually receive on-the-job and classroom training in the operation of the business's equipment, as well as on the company's policies, procedures, and sales techniques, including how to deal with irate customers or late returns.

Some leasing and rental businesses may require that rental clerks know something of the product they rent out. This is particularly true with businesses that lease complex equipment such as farm machinery or medical supplies. Prior sales or business experience is also an asset when applying for a job as a rental clerk. In addition, rental clerks should enjoy working with people.

Getting the Job

Newspaper want ads and Internet job sites generally list jobs for rental clerks. Anyone interested in becoming a rental clerk can also apply directly to any business that rents or leases equipment or services.

Advancement Possibilities and Employment Outlook

Rental clerks learn a great deal about a company and its business practices, which puts them in a good position to become store managers or managers of rental and leasing departments. With further education, rental clerks working for large companies may eventually be promoted to regional supervisor, operations manager, or corporate executive.

According to the U.S. Bureau of Labor Statistics, 451,000 people held jobs as rental clerks in 2004. Employment of rental clerks was expected to increase faster than the average for all occupations between 2004 and 2014. Many companies are employing more clerks in an effort to improve customer service.

Employment for rental clerks is largely dependent on the economy. When financial conditions are good, both individuals and companies may be more inclined to buy items than to rent or lease them; however, some people stick with renting and leasing regardless of economic trends. For example, as advances continue to be made in the fields of computer technology and machinery, some consumers may decide to rent or lease such items rather than risk making a costly purchase of something that could soon be inadequate or obsolete.

Working Conditions

Roughly 50 percent of all rental clerks work part time. Evening and weekend work is likely to be required. Some firms may conduct business strictly during conventional hours.

Working conditions vary depending on the type of merchandise being rented. Most rental and leasing businesses are clean, well lit, and well ventilated. Clerks are typically on their feet most of the time and are often required to lift or carry heavy items.

Earnings and Benefits

Earnings of rental clerks in 2004 varied largely depending on the type of equipment rented or leased. Clerks working for automobile dealers earned $17.87 per hour, whereas clerks working for consumer goods rental establishments such as video rental stores made $7.78 per hour. The median salary of all types of rental clerks in 2004 was $8.79 per hour, according to the Bureau of Labor Statistics. Clerks working for large- or medium-sized companies often receive benefits such as paid holidays and vacations, medical insurance, and retirement plans.

Where to Go for More Information

American Rental Association
1900 Nineteenth St.
Moline, IL 61265
(800) 334-2177
http://www.ararental.org/

Equipment Leasing Association of America
4301 N. Fairfax Dr., Ste. 550
Arlington, VA 22203-1627
(703) 527-8655
http://www.elaonline.com/

Retail Store Sales Worker

Education and Training
On-the-job training

Salary
Median—$8.98 per hour

Employment Outlook
Good

Definition and Nature of the Work

Retail store sales workers sell merchandise to store customers. They work in a variety of settings, including department stores, drugstores, discount stores, and shops that specialize in everything from books and gourmet foods to plants, electronic equipment, or other merchandise.

Salespersons' duties vary from store to store. In some stores salespersons may act mainly as cashiers. When customers make purchases, salespersons typically scan merchandise price tags, total the order, accept payment, make change, wrap purchases, and issue receipts. They may also handle exchanged or returned merchandise, do stock work, unload merchandise, fold clothes, and arrange displays. Sometimes sales workers put price tags on new merchandise or mark down prices on sale items.

In other stores sales workers concentrate on selling merchandise to customers. This is particularly true of clothing stores. Customers who do not know exactly what they want tend to look to retail salespeople for help in making purchasing decisions. Sometimes salespersons demonstrate merchandise, explaining its features and uses. In department or discount stores sales workers usually work in just one department and become experts on the merchandise sold there. In small stores, however, workers need to be familiar with all items offered for sale.

Sales workers in specialty stores may need specialized knowledge. For example, furniture store salespeople need knowledge of interior design. Sales workers employed in an electronics shop need to know the equipment and features available in various price ranges.

Education and Training Requirements

Employers generally prefer to hire high school graduates for full-time sales positions. Some stores hire students for part-time, seasonal, or summer jobs. New workers are usually trained on the job. For jobs in specialty stores employers

A cashier gives change to a customer. Sales workers' duties vary, depending on the store. (*Photograph by Kelly A. Quin. Thomson Gale. Reproduced by permission.*)

sometimes prefer applicants with previous sales experience or specific knowledge of the merchandise. The owner of a plant store, for example, may want to hire an experienced gardener or a person who has taken courses in plant science.

Since many people judge a store by its salespeople, workers in retail sales must be neat, friendly, and eager to help customers. Sales workers must also be able to maintain their composure when dealing with irate customers.

Getting the Job

People interested in working as retail sales workers can apply directly to the stores for which they would like to work. Private and state employment offices may help candidates get jobs. Newspaper want ads and career sites on the Internet often list openings in retail sales.

Advancement Possibilities and Employment Outlook

Some retail store sales workers become department or store managers. Those who work for chain stores may be promoted to administrative jobs in the company's headquarters. Some use their sales experience to find sales jobs in other areas.

According to the Bureau of Labor Statistics, 4.3 million people were employed as retail store sales workers in 2004. Employment of retail salespeople was expected to increase as fast as the average for all occupations between 2004 and 2014. Most openings will occur as experienced workers transfer to other occupations or leave their jobs for other reasons. New jobs will be created as retail sales continue to expand because of the growing population.

Working Conditions

Working conditions in the retail industry vary depending on the store. Most sales workers stand all or most of the day. For some the work may be repetitious, and most stores are hectic during rush hours and holiday seasons.

Retail store sales workers may work full or part time. Full-time workers put in forty hours or more each week. They generally work evenings, weekends, and even some holidays. Stores generally hire part-time workers for the busy periods of the day or during the weeks before big holidays when buying increases. Many workers belong to labor unions.

Earnings and Benefits

Earnings for retail store sales workers vary widely with location, individual experience, and the responsibilities of the job. In 2004 new retail workers started at minimum wage. That same year, according to the Bureau of Labor Statistics, the median hourly income for all retail workers was $8.98. The top-paid 10 percent of workers in this field made more than $17.85 per hour, either on straight salary, commission, or both. A commission is a percentage of the selling price of an item. The earnings of workers paid on commission depend on their volume of sales.

Many stores offer benefits such as paid vacations and holidays and health insurance to full-time workers. Stores usually offer discounts to all workers on merchandise purchased from the store.

Where to Go for More Information

National Retail Federation
325 Seventh St. NW, Ste. 1100
Washington, DC 20004
(800) 673-4692
http://www.nrf.com/

United Food and Commercial Workers
    International Union
1775 K St. NW
Washington, DC 20006
(202) 223-3111
http://www.ufcw.org/

Retail Store Sales Worker Supervisor

Education and Training
High school diploma preferred; sales experience and on-the-job training

Salary
Median—$32,720 per year

Employment Outlook
Fair

Definition and Nature of the Work

Retail store sales worker supervisors manage salespeople, cashiers, stock clerks, and other entry-level employees who work in retail establishments. Sales worker supervisors are employed by general and discount department stores and by specialty stores such as furniture, book, and music stores. In smaller establishments sales worker supervisors may manage the entire sales floor during their shift. In large department stores supervisors generally manage a single department such as shoes or housewares. Sales supervisors typically report to store managers.

Beyond ensuring that employees are doing their jobs, sales worker supervisors hire, fire, and train employees. They also handle customer complaints and questions. Sometimes retail supervisors are entrusted with bookkeeping and purchasing responsibilities. In big department stores they may be responsible for organizing the merchandise on store shelves, reviewing the inventory to make sure everything is in stock, and establishing the sales goals for their departments. Sales worker supervisors in specialty stores may need specialized knowledge. For instance, a supervisor employed in a kitchen supply store should know a good deal about cooking.

Education and Training Requirements

Retail store sales worker supervisors are generally promoted from sales or cashier positions. Employers prefer to hire high school graduates for supervisory positions. New supervisors are often trained on the job. For jobs in specialty stores employers may prefer to hire supervisors with extensive knowledge of the merchandise.

Since many people judge a retail operation by its appearance and its salespeople, sales supervisors must ensure that their store is kept clean and that their employees are neat, well-groomed, and competent. Sales supervisors must also be able to maintain their composure and hold their ground when dealing with irate or unreasonable customers.

Getting the Job

People interested in employment as retail store sales worker supervisors can apply directly to the stores for which they would like to work. Private and state employment offices may offer help in a job search. Newspaper want ads and career sites on the Internet often list openings for retail sales supervisors. Given the high turnover rate in the retail industry, sales employees can sometimes be promoted to supervisor within a year.

Advancement Possibilities and Employment Outlook

Some retail store supervisors become store managers. Those who work for chain stores may be promoted to administrative jobs in the company's headquarters.

According to the U.S. Bureau of Labor Statistics, 946,000 people were employed as retail store sales worker supervisors in 2004. Employment of sales supervisors was expected to increase slower than the average for all occupations between 2004 and 2014. As retail operations expand, companies will likely give existing supervisors more responsibility instead of hiring new supervisors. Most openings will occur as experienced workers transfer to other occupations or leave their jobs.

Working Conditions

Working conditions vary depending on the store. Some retail store sales worker supervisors stand all or most of the day and others sit at a desk for a good part of their shift. The work may be repetitious, and many stores get hectic during rush hours.

Retail store sales worker supervisors usually put in forty hours or more each week, including evenings, weekends, and even some holidays. Supervisors may be especially harried in the weeks leading up to major holidays because they are usually in charge of hiring part-time employees for the season and must deal with a large influx of customers.

Earnings and Benefits

Earnings for retail store sales worker supervisors vary widely with location, individual experience, and the responsibilities of the job. The median annual wage for sales worker supervisors in 2004 was $32,720. The top-paid 10 percent made more than $58,400.

Many stores offer benefits such as paid vacations, paid holidays, and health insurance to full-time workers. Employers usually offer discounts to their workers on merchandise purchased from the store.

Where to Go for More Information

National Retail Federation
325 Seventh St. NW, Ste. 1100
Washington, DC 20004
(800) 673-4692
http://www.nrf.com/

United Food and Commercial Workers
International Union
1775 K St. NW
Washington, DC 20006
(202) 223-3111
http://www.ufcw.org/

Sales Demonstrator and Product Promoter

Definition and Nature of the Work

Sales demonstrators show merchandise to customers in order to interest them in buying a product or a line of products. Product promoters try to persuade retail stores to sell products and market them in a specific way. Both demonstrators and product promoters work for the manufacturers of cosmetics, food, home care products, and household appliances. Many are employed on a temporary basis for a specific period of time.

Most demonstrators work in department stores, in supermarkets, and at conventions and exhibits. Some travel to homes. Others demonstrate products on television during "infomercials" or on home shopping programs. Product promoters, on the other hand, usually travel between retail operations spread out over a designated region. Demonstrators and product promoters who work for the manufacturers of industrial hardware and machinery demonstrate their products at conventions, trade shows, and county fairs.

Demonstrators and product promoters usually have a prepared speech that they deliver as they demonstrate the product, but their activities vary according to the type of merchandise they sell. For example, many demonstrators work in supermarkets introducing new food products. Some of these demonstrators hand out free samples while telling customers about the product; others actually cook the food in front of the customers. All demonstrators must be prepared to answer customers' questions about the featured merchandise.

Product promoters often bring promotional materials with them on their sales stops and pass them on to business owners. A liquor promoter, for instance, may

Education and Training
High school and on-the-job training

Salary
Median—$9.95 per hour

Employment Outlook
Good

Some sales demonstrators and product promoters work at conventions and exhibits. They tell visitors about a company and may hand out free samples of its products. (© Martha Tabor/Working Images Photographs. Reproduced by permission.)

give a bar owner a neon sign or ashtrays showing the product logo. A soft drink promoter may provide a grocery store with banners, signs, or standing cardboard displays that prominently show off the drink in the middle of the store.

Both demonstrators and product promoters make reports about reactions to their employers' products and then present these reports to their managers. They may also participate in the design of an exhibit or presentation.

Education and Training Requirements

Demonstrators and product promoters are trained on the job, either by working with an experienced employee or through a formal company training program that includes classroom instruction. Employers usually require applicants to have a high school education. Demonstrators and product promoters of specialized items such as teaching aids and scientific apparatus may need course work at the college level in that specialty. Employers may also prefer to hire those who have previous experience in sales.

Getting the Job

A person interested in product demonstration or promotion can get a start in the field by registering with a temporary help or modeling agency; both types of agencies place workers in temporary demonstrator and product promotion jobs requiring little or no special training. Jobs in this field are advertised in newspapers want ads and on Internet job sites as well. Interested individuals should also contact manufacturing companies that employ and train their own demonstrators and product promoters.

Advancement Possibilities and Employment Outlook

More than half of all demonstrators and product promoters work part time. Demonstrators and product promoters who work on a part-time or temporary basis usually advance as they gain experience by receiving more complicated assignments that offer higher wages. Those who work full time, especially those with a college degree, can advance to executive positions in sales, advertising, or public relations.

According to the U.S. Bureau of Labor Statistics, 120,000 people held jobs as demonstrators and product promoters in 2004. Employment of demonstrators and product promoters was expected to increase as fast as the average for all occupations between 2004 and 2014. Employment opportunities in this field grow with an increasing number of trade shows and in-store promotions at malls and department stores. In fact, the supply services industry is one of the fastest growing industries in the nation. Additional openings will arise from a need to replace workers who leave the field.

Working Conditions

Demonstrators are on their feet most of the working day, and product promoters spend a great deal of time in the car driving from one retail operation to the next. Working hours vary from a few hours a week for part-time workers to more than fifty hours a week for those demonstrating technical products on a full-time basis. Demonstrators and product promoters often work evenings and weekends.

Successful demonstrators and product promoters have pleasant, enthusiastic personalities and get along well with people. They have the patience needed to repeat the same speech and answer the same questions many times. They are also effective speakers. Some demonstrators and product promoters belong to labor unions.

Earnings and Benefits

Earnings for demonstrators and product promoters vary greatly. The median salary was $9.95 per hour in 2004, according to the Bureau of Labor Statistics.

Full-time store demonstrators earn salaries comparable to those of full-time sales workers. They can also earn commissions, or percentages of sales, based on their individual skills and experience. Demonstrators and product promoters with college and advanced degrees may earn more. Employers often pay for job-related travel expenses.

Where to Go for More Information

Direct Selling Association
1667 K St. NW, Ste. 1100
Washington, DC 20006
(202) 452-8866
http://www.dsa.org/

Trade Show Exhibitors Association
2301 S. Lake Shore Dr., Ste. 1005
Chicago, IL 60616
(312) 842-8732
http://www.tsea.org/

Stock Clerk

Definition and Nature of the Work

Stock clerks typically work in stores, warehouses, and factories, where they control the flow of supplies in and out of stockrooms. They receive and store merchandise or equipment that is retained for future use and issue these items from the stockroom when they are needed. In addition, they keep track of the number of items in storage and reorder items that are in short supply. The main goal of a stock clerk is to prevent production slowdowns or sales losses by making sure there are adequate supplies of merchandise or equipment on hand.

When stock clerks receive deliveries, they unpack the boxes, inspect the items, and return unsatisfactory or damaged goods to the wholesaler or distributor. Acceptable merchandise is then arranged on shelves and racks, in bins, or on the floor of the stockroom. Stock clerks are also responsible for marking goods with

Education and Training
On-the-job training

Salary
Median—$9.66 per hour

Employment Outlook
Poor

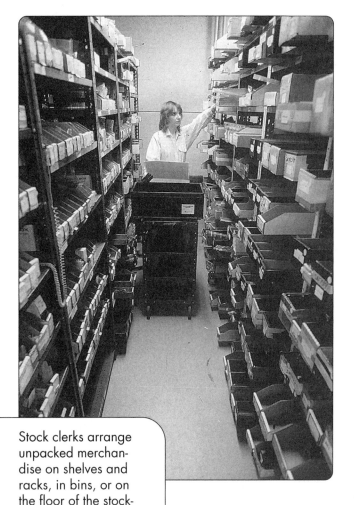

Stock clerks arrange unpacked merchandise on shelves and racks, in bins, or on the floor of the stockroom so it can be easily retrieved when they receive requests or orders for items. (© Terry Wild Studio. Reproduced by permission.)

the proper identifying codes and prices so that supplies can be retrieved easily. When stock clerks receive requests or orders for items from the stockroom, they send the appropriate merchandise to the right department. In large stockrooms, automated material-handling equipment is used to help store and retrieve goods.

Stockroom clerks typically use handheld scanners and computers to keep track of the items. When an item enters or leaves the stockroom they scan a bar code affixed to the item. The scanner then feeds the information into a computer, which keeps records of the merchandise in the stockroom. Periodically stock clerks may use the scanner to go over all the merchandise in the stockroom or on the sales floor to see if the computer's inventory records are correct. When inventory is down, they reorder items in short supply. In some stockrooms, however, computers automatically order items. Stock clerks who work with food, drugs, or other perishable items are responsible for maintaining the proper temperature and humidity in the stockroom. They also may date the goods and rotate them so they do not spoil.

In large companies several different employees handle the work that is done by one stock clerk in a smaller firm. For instance, shipping and receiving clerks may examine shipments, return damaged goods, and report quality and quantity problems to a supervisor. The records kept by stock clerks may be used by stock control workers to compile reports that establish or recommend stock level or replenishment needs. Inventory clerks may keep track of supplies on hand and order additional supplies as needed. Markers may label the goods with codes. Order fillers may pull items from the stockroom at the request of various people or departments in a company, and messengers may be employed to deliver orders to those people or departments. In large factories procurement clerks handle the purchasing of new equipment.

Education and Training Requirements

There are no specific educational requirements to become a stock clerk, but interested individuals should have basic reading, writing, and mathematical skills. Familiarity with computers is desirable as well. Employers often look for applicants with typing or data-entry skills and filing abilities because recordkeeping is an important part of the stock clerk's job. Candidates can be trained on the job in one to three months, beginning with basic tasks such as unpacking and counting merchandise and advancing to taking inventory and keeping records. As more automated and computerized equipment is used, training and retraining may take longer.

Getting the Job

Internet job sites and newspapers often carry want ads for stock clerks. Those interested can also apply directly to factories, wholesale and retail businesses, mail order houses, government agencies, hospitals, and other places that process a large volume of merchandise. Private or state employment offices may list job openings as well.

Advancement Possibilities and Employment Outlook

Stock clerks can advance in a variety of ways. Those who work for large businesses can become invoice clerks, stock control clerks, procurement clerks, or stockroom supervisors. In many cases further education is required for supervisory positions, as well as for positions as buyers and purchasing agents.

According to the U.S. Bureau of Labor Statistics, 1.6 million people were employed as stock clerks in 2004. Employment of stock clerks was expected to decline between 2004 and 2014. The increased use of computers and other automated equipment in stockrooms will limit job growth, but some openings will occur each year to replace workers who leave the field. The greatest number of openings will likely be in grocery stores and department stores due to the high number of items that these establishments sell.

Working Conditions

Many stockrooms are well lighted, heated, and clean; others may be uncomfortably damp, drafty, and dim. Stock clerks usually work forty hours a week, with possible overtime during holiday seasons or when inventory is taken. These workers do a great deal of standing and walking during the working day. They bend, stoop, and climb, sometimes while lifting and carrying stock weighing as much as one hundred pounds. Stock workers risk injury when climbing ladders and lifting heavy objects. Many stock clerks are union members.

Earnings and Benefits

Beginning stock clerks frequently start out at the minimum wage and advance from there. Stock clerks earned a median hourly wage of $9.66 in 2004, according to the Bureau of Labor Statistics. Full-time workers usually receive benefits that include paid vacations and holidays, health insurance, and retirement plans.

Where to Go for More Information

International Brotherhood of Teamsters
25 Louisiana Ave. NW
Washington, DC 20001
(202) 624-6800
http://www.teamster.org/

United Food and Commercial Workers
    International Union
1775 K St. NW
Washington, DC 20006
(202) 223-3111
http://www.ufcw.org/

Supermarket Worker

Definition and Nature of the Work

Supermarkets employ workers in a variety of jobs. Many supermarkets are part of chain operations that include branch stores, several warehouses, and a central location for their business office. The business offices of supermarket chains employ workers such as accountants, bookkeepers, clerks, typists, and secretaries. Other supermarket workers hold jobs in warehouses or work as truckers. This job description focuses on those who work in the branch stores of chain supermarkets and in independent food stores.

Stock clerks receive and store merchandise and keep the shelves on the sales floor filled with goods. They typically use scanners to take merchandise counts so that they can reorder items that are in short supply. When stock clerks are not busy with these tasks, they perform general cleaning duties such as mopping and sweeping. They also may perform courtesy tasks that include locating specific items for customers and bagging groceries.

Education and Training
On-the-job training
minimum

Salary
Median—varies by
position from $7.90 per
hour to $15.08 per hour

Employment Outlook
Fair

Supermarket workers have a variety of jobs. Checkers use cash registers or scanners to total up customers' purchases. (© Chuck Savage/Corbis.)

Produce clerks must keep fruits and vegetables in fresh condition. They date produce when it arrives and see that goods are sold in the order in which they are received. They also maintain the correct temperature and humidity in the stockroom. In some stores produce clerks wrap merchandise before putting it in display cases. On the sales floor produce clerks keep unwrapped fruits and vegetables wet so that they stay fresh. They may use sprinkling cans or hoses to wash produce. Most large grocery stores, however, have installed automatic sprinkler systems. When fruits and vegetables are no longer in satisfactory condition, produce clerks must remove and replace them.

Some workers are also employed as bakery and delicatessen clerks. They bake, ice, slice, weigh, or package prepared foods for customers. They are also responsible for keeping their work areas clean and safe.

The meat department employs butchers and meat wrappers to prepare meat for sale. Butchers take the large pieces of meat purchased by the supermarket and saw or cut them into small portions such as steaks and chops. The prepared meat is then packaged by meat wrappers, who use special machines to wrap, weigh, and label the meats.

On the sales floor, checkers operate scanners or cash registers to add up customer purchases. As customers' merchandise moves across the checkout counter on a conveyor belt, checkers scan the price of each item or, in the case of produce or large items, enter the proper amount into the cash register manually. They accept payment, make change, and cash checks; if the store does not employ baggers, the checker bags the merchandise as well. Checkers must also keep their counters clean and restock items sold at the checkout counter. Heavy cleaning tasks such as scrubbing and waxing floors and washing windows are typically handled by outside cleaning crews.

About one-fourth of all supermarket workers are store or department managers. They supervise workers and make sure operations run smoothly. They also deal with customer complaints and requests.

Education and Training Requirements

Requirements vary depending on the job. Cashiers, stock clerks, and other clerks receive their training on the job. Many stores hire high school students to work these jobs on a part-time basis. Applicants for the job of butcher should have a high school diploma and specialized training in the use of power tools. To become the manager of a store, candidates usually need a college education with emphasis on courses in business and marketing.

Getting the Job

Prospective supermarket workers should apply directly to the stores for which they would like to work. Many stores post want ads on their doors or in windows when openings occur. The want ads in newspapers and career sites on the Internet also list jobs for supermarket workers.

Advancement Possibilities and Employment Outlook

Clerks may become checkers or department managers. With further education they may become assistant managers or store managers. In larger stores employees with promise may be assigned to many different jobs in preparation for an entry-level management position.

According to the U.S. Bureau of Labor Statistics, 2.4 million people were employed by grocery stores and supermarkets in 2004. Employment of grocery store workers was expected to increase slower than the average for all occupations between 2004 and 2014. Widespread use of computerized inventory and checkout systems may result in a decrease in the number of some jobs; however, because of the high turnover rate in this field, some openings will always occur.

Working Conditions

Many supermarket workers are employed part time. Full-time workers usually put in a thirty-five- to forty-hour week. Many full-time workers are assigned to split shifts to accommodate rush hours. An increasing number of supermarkets are open twenty-four hours a day, but they usually employ only a few workers for late night and early morning hours.

Most supermarket workers have to stand and walk during most of their working day. Some, such as stock clerks and baggers, lift and carry objects weighing up to eighty pounds. Butchers also lift heavy objects and are subject to cuts from knife and saw blades. In addition, they spend many hours at a time in refrigerated rooms.

Employees who deal with customers are expected to remain pleasant and courteous at all times. Because they work with food, they must be clean and neat. Many supermarkets supply uniforms for their workers. Many supermarket employees belong to labor unions.

Earnings and Benefits

Earnings vary with an individual's level of responsibility and experience. In general grocery store workers earned less in their jobs in 2004 than workers in comparable jobs in other industries. According to the Bureau of Labor Statistics, supermarket cashiers earned a median income of $7.90 per hour in 2004; managers made nearly double that amount. Full-time supermarket workers usually receive benefits that include paid holidays, sick leave, and vacations, health insurance, and retirement plans.

Where to Go for More Information

National Grocers Association
1005 N. Glebe Rd., Ste. 250
Arlington, VA 22201-5758
(703) 516-0700
http://www.nationalgrocers.org/

United Food and Commercial Workers
   International Union
1775 K St. NW
Washington, DC 20006
(202) 223-3111
http://www.ufcw.org/

Telemarketer

Education and Training
On-the-job training

Salary
Average—$23,520 per year

Employment Outlook
Poor

Definition and Nature of the Work

Telemarketers are sales and marketing representatives who do business strictly by telephone. A wide variety of products and services from office supplies to savings accounts to resort memberships are sold through telemarketing. Some specialists sell directly, while others gather information that will help identify potential customers or determine the success of new products.

Many telemarketers are required to call people from a long list of names. Once telemarketers engage a potential customer on the phone, they must read a scripted sales pitch to the customer in an attempt to sell him or her a product. In some instances telemarketers make up their own sales script but more often than not the script is provided to them by their employers. Telemarketers may also be responsible for generating their own list of names from telephone directories and lists purchased by their company.

The duties of telemarketers may include confirming orders placed with field representatives and conducting marketing surveys to find sales prospects. In some cases telemarketing is only one part of a company's overall sales operation, and the telephone specialists work as a team with direct-mail or field experts. In these instances telemarketers typically target people who have already purchased merchandise from the company.

Education and Training Requirements

Telemarketing requires no particular educational credentials and training is generally provided on the job. Specialists in the field come from a variety of backgrounds. The most successful workers have good telephone personalities and strong sales skills.

Telemarketers sell products or services to customers over the telephone. (© Tom and Dee Ann McCarthy/Corbis.)

Getting the Job

Jobs for telemarketers are likely to be advertised on career sites on the Internet and in newspapers. Anyone interested in telemarketing can usually find job openings under headings such as "Telephone Sales," "Marketing Research," or "Marketing Services."

Advancement Possibilities and Employment Outlook

Telemarketers may become supervisors or sales managers. Specialists also may become telemarketing directors for large companies.

According to the U.S. Bureau of Labor Statistics, 415,000 people held jobs as telemarketers in 2004. Employment of telemarketers was expected to decline between 2004 and 2014. Since the early 1990s the federal government and many state governments have set forth laws and regulations placing restrictions on the telemarketing industry. The most damaging of these laws and regulations was the creation of the National Do-Not-Call Registry. U.S. consumers with no interest in receiving telemarketing calls from for-profit companies could list their number on this national registry. If telemarketers called any numbers on the registry, they faced stiff fines.

People who wish to become telemarketers should choose their employers carefully because some short-lived telemarketing firms operate illegally, failing to deliver the promised goods and then closing or relocating abruptly. The best opportunities for a long-term career are with a company that has been in business for some time and has a reputation for honesty.

Working Conditions

Telemarketers generally work in groups, usually in a special telephone room. They may work days or evenings, and the job may be sedentary if it is confined to telephone calling. Telemarketers are under pressure to meet sales quotas and face repeated and often nasty rejections from the prospective customers they call.

Earnings and Benefits

Some telemarketers are salaried whereas others work partly or totally on a commission basis. According to a Bureau of Labor Statistics survey, telemarketers earned an average income of $23,520 per year in 2004. Skilled sales representatives who receive commissions may earn much more. Bonuses are sometimes awarded for exceeding quotas.

> **Where to Go for More Information**
>
> American Marketing Association
> 311 S. Wacker Dr., Ste. 5800
> Chicago, IL 60606
> (800) 262-1150
> http://www.marketingpower.com/

Vending Machine Servicer and Repairer

Education and Training
On-the-job training

Salary
Median—$26,333 per year

Employment Outlook
Fair

Definition and Nature of the Work

Vending machine servicers, also known as vending machine route workers, are the people who stock and service vending machines. There are millions of vending machines in the United States today that dispense everything from candy bars and hot soup to pencils and toiletries. Although vending machine servicers are employed by vending companies, they work alone and at their own pace. Workers travel their own routes and are in charge of all the machines on that route. Servicers install the machines, collect the money from them, and replace the items that have been bought. They also keep records of the money they collect and the merchandise that is sold from the machines.

Vending machine servicers usually transport their goods by truck or van, so they must be good drivers. They are responsible for delivering merchandise safely. Servicers may also make simple adjustments to the machines to keep them running smoothly. Broken machines are removed and taken to a repair shop. Workers who do these complex repairs are called vending machine repairers.

Servicers and repairers may be their company's only representative in the field. They must be prepared to deal with customer requests and complaints. Servicers may have to determine whether the machines are profitable. If a servicer notices that a machine is not used very much, he or she may suggest that it be removed or replaced with a machine that offers a product in greater demand by customers.

Vending machine servicers and repairers work alone and at their own pace, installing vending machines, collecting the money from them, and replacing items that have been bought. (© Martha Tabor/Working Images Photographs. Reproduced by permission.)

Education and Training Requirements

Employers prefer applicants who have a high school education. Applicants must have a driver's license to be a servicer, and most employers require a clean driving record. Many states require that servicers have a chauffeur's license.

Formal preparation is not needed because most of the training takes place on the job. New employees learn the job by traveling with experienced workers. The training period lasts several weeks, and then new servicers are given their own route. Some companies also provide classroom training for workers.

Vending machine repairers are sometimes required to have prior training in electronics or machine repair. Many vocational high schools and junior colleges offer basic training courses in electronics and machine repair. Servicers and repairers are also encouraged to attend training sessions sponsored by machine manufacturers.

Getting the Job

To get a job as a servicer or repairer, interested individuals should apply directly to the vending companies for which they would like to work. Newspaper want ads and career sites on the Internet may also list openings. Private employment agencies and state employment offices sometimes provide help in finding a job.

Advancement Possibilities and Employment Outlook

Vending machine servicers or repairers may become route supervisors or branch managers. Sometimes the experience that servicers or repairers receive helps them get good jobs in other business fields.

According to the U.S. Bureau of Labor Statistics, employment of vending machine servicers and repairers was expected to grow more slowly than the average for all occupations between 2004 and 2014. Though the number of vending machines will likely increase, newer vending machines hold more food and break down less often, requiring fewer workers to maintain them.

Working Conditions

Vending machine servicers and repairers generally work forty hours a week. They work irregular hours if customers are open on weekends or at night or if repairs must be made right away. Servicers and repairers must be able to drive a truck in all kinds of weather, including torrential downpours, snow, and icy conditions. Physical labor is a part of the job because servicers must load and unload merchandise. Many vending machine servicers and repairers belong to labor unions.

Earnings and Benefits

Earnings vary depending on experience and location of the work. Vending machine repairers and servicers earned a median annual income of $26,333 in 2004, according to the Bureau of Labor Statistics. Some workers are paid a commission in addition to their base salaries, and many receive benefits, including paid holidays and vacations, health insurance, and retirement plans.

Where to Go for More Information

International Brotherhood of Teamsters
25 Louisiana Ave. NW
Washington, DC 20001
(202) 624-6800
http://www.teamster.org/

National Automatic Merchandising
  Association
20 N. Wacker Dr., Ste. 3500
Chicago, IL 60606-3102
(312) 346-0370
http://www.vending.org/

Warehouse Worker

Definition and Nature of the Work

Warehouse workers receive, store, and ship merchandise that is kept in warehouses—buildings in which all kinds of goods are stored and protected from theft or deterioration. Commodities such as steel or wood sit in warehouses before they are used to create manufactured goods. Manufactured goods are often stored in warehouses between the time they are produced and the time they reach retail stores or customers. Many manufacturers, wholesalers, retailers, and transportation companies, as well as federal, state, and local government agencies, have their own private warehouses. Independently owned warehouses, sometimes called public warehouses, charge a fee for storage. Many warehouses are located in large cities with access to ports and freight terminals.

Some warehouses are known as specialty warehouses. Examples include refrigerated warehouses, which are used to store frozen foods, and bonded warehouses,

Education and Training
On-the-job training

Salary
Varies—see profile

Employment Outlook
Good

which are owned by people who post bonds to ensure payment of import duties or internal revenue taxes that may be due on the stored merchandise.

The exact duties of warehouse workers vary depending on the place of employment. Generally handlers in the warehouse load and unload merchandise as it is received or when it is being shipped to customers. When merchandise arrives at the warehouse, it is unloaded from trucks, ships, or railroad sidings onto warehouse platforms. In some warehouses handlers load and unload merchandise by hand; in others workers operate forklifts, which are small trucks used to hoist and carry merchandise stacked on wooden platforms and pallets. Automated material-handling equipment, conveyor belts, automated high stackers, and guided vehicles help store and retrieve goods in larger warehouses. Groups of warehouse workers are supervised by individuals known as gang leaders. These gang leaders are generally in charge of all warehouse activities.

Warehouse stock clerks keep records as goods enter and leave the warehouse. Much of this information is contained in bar codes. Stock clerks use handheld scanners and readers to read the codes, which are then transferred to a computer that is used for inventory control. Checkers and shipping receivers make sure that merchandise arrives in good condition. They also make sure that the entire delivery, not just part of it, arrives intact.

Warehouse record clerks are responsible for keeping records of all incoming and outgoing shipments. They check each shipment against shipping invoices or bills of lading. In public warehouses record clerks prepare storage receipts for customers: this task is regulated by law, and the receipts can be used by the owner of the stored goods as security for loans.

Order fillers find and assemble the merchandise for outgoing shipments from the customer's itemized list. They sometimes deliver the goods to the shipping room or loading platform by truck. In the shipping room, shipping clerks pack, wrap, or crate the merchandise, write shipping orders, and also weigh, address, or attach postage or bills of lading to the packages.

Education and Training Requirements

Some employers prefer to hire workers who have a high school education. For jobs involving record keeping, applicants may be required to have legible handwriting, typing, or data-entry skills. Workers are generally trained on the job for several weeks. Because warehouse workers may be required to lift heavy packages, applicants must be fairly strong and in good health to get the job.

Getting the Job

Individuals interested in becoming warehouse workers can apply directly to the warehouses for which they would like to work. The state employment office, Internet career sites, and newspaper want ads may list openings for this position.

Advancement Possibilities and Employment Outlook

Warehouse workers who handle merchandise can become checkers or gang leaders. Some become warehouse supervisors, but supervisory jobs are quite scarce.

According to the U.S. Bureau of Labor Statistics, employment of warehouse workers is expected to grow as fast as the average for all occupations between 2004 and 2014. The increased use of computers, automated handling equipment, and automated inventory-tracking technology will eventually eliminate some jobs. However, the warehousing industry grows with the economy. As consumers make more money and acquire more things, more warehouse workers will be needed to handle and store those things on their way to market. In addition, more warehouses will likely be needed to store the growing number of things bought over the Internet. High turnover in the field along with the retirement of experienced workers should also create some openings.

Working Conditions

Warehouse work is physically strenuous. Workers are typically required to lift heavy packages, bend, stoop, or operate heavy equipment. Warehouses are often block-long buildings and some workers have to walk long distances repeatedly throughout the day. Depending on the type of merchandise stored, warehouses are fairly clean, well ventilated, and well lighted. However, warehouse workers who work on loading platforms may be exposed to all kinds of weather, and those who work in refrigerated plants must wear protective clothing. To reduce the risk of accidents, workers are required to follow strict safety regulations.

Warehouse workers generally work about forty hours a week. Overtime is often available at premium rates, and the work is usually steady all year. Many workers in this field are union members.

Earnings and Benefits

Earnings vary depending on the location of the warehouse and the type of work performed. According to the U.S. Bureau of Labor Statistics, in 2004 warehouse stock clerks earned a median wage of $12.32 per hour, warehouse shipping clerks received a median wage of $12.47 per hour, and warehouse supervisors earned a median of $20.52 per hour. Benefits generally include paid holidays and vacations, health and life insurance, and retirement plans.

Where to Go for More Information

American Moving and Storage Association
1611 Duke St.
Alexandria, VA 22314
(703) 683-7410
http://www.amconf.org/

International Association of Refrigerated Warehouses
1500 King St., Ste. 201
Alexandria, VA 22314
(703) 373-4300
http://www.iarw.org/

International Warehouse Logistics Association
2800 S. River Rd., Ste. 260
Des Plaines, IL 60018
(847) 813-4699
http://www.iwla.com/

Auctioneer

Definition and Nature of the Work

Auctioneers sell various kinds of property at public sales. Auction sales may be held for individuals or businesses or by court order. Most auctioneers specialize in one type of merchandise, such as antiques, livestock, real estate, industrial equipment, or inventory liquidation. Many of these workers are self-employed, meaning they are hired on a job-by-job basis. Others, such as those employed by art and antique galleries, may be retained on a long-term basis.

Auctioneers appraise the merchandise before a sale and arrange it according to type or estimated worth. When the sale begins, items are brought up to the auction block or platform either by assistants or by the auctioneers. Auctioneers describe each item to the audience and ask for opening bids. Once the first bid is made, other people at the sale may offer higher bids for the item. When it looks as if the highest bid has been made and there are no further bids, auctioneers announce that the item is sold and then go on to the next item. If an item does not attract a bid acceptable to the seller, auctioneers may withdraw it from the sale.

Auctioneers are paid on a commission basis, which means they are given a percentage of the selling price of each item; therefore, they try to get the highest possible price for each item. When an item is sold, one of the auctioneer's assistants hands it to the buyer while another acts as cashier and record keeper. Auctioneers usually speak dramatically and very rapidly. They use their own jargon to keep the audience excited and entertained.

Auctioneers conduct many different types of auctions. Gallery auctions usually involve the sale of antiques and works of art in a gallery or showroom. Gallery sales operate in much the same manner as real estate auctions., but real estate auctions usually take place on the property or estate that is being auctioned. Industrial auctions, a highly specialized area of auction sales, involve the sale of industrial property. At produce auctions, auctioneers sell fruits and vegetables to food brokers, retailers, and wholesalers. Other wholesale auctions involve the sale of tobacco, livestock, and grains. Produce and wholesale auctions are often conducted by telephone or over the Internet, with auctioneers relaying the sellers' descriptions of their goods to the bidders.

Auctioneers are usually responsible for advertising sales in newspapers, on the radio, in trade magazines, via the Internet, and by mailing out circulars and tacking up handbills. Gallery sales are often advertised through catalogs that have descriptions of the objects up for an auction.

Education and Training Requirements

An individual interested in becoming an auctioneer can receive formal training in the field by attending a reputable auction school. A high school education is recommended because auctioneers need a great deal of general information in order to make intelligent appraisals. Auction schools usually offer two- and four-week training programs that cover elocution, proper breathing tech-

Auctioneers have a talent for organizing and promoting, effective public speaking skills, and a knack for entertaining audiences. (© Phil Schermeister/Corbis.)

niques, auctioneer jargon, and appraisal. After attending auction school, beginning auctioneers can sometimes become apprenticed to experienced auctioneers. Auctioneers who specialize in art objects and antiques often take college courses in the fine arts.

Getting the Job

Interested individuals can enter the field as an auctioneer's assistant by applying directly to auction houses and self-employed auctioneers. Some jobs are advertised on career sites on the Internet and in newspapers that circulate in areas where a large number of auction sales are held.

Advancement Possibilities and Employment Outlook

Auctioneers with good reputations receive lucrative assignments and high commission rates. Many experienced auctioneers eventually go into business for themselves, increasing their earnings and booking more profitable sales.

The employment outlook for auctioneers will likely depend on the field in which they work. For instance, real estate auctioneers specializing in farm estate sales will likely receive much business in the future if livestock prices tumble and banks foreclose on farm owners who cannot make their payments. In general, the Internet will continue to take business away from auctioneers. Auction sites such as eBay allow people to bid on just about anything over the Internet—without the need for an auctioneer. Jobs in auctioneering, however, will become available as trained workers retire or leave the field.

Working Conditions

Auctioneers are in an exciting and demanding line of work. Their work is highly diversified and requires good organizational and promotional skills, effective public speaking, and a knack for entertaining audiences. Auctioneers need physical strength because they frequently carry heavy objects up to the auction block.

They also need stamina because they conduct auctions while standing and talk nonstop for long periods of time.

Where to Go for More Information

National Auctioneers Association
8880 Ballentine St.
Overland Park, KS 66214
(913) 541-8084
http://www.auctioneers.org/

National Auto Auction Association
5320-D Spectrum Dr.
Frederick, MD 21703-7337
(301) 696-0400
http://www.naaa.com/

Auctioneers may work evenings and weekends. Some, especially those who are self-employed, work more than forty hours a week. Many work only part time and have other jobs as well.

Earnings and Benefits

Earnings for auctioneers vary greatly. According to Salary-Expert.com, auctioneers made an average wage of $46,062 per year in 2006. Most auctioneers work on a commission basis, with rates ranging from less than 6 percent to more than 30 percent of the item sold, depending on the value of the property up for sale and the experience and reputation of the auctioneer.

Food Broker

Education and Training
High school minimum; on-the-job training and possibly college recommended

Salary
Median— $45,400 to $46,829 per year

Employment Outlook
Good

Definition and Nature of the Work

Food brokers are independent sales agents who own their own businesses. They negotiate sales for producers and manufacturers of food and food products. Food brokers provide a service to both food producers and buyers by selling to chain wholesalers, independent wholesalers, and retail stores. Producers and manufacturers often find it less expensive to sell through food brokers rather than directly because it saves the cost of paying a sales staff to market their products. Since brokers represent a large number of producers, the wholesalers and retailers also save time, energy, and money by dealing with one broker rather than with many manufacturers' representatives.

Brokers usually sell in a specified geographic area. However, the products they sell may be grown, processed, or manufactured anywhere in the world. Those who work in heavily populated areas usually cover a small geographic area; in rural areas brokers cover a large territory. Many food brokers employ clerical and sales workers. These sales workers travel to meet with retail store owners, managers, and sometimes wholesalers. Food brokers who own a brokerage house may be closely involved in sales or work primarily as administrators and supervisors.

Another service that food brokers provide is keeping producers and manufacturers up-to-date on local market conditions. Brokers try to increase their sales volume and achieve the greatest possible distribution of their products, which involves strong sales of established products and vigorous marketing of new products. Food brokers may help wholesalers or store managers develop sufficient inventories of various products and offer suggestions on store displays and other means of promotion. Additional responsibilities typically include moving merchandise, rearranging product displays, replacing spoiled merchandise, keeping accurate records of their sales, and preparing reports on market conditions for producers and manufacturers.

Education and Training Requirements

Individuals interested in becoming food brokers need at least a high school education, but most people who enter this field have attended college. Any sales experience gives applicants good preparation for the job. Working in a grocery store or supermarket is particularly useful.

Most brokers begin as food sales workers and are usually trained on the job by experienced sales workers. Experienced workers often accompany newcomers on sales calls to help them become acquainted with their buyers. Food brokers may also be trained by the sales managers of companies whose products they sell.

Getting the Job

Individuals interested in becoming food brokers can apply directly to brokerages. These firms sometimes list openings with state employment offices, in want ads in local newspapers, or with career sites on the Internet. Brokers are usually willing to hire workers they think will be able to increase sales volume.

Advancement Possibilities and Employment Outlook

The owners of food brokerage firms may expand their businesses and thereby increase profits. Food brokers may advance to supervisory jobs such as sales manager within a firm. Some start their own food brokerages; others take jobs as manufacturers' representatives for companies in related industries.

A food broker is a type of manufacturer's sales worker. According to the U.S. Bureau of Labor Statistics, employment of manufacturer's sales workers was expected to increase as fast as the average for all professions from 2004 to 2014. As the economy and the American population grow, more food brokers will be needed to negotiate the sale of food items. Many new food brokers will also be needed to replace those who leave the field. The need for food brokers will decrease, however, as advances in information technology allow existing brokers to be more efficient at their jobs.

Working Conditions

Food brokers work mainly in their offices. Occasionally they may travel to meet with customers, food producers, or manufacturers. Traveling rarely takes them away from home overnight. Brokers must be persuasive and enjoy competition. They must like dealing with people and be genuinely interested in helping their customers sell the products they have purchased. Because brokers work on a commission or bonus basis, they generally put in long hours so that they can make many sales.

Earnings and Benefits

As stated, food brokers are a subset of manufacturer's sales workers. The Bureau of Labor Statistics reported that manufacturer's sales workers who did not specialize in technical or science products earned a median wage of $45,400 per year in 2004. According to SalaryExpert.com, food brokers made an average annual wage of $46,829 in 2006. Food brokers are paid on a commission basis by manufacturers and producers, so they earn money only when they make a sale. However, most well-established food brokers receive a steady income from regular customers. As is the case with others who own their own businesses, the earnings of food brokers depend on the volume of sales. Brokers must also provide their own benefits.

Where to Go for More Information

Broker Management Council
P.O. Box 150229
Arlington, TX 76015
(817) 561-7272
http://www.bmcsales.com/

National Association of Manufacturers
1331 Pennsylvania Ave. NW
Washington, DC 20004-1790
(202) 637-3000
http://www.nam.org/

National Association of Wholesaler-
  Distributors
1725 K St. NW, Ste. 300
Washington, DC 20006-1419
(202) 872-0885
http://www.naw.org/

Insurance Agent and Broker

Education and Training
College preferred; training plus license mandatory

Salary
Median—$41,720 per year

Employment Outlook
Fair

Definition and Nature of the Work

Insurance agents are hired by insurance companies to find customers and sell them insurance policies. The three main categories of insurance are life, health, and property-liability. Each protects its policyholder against possible financial loss. Life insurance pays the holder's family a certain sum in the event of the holder's death. Health insurance protects policyholders against large medical bills covered under the policy if the need should arise. Property-liability insurance, sometimes called casualty insurance, covers damage to or theft of property that may occur, for instance, as the result of an auto crash, a fire, or a home burglary.

Insurance agents assist their clients, who may be individuals or companies, in selecting the right policy for their needs. The agents explain and write the policies, which are agreements between the client and the insurance company, and help their clients fill out the necessary forms to obtain the desired insurance. Agents who sell life insurance may schedule physical examinations for clients. Agents must make themselves available to answer questions and to assist clients in filing claims.

Agents work in several different ways. They may work for only one company, or they may act as independent agents who are hired by two or more insurance firms. Agents often specialize in a certain type of insurance and may sell strictly to individuals or to businesses.

Insurance brokers do very much the same kind of work that agents do. Brokers, however, do not work for specific insurance companies. They place clients with the insurance companies that are most suitable for the clients' needs.

Insurance agents and brokers assist customers in finding the right kind of policy for their needs. (© Martha Tabor/Working Images Photographs. Reproduced by permission.)

Because of changes in the financial services industry, many insurance agents and brokers now offer a number of financial-planning services. Some are also licensed to sell securities, such as mutual funds or annuities.

Education and Training Requirements

Almost all insurance agents and brokers have finished high school and most have college training. Most insurance companies and independent agencies hire only college graduates. Courses in business, mathematics, accounting, and economics are helpful. Some colleges actually offer courses in insurance. Proficiency in computer business applications is also important because they are used to provide financial information and calculate premiums (the amount paid by a client—usually each month or every six months—for insurance coverage). All agents and brokers must be licensed by the state in which they work. To obtain a license, candidates must pass a written test. Agents and brokers who plan to sell mutual funds and other securities must obtain a separate state license.

The insurance business offers a wide variety of training courses. Many insurance companies and agencies offer classes to help trainees study for the licensing test. Once licensed, new insurance agents and brokers learn by observing experienced workers, but training does not stop after licensing. There are many conferences and further courses to help insurance agents and brokers stay up-to-date on the latest trends in their field. In fact, insurance companies and agencies usually encourage and help their employees further their education on topics such as tax law. These courses also help with advancement. As the number of financial products being offered increases, employers are placing a greater emphasis on higher education.

Getting the Job

Probably the best way to enter the insurance field is to talk to agents and brokers in several different firms. Because there are so many directions a career in this field can take, it is very helpful to seek advice from the experts before making any definite decisions. Interested individuals should also find out how to get a license.

Once prospective agents or brokers decide on a particular area and type of position in the field, they should apply directly to insurance companies, agencies, or brokerages that specialize in that type of insurance. Career sites on the Internet and ads in newspapers may also list openings for jobs with insurance agencies.

Advancement Possibilities and Employment Outlook

The insurance business offers many opportunities for advancement. Courses are given to new and experienced workers who want to improve their skills. Many of the courses qualify workers for advancement or serve as a sign of achievement. After further training, insurance agents can go on to positions as underwriters. Some agents become managers or agency heads; others start their own agencies or brokerages.

According to the U.S. Bureau of Labor Statistics, insurance agents and brokers held 400,000 jobs in 2004. Employment of insurance agents and brokers was expected to grow more slowly than the average for all occupations between 2004 and 2014. Insurance agencies and companies will likely be hiring fewer agents to cut costs, which have been rising steadily in the insurance industry for decades. Computers and the Internet are also allowing existing agents to handle greater numbers of sales and to find new clients more easily. Therefore, most jobs will result from the need to replace agents and brokers who retire or leave the field.

Working Conditions

Working conditions vary with the type of insurance being sold. Life insurance agents and brokers, for example, need to be more sales oriented than workers who sell other kinds of insurance. Clients are more likely to see the need for health and property-liability insurance than for life insurance.

All agents and brokers spend much of their working time outside the office. Their workweeks include evenings and weekends and often extend beyond the standard forty hours. Because some agents and brokers work partly or completely on commission, they must work longer hours to earn higher pay. The job demands independence and responsibility. Insurance agents are very much on their own.

Earnings and Benefits

Because agents and brokers usually work on commission (a percentage of sales), their incomes vary widely. Those who work longer hours generally earn more. As a rule experienced workers earn much more than new agents or brokers. Most employers take this into account and pay new workers a base salary plus commission while they learn and build up their clientele. According to the Bureau of Labor Statistics, insurance agents and brokers earned a median annual salary of $41,720 in 2004. The top-paid 10 percent of workers in this field earned more than $108,800.

Insurance agents can expect paid holidays and vacations, health insurance, and retirement plans. Agents who work entirely on commission may have fewer benefits. Self-employed agents and brokers must provide their own benefits.

Where to Go for More Information

Insurance Information Institute
110 William St.
New York, NY 10038
(212) 346-5500
http://www.iii.org/

National Association of Insurance Women
6528 E. 101st St., PMB #750
Tulsa, OK 74133
(800) 766-6249
http://www.naiw.org/

Property Casualty Insurers Association
  of America
2600 S. River Rd.
Des Plaines, IL 60018
(847) 297-7800
http://www.pciaa.net/

Manufacturers' Sales Worker

Education and Training
Typically college plus training

Salary
Median—$45,400 to $58,580 per year

Employment Outlook
Good

Definition and Nature of the Work

Manufacturers' sales workers sell products to businesses. Sometimes called manufacturers' representatives, these sales workers work for many different industries. They sell computers, pharmaceutical supplies, equipment for industrial processes, and many other products to wholesale buyers, purchasing agents, and retail buyers.

The duties of the job vary widely, depending on the product being sold, the market, and the manufacturer. However, all manufacturers' sales workers must be familiar with their product and its major selling points. They also need to know the priorities of their customers and the unique qualities of their product that set it apart from other products. They seek out new customers to widen their selling market; for example, a sales worker employed by a pharmaceutical company might go directly to doctors' offices and drugstores. In addition, manufacturers' sales workers attend conferences and trade meetings to talk with potential customers. A sales worker for a pharmaceutical firm might arrange a display at a doctors' convention. Sales workers maintain contact with their customers for additional orders and to introduce new products. Most sales workers also do paperwork such as arranging the terms of sales and establishing customers' credit ratings.

A manufacturers' sales worker meets with a building contractor to sell him building supplies. (© Martha Tabor/Working Images Photographs. Reproduced by permission.)

Some manufacturers' sales workers sell products that need to be reordered frequently. These salespeople usually travel the same route on a regular basis to take reorders. Those who sell to retail outlets may suggest marketing techniques for their products.

Other sales workers, such as those who deal with industrial machinery, sell products that are seldom, if ever, reordered. Generally these workers spend a great deal of time making a single sale. Each sale may be worth thousands or hundreds of thousands of dollars. Sales workers in this situation usually work with several customers at one time.

In fields such as computer sales, manufacturers' sales workers must possess a great deal of technical knowledge. Some companies hire technical support workers to assist sales workers. Technical support workers are people who, although not directly involved in sales, accompany sales workers to provide technical information. Depending on the product, technical support workers may be engineers, scientists, or computer experts. They may also work with the customer after the sale is made, perhaps by supervising the installation of equipment or by providing training to workers at the customer's plant or office or by designing systems that will let the customer get the best use from the product.

Education and Training Requirements

Education requirements for manufacturers' sales workers vary depending on the product they sell. Many companies prefer to hire applicants who have a college degree. Manufacturers generally will seek graduates with degrees in fields relating to the products they will be selling. For example, drug manufacturers tend to hire applicants who have a degree in biology or chemistry. Manufacturers also look for candidates who have some technical training or work experience in the industry to which they sell.

Once applicants are hired, they are trained either at the manufacturing plant or at a branch office. The length of time needed to complete the training period varies from one company to another. In some companies beginners are trained for two years or more.

Getting the Job

College placement offices can offer students help in finding jobs as manufacturers' sales workers. Interested individuals should also apply directly to the manufacturers for which they would like to work. Jobs are frequently listed in newspaper want ads or on career sites on the Internet.

Advancement Possibilities and Employment Outlook

Manufacturers' sales workers may advance to supervisory positions such as sales training manager or sales manager. Some advance to other administrative jobs in their company.

According to the U.S. Bureau of Labor Statistics, employment of manufacturers' sales workers was expected to increase as fast as the average for all professions from 2004 to 2014. The number of products available to consumers will likely increase in coming years, and more sales workers will be required to peddle these products. New sales representatives will also be needed to replace those who leave the field; however, the need for manufacturers' sales workers will be tempered by advances in information technology that will allow existing salespeople to be more efficient at their jobs.

Working Conditions

Many manufacturers' sales workers must do a great deal of traveling. They generally travel before or after their workday so that they will not lose selling time. Because they work for commissions or bonuses, sales workers usually try to work with customers for as many hours each day as they can. Sales workers must be friendly and enthusiastic about their work and be able to adjust easily to the personalities of their various customers.

Earnings and Benefits

Earnings for manufacturers' sales workers vary widely, depending on the industry, the employer, and the education required. The Bureau of Labor Statistics reported that manufacturers' sales workers who sold technical and scientific products earned a median annual income of $58,580 in 2004. Those who did not specialize in technical or science products earned a median of $45,400 per year. Benefits usually include health and life insurance, paid holidays and vacations, and retirement plans. Many sales workers are given a company car for business use or are reimbursed for the use of their own car and other travel expenses.

Where to Go for More Information

National Association of Wholesaler-
   Distributors
1725 K St. NW, Ste. 300
Washington, DC 20006-1419
(202) 872-0885
http://www.naw.org/

Professional Society for Sales and
   Marketing Training
5905 NW 54th Circle
Coral Springs, FL 33067
(800) 219-0096
http://www.smt.org/

Sales and Marketing Executives
   International
P.O. Box 1390
Sumas, WA 98295-1390
(312) 893-0751
http://www.smei.org/

Real Estate Sales Agent and Broker

Definition and Nature of the Work

Real estate brokers own real estate firms and employ real estate sales agents to help sell or rent property for the owners. Brokers charge fees, and sales agents earn commissions on the sale or rental of property. Brokers may also manage, appraise, or develop real estate or even combine their real estate business with an insurance agency or law practice. Members of the National Board of Realtors may call themselves realtors.

Most sales agents and brokers sell private homes. Some specialize in commercial property such as apartment buildings, offices, or factories. Relocation specialists offer packages of home buying and selling services for people moving from one geographic area to another. They may work with individuals or for companies transferring a number of employees.

Real estate sales agents and brokers work from a file of properties that are listed for sale or rent. They use computers and the Internet to locate or list available properties and to identify available sources of financing.

Real estate sales agents and brokers obtain new listings for their agency by locating property owners interested in selling through the brokerage. Much of their business is generated through word of mouth. When they must find new clients, some realtors call homeowners who are trying to sell their homes privately through newspaper ads. They may also contact all the homeowners in a certain area and ask them if they wish to sell. Many real estate agents and brokers send postcards listing their recent sales to other homeowners in the neighborhood. Agents and brokers often visit newly listed properties so that they can familiarize themselves with the features of each property.

In any sale the agents have to negotiate with both the seller and the buyer. Sellers usually begin by asking more for their property than buyers are willing to pay. Agents must be able to convince sellers to set a realistic price. However, most of the agents' efforts focus on the buyer. Agents try to learn what will motivate the buyer to make a purchase, and they must be able to convince buyers that the property in question suits their needs, their desires, and their budget.

Buyers generally offer somewhat less for a property than the seller asks unless the real estate market is hot. If the market is hot, then buyers may compete with one another and drive the price of a property above the asking price. In both cases agents help negotiate the final price. Agents and brokers help buyers arrange to finance the home and perform title searches. Agents arrange for the inspection of the home to ensure nothing is wrong with the property, and they are generally present at closings when final contracts of sale are signed.

Those real estate sales agents who sell homes must be prepared to answer questions about the tax rates in the area, the quality and location of the schools, and the availability of public transportation and shopping. Agents who handle commercial property must be familiar with business trends, the labor market, taxes, freight transportation, and marketing facilities.

Education and Training Requirements

To get a job as a real estate sales agent, a candidate must obtain a license from the state by passing a written test. The test covers real estate transactions and laws regarding the sale of property. Brokers generally must pass a more compre-

Education and Training
High school plus sixty to ninety hours of training and license

Salary
Median—$35,670 to $58,720 per year

Employment Outlook
Good

hensive test and may also be required to have several years' experience selling real estate. Most states require that licensed real estate workers have between sixty and ninety hours of formal training. Courses in real estate are available at two- and four-year colleges. In addition, professional associations sponsor courses to prepare prospective agents and brokers for the state test.

Some employers hire high school graduates to work as office assistants while they prepare for the state test. Other employers prefer applicants who are already licensed and who have a bachelor's degree or some college training in business or real estate. Personality traits such as maturity and enthusiasm are also important.

Getting the Job

Interested individuals should apply directly to the real estate brokers for whom they would like to work. Newspaper want ads and career sites on the Internet often list job openings in the real estate field.

Advancement Possibilities and Employment Outlook

Quite often experienced sales agents obtain a broker's license and go into business for themselves. Successful sales workers generally stay in sales of one kind or another because the financial rewards are very good. Some, however, become appraisers or go into property management.

According to the U.S. Bureau of Labor Statistics, 460,000 people were employed as real estate sales agents and brokers in 2004. Employment in this field was expected to increase as fast as the average for all occupations between 2004 and 2014. The use of computer databases, fax machines, and the Internet may eliminate some of the demand for agents in the future, as these technological advances enable fewer agents and brokers to serve greater numbers of clients. The Internet also allows buyers and sellers to find one another without the help of the realtor. As the house-buying population grows, however, the demand for real estate sales agents and brokers will grow with it. Jobs are usually plentiful in this competitive field because there is a high turnover rate. Many beginners transfer to other fields because they fail to find profitable listings or are unable to make enough sales to generate a decent income.

Working Conditions

Real estate sales agents and brokers meet clients, arrange closings, and handle other paperwork in the office. They spend a great deal of time on the telephone locating property up for sale and negotiating with clients and property owners. They also spend time in the field checking out new properties and showing real estate to prospective buyers. Most agents work nights and weekends to arrange meetings that are convenient to buyers and sellers. Their work time is flexible, however, and they can set their own hours.

Real estate sales agents and brokers should enjoy interacting with different kinds of people. Many agents are fairly independent in their work and find satisfaction in locating the right property for the right buyer.

Earnings and Benefits

When a piece of property is sold, the seller pays a percentage of the selling price to the broker. The sales agent receives a percentage of that fee, often about 50 percent, as a commission. However, the rate of commission varies, depending on the policy of the firm, the total selling price, and the type of property. Because sales agents are paid on a commission basis, their earnings vary greatly. The Bureau of Labor Statistics reported that the median annual income for real estate agents in 2004 was $35,670. The top-paid 10 percent earned in excess of $92,770 per year. Brokers earned a median income of $58,720 per year in 2004, and the top-paid 25 percent of brokers made more than $99,820. Some brokers provide sales workers with benefits such as life and health insurance.

Where to Go for More Information

National Association of Real Estate Brokers
9831 Greenbelt Rd.
Lanham, MD 20706
(301) 552-9340
http://www.nareb.com/

National Association of REALTORS
30700 Russell Ranch Rd.
Westlake Village, CA 91362
(805) 557-2300
http://www.realtor.com/

Retail Butcher

Definition and Nature of the Work

Retail butchers prepare meat, fish, and poultry to sell to customers in stores. Some butchers work in supermarkets; others work in butcher shops. Many butchers own their shops and employ assistants. Butchers are sometimes called meat cutters, unless they deal only in fish. Fish specialists may be referred to as fish mongers or fish cleaners.

Butchers unload meat carcasses from delivery trucks and then cut the carcasses into small pieces that can be sold to customers. They use several kinds of equipment to prepare the meat: power machines such as band saws are used to cut through heavy bones, and other special knives such as slicers, cleavers, and even handsaws are used on the smaller pieces.

Retail butchers begin their task by sawing the carcass in half and then cutting it into quarters. Those quarters are divided up into various "cuts" of meat such as steaks, chops, or roasts. Next, butchers remove fragments of bone from the meat with a knife or a machine that brushes off the bone chips. Meat trimmings are ground into hamburger. Retail butchers also prepare sausages and cured meats (such as corned beef) and clean and cut fish and poultry before it is sold.

Some butchers wait on customers. In small stores butchers cut meat portions to each customer's request, weigh and wrap them, and process the customer's payment. In supermarkets butchers work behind the scenes. Meat is packaged and placed in display cases from which customers make selections. Butchers may be asked to prepare special orders for customers in supermarkets.

Education and Training Requirements

Any person interested in becoming a butcher can learn the trade through on-the-job training or through a union apprenticeship. Employers prefer to hire high school graduates. Beginners learn by watching and helping experienced butchers. Those interested may attend classes to supplement their training.

Getting the Job

Candidates can apply directly to the butchers and supermarkets for which they would like to work. Openings are often listed with the state employment office. Jobs are also listed in the classified ads of local newspapers or on the Internet.

Education and Training
On-the-job training or apprenticeship

Salary
Median—$27,030 per year

Employment Outlook
Good

Advancement Possibilities and Employment Outlook

Some butchers become meat buyers for supermarkets. Some become store or department managers. Experienced butchers may open their own retail shops. To do so, they must come up with considerable sums of money to get their businesses started.

According to the U.S. Bureau of Labor Statistics, employment of butchers was expected to increase about as fast as the average for all occupations between 2004 and 2014. New automated equipment allows less skilled meat processing workers to pre-cut and package the meat shipped directly to supermarkets, thereby lowering the need for skilled retail butchers. The increase in population in the United States, however, will increase the demand for meat. A limited number of openings will occur as experienced workers retire or leave their jobs for other reasons.

A retail butcher weighs New York strip steaks that will be packaged and sold to customers. (© Henny Ray Abrams/Reuters/Corbis.)

Working Conditions

Because meat, fish, and poultry must be refrigerated, butchers work in cold rooms. They need physical strength to lift, carry, and handle heavy carcasses. The floors in meat-cutting rooms are slick with blood and fat and the instruments butchers use are sharp. To avoid cuts and amputations, they must use care and know how to handle their tools. Butchers usually work forty hours a week. They generally have secure jobs.

Earnings and Benefits

Retail butchers who are union members receive wages set by union-employer negotiations. The median annual income for butchers employed by grocery stores was $27,030 in 2004, according to a report by the Bureau of Labor Statistics. Benefits usually include health insurance, paid holidays and vacations, and retirement plans.

Where to Go for More Information

American Meat Institute
1150 Connecticut Ave. NW, 12th floor
Washington, DC 20036
(202) 587-4200
http://www.meatami.org/

United Food and Commercial Workers
 International Union, CLC
1775 K St. NW
Washington, DC 20006
(202) 223-3111
http://www.ufcw.org/

Small Business Owner

Education and Training
Varies—see profile

Salary
Varies—see profile

Employment Outlook
Good

Definition and Nature of the Work

Small business owners manage their own companies. Small businesses include not only retail stores such as gift shops and bookstores but also real estate, advertising, and employment agencies; self-service laundries; manufacturing firms; and franchise operations such as fast food restaurants and gas stations. In addition, many freelancers and consultants in various fields run their own businesses. Although different standards were applied to different industries, in 2006 the U.S. Small Business Administration classified most basic retail and service operations as small if their yearly revenues were below $6.5 million.

Although the responsibilities and duties of small business owners vary depending on the nature of the company, most owners must be involved in planning, managing money, and buying materials. *(Photograph by Kelly A. Quin. Thomson Gale. Reproduced by permission.)*

The three most common types of small businesses are sole proprietorships, partnerships, and corporations. In a sole proprietorship one person owns the business. A partnership is essentially an agreement involving two or more people who wish to work together in their own business. In a sole proprietorship the company's profits are kept by the owner; in a partnership the profits are divided among the partners. The owners are responsible for the firm's debts.

A corporation has a more formal structure. In a small corporation the owners are usually the officers of the corporation and are paid a salary. The structure of a corporation offers small business owners two advantages. A corporation can sell stock to bring investment capital into the business. Moreover, the officers of a corporation cannot be held personally liable for the firm's debts.

The responsibilities and duties of small business owners depend on the nature of their companies. Most frequently the owners' primary functions involve planning, money management, and marketing. To keep their companies in business, owners must know when they should take financial risks. They need to be aware of the size of the market for the product or service they provide, and they must adapt to changing market conditions by creating new products, improving services, or promoting their company in a new and innovative way. Small business owners must offer their products at competitive prices by keeping costs down and buying services and equipment within their budget.

Business owners who employ technical or other workers must hire, train, and supervise their employees. Some owners run the entire operation themselves. For example, the owner of a shop that sells and repairs bicycles may buy the inventory, make the repairs, sell to customers, and handle the store's accounts. The store owner may also unpack merchandise, build displays, and clean the shop.

Franchise holders buy a license from a parent company that permits them to sell the company's goods or services. The conditions under which franchises are sold vary from one company to the next. Many agreements provide for exclusive sales rights in a stipulated territory and use of the company name and method of operation. Franchise holders are generally required to invest a large sum of money in their operation. They may also be required to buy supplies and equipment from the parent company. In return, franchise holders receive a large share of the profits from their operation.

Education and Training Requirements

Small business owners must be competent managers who possess a thorough knowledge of their field. Interested individuals should have a combination of formal education and practical training suited to the kind of business they want to operate. A person interested in running a store, for instance, needs experience in retailing, along with high school or college courses in bookkeeping, accounting, and business. More technical training or an apprenticeship may be required to work in some fields. To open a machine shop, for example, a person must complete a formal apprenticeship and have many years of experience as a machinist. Prospective small business owners should also be familiar with tax laws and with state and federal laws regulating businesses.

Getting the Job

There are several ways to start a business. Candidates may buy an established enterprise or become a partner or shareholder in one. Small business owners can purchase a franchise or begin completely on their own. To find a partner, prospective business owners should attend networking events in their industry and get to know the business people in their community.

People who want to start a business need money to invest. After the initial starting costs are met, they still need enough money to cover costs until the business begins to pay for itself. Some of that money should come directly from the business owner; additional funding may be borrowed from investors, family members, and lending institutions. Another option is to sell stock in the company to raise money.

Advancement Possibilities and Employment Outlook

Success in a small business depends on knowing what the customer wants and making the product or service easily available at a reasonable cost. Those who succeed may expand their business or branch out into other fields. However, most small businesses remain small, and the owners consider themselves successful if they can support themselves from the profits of the business.

The outlook is always good for those who can find a market for their product and can afford to take financial risks. The continued growth of franchises means that there will be many business opportunities in this area.

Working Conditions

Most people who start their own businesses do so because they place a high value on their independence. They are prepared to work long hours and take certain economic risks rather than work for someone else. Other people start home-based businesses because they want to work from home.

To be successful, small business owners must have an entrepreneurial temperament; that is, they must be willing to take risks in return for the prospect of greater rewards.

Small business owners generally work well over forty hours a week. Some continue to hold salaried jobs with other employers until their business is established. Small business owners may face economic uncertainty at times, but those who succeed gain a great sense of personal satisfaction.

Earnings and Benefits

Theoretically a small business owner with very low expenses could make over $6 million per year in accordance with the U.S. Small Business Administration's 2006 standards. In reality the earnings of small business owners depend solely on the success of the business itself. Some owners do well. Others make no more money than they would working at a salaried job. Many owners lose money and go out of business.

Generally, small businesses must be in operation for several years before they show a clear profit. Small business owners usually must reinvest profits in the company. Over a period of time many owners build up a substantial financial interest in their business. If the company is profitable, the owner may sell it for cash.

Small business owners working in proprietorships and partnerships must provide their own health and life insurance and retirement benefits. Corporate officers receive the same benefits given to other company employees.

Where to Go for More Information

National Federation of Independent Business
53 Century Blvd., Ste. 250
Nashville, TN 37214
(800) 634-2669
http://www.nfibonline.com/

National Retail Federation
325 Seventh St. NW, Ste. 1100
Washington, DC 20004-2608
(800) 673-4692
http://www.nrf.com/

United States Small Business Administration
409 Third St. SW
Washington, DC 20416
(800) 827-5722
http://www.sba.gov/

Title Examiner

Definition and Nature of the Work

Title examiners search, analyze, and evaluate records on titles to land, homes, and other buildings. They make sure that the title to a property is free of restrictions that may affect its sale or use. The findings of a title search and examination are needed to issue title insurance, grant mortgage loans, buy and sell property, acquire rights of way, and obtain and protect mineral rights.

Titles are documents that show evidence of ownership to a piece of property. Local government agencies and other organizations keep these records. Title examiners search for copies of these records and other documents, including vital statistics and street and land map books, to determine the legal status of a title. Entry-level employees known as title searchers often assist title examiners in their investigation.

Title examiners verify ownership and the legal description of a property and check for zoning ordinances that may restrict the use of the property. They copy or abstract required information from documents such as mortgages and trust deeds. Sometimes they rely on title abstractors to do this work.

Having gathered this information, the title examiner then reviews the data and submits a report on the title to the property. If any problems—such as the existence of unpaid property taxes—are identified, the title examiner will meet with the client to discuss the findings of the report.

Some title examiners are also involved in preparing official descriptions of properties. They may assist in the preparation of leases, grants, deeds, and easements. Examiners who are employed by title insurance companies prepare and issue the policies that guarantee the legality of a title.

Education and Training
High school mandatory, along with training; college preferred

Salary
Average—$39,420 per year

Employment Outlook
Fair

Education and Training Requirements

Individuals interested in becoming title examiners must have a high school diploma. Most employers prefer to hire applicants with at least two years of college. A bachelor's degree is recommended. Useful college courses include law, business administration, real estate, banking, finance, and mathematics. Generally, to qualify for title examiner positions, candidates must have two to four years of experience in title searching and abstracting. Some large companies provide their own training programs for people wishing to become title examiners.

Getting the Job

Most title examiners begin by gaining experience in title searching and abstracting. Potential employees can apply directly to title companies, real estate agencies, mortgage companies, land development corporations, and oil companies for entry-level positions. Applicants interested in a job with local, state, or federal government agencies can obtain information from local, state, or federal civil service agencies. Students can also obtain information about job openings from their school placement office. Openings are often listed on Internet job sites and in newspaper want ads as well.

Title examiners search, analyze, and evaluate records to ensure that titles—documents that show evidence of ownership to a piece of property—are free of restrictions. (© Martha Tabor/ Working Images Photographs. Reproduced by permission.)

Advancement Possibilities and Employment Outlook

Many title examiners begin by working as title clerks, abstractors, and title searchers. With experience they may become title examiners and senior title examiners. Senior examiners are responsible for complex title searches or those that involve large amounts of money. Some title examiners become managers and administrators responsible for assigning title examinations to different examiners.

According to the U.S. Bureau of Labor Statistics, employment of title examiners was expected to grow more slowly than the average for all jobs between 2004 and 2014. Positions will become available as people retire or leave the field.

Working Conditions

Many title examiners work independently; others have title searchers and abstractors to assist them. Frequent local travel is required because much of the necessary information for this job is stored in government offices and at other locations. Title examiners examine the data they collect in comfortable, well-lighted offices. The work is detailed and may be repetitious at times. Individuals in this occupation generally work a forty-hour week; however, overtime may be required to complete work before sale closings.

Where to Go for More Information

Real Estate Educators Association
19 Mantua Rd.
Mount Royal, NJ 08061
(856) 423-3215
http://www.reea.org/

Earnings and Benefits

Earnings vary according to the type and size of the company, its geographic location, and the experience of the title examiner. According to a survey conducted by the Bureau of Labor Statistics, in 2004 title examiners earned an average annual salary of $39,420. Benefits usually include paid vacations and holidays, health insurance, and retirement plans.

Wholesale Sales Worker

Definition and Nature of the Work

Wholesale sales workers sell merchandise to retail outlets and other businesses. These individuals work in many industries ranging from plumbing supplies to clothing, drugs, and health care products. Sales workers represent wholesale houses, which buy products made by many manufacturers and distribute them to retail stores. Because it is difficult for retailers to deal with dozens or even hundreds of different manufacturers, they often prefer to buy from wholesalers.

Many wholesalers sell the same products at about the same prices so they must compete for business. Buyers usually choose to deal with the wholesaler that provides the best service. It is important, therefore, for wholesale sales workers to establish good working relationships with their customers. The specific duties of wholesale sales workers vary from one industry to another; however, all salespeople try to provide dependable service, prompt delivery, and a wide array of products.

Most wholesale sales workers travel to their customers. They are usually assigned to a geographic area. Depending on the number of customers they have, their territory can range in size from one section of a large city to various cities in several states. Sales workers call on customers with catalogs, samples, promotional literature, and multimedia presentations. They inform their customers of price changes and new items. Many wholesale sales workers also perform customer services. For example, they check stock, reorder items, streamline inventory and ordering systems, and suggest advertising and display techniques. Those who sell technical, mechanical, and electrical equipment may help install and maintain it.

In addition to their selling and servicing tasks, wholesale sales workers must spend several hours a day on a computer keeping records of sales and expenses, writing reports for manufacturers and wholesalers, making appointments, and entering orders. They may also accept payment and arrange credit terms for

In addition to selling merchandise to retail outlets and other businesses, wholesale sales workers usually check stock, reorder items, and streamline inventory and ordering systems. (© Terry Wild Studio. Reproduced by permission.)

customers. Sales workers must attend sales meetings, seminars, and conventions and study trade literature to keep up with new products and new techniques for selling them.

Education and Training Requirements

Education and training requirements vary, depending on the specific job and employer. Applicants for jobs selling technical products are often required to have college training in a related area. Companies that sell pharmaceutical products prefer applicants who have a degree in the biological sciences. Companies that sell technical equipment often require workers to have an engineering degree. In general, job experience in the industry in which one works is always valuable. A plumbing supplies sales worker with experience as a plumber's apprentice is likely to understand customers' problems better than someone without any plumbing knowledge. Previous sales experience is useful as well.

Most wholesale sales workers are trained formally on the job by their employers. Depending on the type of products sold by the company, training programs vary in length from a few weeks to several years. These programs usually offer instruction in selling techniques along with information on merchandise features and uses.

Getting the Job

People interested in becoming wholesale sales workers should apply directly to wholesale houses. Private employment agencies sometimes list openings in the field. Newspaper want ads and career sites on the Internet may provide job leads as well.

Advancement Possibilities and Employment Outlook

There are several avenues of advancement for wholesale sales workers who have experience and proven ability. They can be promoted to supervisory and managerial positions such as sales training manager or company sales manager. With a college degree they may also enter other related areas, including buying and marketing.

According to the U.S. Bureau of Labor Statistics, employment of wholesale sales workers was expected to increase as fast as the average for all professions from 2004 to 2014. The number of products available to consumers will likely increase in coming years and more sales workers will be required to peddle these products. New sales representatives will also be needed to replace those who leave the field. However, the need for wholesale sales workers will be tempered by advances in information technology that will allow existing salespeople to be more efficient at their jobs.

Working Conditions

Most wholesale sales workers put in long, irregular working hours that often stretch into evenings and weekends. They spend much of their working time on their feet and may have to carry heavy sample cases and catalogs. A great deal of traveling is also required, and workers may be away from home for days at a time. Wholesale sales workers frequently work under a variety of pressures, including deadlines and cancellations of large orders.

Earnings and Benefits

The Bureau of Labor Statistics reported that in 2004 wholesale sales workers who sold technical and scientific products earned a median annual income of $58,580. Those who did not specialize in technical or science products earned a median wage of $45,400 per year. Many wholesale sales workers work on a salary plus commission basis. (A commission is a percentage of the money received from a sale.) Some work strictly on commission. Those who sell seasonal products may draw wages against future commissions during slack periods. Many employers provide fringe benefits to their workers, including paid vacations and insurance plans. Most companies cover travel expenses for their workers or provide them with automobiles and expense accounts.

Where to Go for More Information

National Association of Wholesaler-
    Distributors
1725 K St. NW, Ste. 300
Washington, DC 20006-1419
(202) 872-0885
http://www.naw.org/

Professional Society for Sales and
    Marketing Training
5905 NW 54th Circle
Coral Springs, FL 33067
(800) 219-0096
http://www.smt.org/

Sales and Marketing Executives
    International
P.O. Box 1390
Sumas, WA 98295-1390
(312) 893-0751
http://www.smei.org/

Advertising Account Executive

Definition and Nature of the Work

Advertising account executives, also known as advertising sales agents, work for advertising agencies. Account executives are the link between the agency and its clients. They sell the agency's services to the client—the client is usually a company—and work closely with that company's advertising manager. Account executives utilize the agency's various departments—including copywriting, art, and marketing—to create effective advertising campaigns for their clients. In some large agencies account executives report to account supervisors. Generally, however, account executives are supervised by the top management or owners of the agency. In small agencies the owner or partners handle creative work such as copywriting and art and also do the work of an account executive.

Account executives must do extensive research before they can develop a plan for an advertising campaign suited to a client's needs and goals. Usually their first step is to decide on a target market based on information supplied by the client and by the agency's market research department. Having established a target market, account executives start developing the overall creative concept that will be used to promote the item. Before they can do this, however, they must become thoroughly familiar with the company's product.

Take the case of a company that makes ice cream. The advertising account executive must learn all about the client's ice cream, including its ingredients, what flavors are available, the way it is made, how it tastes, how it has been advertised in the past, and its share of all ice cream sales. In addition, account executives gain valuable information for an effective advertising campaign by studying competitors' advertising strategies. In this case the executives would examine the advertising tactics of the region's top-selling ice cream manufacturers.

The completed plan typically includes budgeting and scheduling information, projections of sales resulting from the campaign, and specific information on the sales approach and media to be used—all of which are prepared by the advertising account executive. The final step for account executives is selling the client on the advertising campaign. They may spend a considerable amount of time resolving differences and making changes in the plan until the client grants approval.

Although clients may be consulted frequently in the course of advertising campaigns, it is the account executives who actually direct them. They see that ad campaigns appear on schedule and stay within the limits of the proposed budget. They meet with the artists, writers, photographers, and others who create the ads. During campaigns account executives keep one eye on the creative quality of the ads and the other on the sales figures. If an ad campaign does not achieve the expected results, they must make changes or risk losing the account. A successful campaign, on the other hand, usually guarantees repeat business from the client and may lead to campaigns for new clients.

Education and Training Requirements

Prospective advertising account executives need at least a bachelor's degree to enter the field. A major in advertising, marketing, business administration, or the liberal arts is useful preparation. Many large advertising agencies prefer applicants who have a master's degree in business administration.

Any job experience in sales, advertising, market research, or advertising research is helpful for landing a job as an entry-level account executive. Summer work, part-time jobs, and internships are a good way to start. Large advertising agencies usually offer a specialized training program for account executives. In smaller agencies new hires learn the business from seasoned executives.

Getting the Job

Competition is fierce for entry-level positions at top advertising agencies. Qualified candidates should apply directly to the ad agencies for which they would like to work. School placement offices sometimes help their students find positions. Private employment agencies, newspaper want ads, and career sites on the Internet also provide job listings in this field.

Advancement Possibilities and Employment Outlook

With skill, experience—and sometimes luck—an account executive can advance to the highest positions in an agency. Executives may become account supervisors of one or more accounts or go to work for a former client as an advertising manager. Many account executives start their own agencies.

According to the U.S. Bureau of Labor Statistics, advertising account executives held about 154,000 jobs in 2004. Employment of account executives was expected to grow as fast as the average for all occupations between 2004 and 2014. As the population expands and more outlets for advertising become available on the Internet and through cable television, ad agencies will likely hire more account executives. It is important to keep in mind, however, that the need for new hires may decrease somewhat if advances in office technology make existing account executives more productive. Competition within the advertising industry is notoriously keen.

Working Conditions

Advertising account executives work under a great deal of pressure in a highly competitive environment. They put in long hours and are ultimately responsible for seeing that artists and copywriters meet their schedules. In addition, the position of advertising account executive offers little job security. If an advertising agency loses a big account, the people who worked on that account may lose their jobs.

Account management does have its perks, however. Executives have expense accounts for clients, do a lot of wining and dining to win business, and occasionally go on location to assist in filming commercials.

Earnings and Benefits

Salaries vary depending on the location of the agency and the account executive's experience and education. The Bureau of Labor Statistics reported that in 2004 the median annual salary for advertising account executives was $40,300. Those who demonstrated an ability to run consistently successful campaigns earned much more. The top-paid 10 percent of account executives made $89,720 or more per year. Benefits include paid vacations and holidays as well as health insurance and retirement plans.

Where to Go for More Information

American Academy of Advertising
College of Mass Communications
Texas Tech University
Box 43082
Lubbock, TX 79409
(806) 742-3385
http://advertising.utexas.edu/AAA/

American Advertising Federation
1101 Vermont Ave. NW, Ste. 500
Washington, DC 20005-6306
(202) 898-0089
http://www.aaf.org/

American Association of Advertising
   Agencies
405 Lexington Ave., 18th Fl.
New York, NY 10174-1801
(212) 682-2500
http://www.aaaa.org/

Advertising Manager

Education and Training
Bachelor's degree minimum; master's degree preferred

Salary
Median—$63,610 to $107,030 per year

Employment Outlook
Very good

Definition and Nature of the Work

Companies employ advertising managers to publicize their goods or services. Just as most companies have departments that handle marketing, accounting, production, and human resources, they also have a department that handles advertising. Advertising managers head these departments. They work closely with marketing directors to identify their company's target market, outline goals, and set budgets for their ad campaign. The main goal of an advertising manager is to find the most effective means of informing customers about their firm's products and services.

Some companies handle part or all of their own advertising. In such cases all display, point-of-sale, and direct-mail advertising are created by the company's advertising department rather than by an outside ad agency. In a company that has a large advertising department, the advertising manager oversees the department's work and coordinates the efforts of staff members who create and place the ads. In a small department, however, the manager may actually perform some of the department's tasks, including creating the art and copy and handling work such as media buying.

Companies that do not handle their own advertising use the services of advertising agencies to plan and create their ad campaigns. In these cases advertising managers typically work with account executives at ad agencies to come up with the best ad campaigns. When projects are outsourced to an ad agency, advertising managers select the agency, explain their companies' ideas to agency account executives, and supervise the advertising agencies' handling of the account. Based on their own market research, advertising managers may know what advertising media they want to use. Authority to approve agency plans often lies with the advertising managers, but in some cases top management has final approval of all ad campaigns.

After an ad campaign is launched, advertising managers keep track of its effectiveness. If a campaign fails to produce the desired results, managers may decide to make changes to it or scrap it altogether.

An advertising manager works with a marketing director to develop goals and an advertising budget for a specific product. (© John Henley/Corbis.)

Education and Training Requirements

Advertising managers are highly skilled workers with many years of experience. Some become managers after years of working for advertising agencies as advertising account executives. Others work their way up in the advertising departments of large companies.

To get into the field of advertising, candidates need a college education. Courses in the liberal arts, communications, business administration, journalism, and marketing are useful. Many employers require advertising managers to have a master's degree, and a growing number of managers are also completing certification programs.

Getting the Job

Interested individuals should apply directly to the companies for which they would like to work. Newspaper want ads, career sites on the Internet, and trade journals often list openings for entry-level jobs in advertising departments. Private employment agencies may also provide help in finding jobs.

Advancement Possibilities and Employment Outlook

Advertising managers are already in top positions. Some take jobs with larger corporations, where they have greater responsibilities and more challenging work. Others go to work for advertising agencies or start their own agencies. As with all top management positions, there is stiff competition for the position of advertising manager.

According to the U.S. Bureau of Labor Statistics, employment of advertising managers was expected to grow faster than the average for all occupations between 2004 and 2014. The number of products and services competing for American dollars will likely increase in coming years. As the marketplace becomes more competitive, more advertising managers will be needed to ensure products find their way into the hands of customers.

Working Conditions

Advertising managers work under considerable pressure. Each of their campaigns is expected to produce a visible increase in their companies' sales volume. They generally work long hours in order to meet deadlines and to properly coordinate the activities of many different workers in their department.

Earnings and Benefits

Salaries vary according to the size and location of the agency. The U.S. Bureau of Labor Statistics reported that in 2004 advertising managers earned a median annual salary of $63,610. Those in the high-tech industry made much more. For example, the median salary for advertising managers at computer systems design companies was $107,030 per year. Managers generally receive benefits such as paid holidays and vacations, health and life insurance, and retirement plans. Many managers also receive bonuses and stock in the company and participate in profit-sharing plans.

Where to Go for More Information

American Academy of Advertising
College of Mass Communications
Texas Tech University
Box 43082
Lubbock, TX 79409
(806) 742-3385
http://advertising.utexas.edu/AAA/

American Advertising Federation
1101 Vermont Ave. NW, Ste. 500
Washington, DC 20005-6306
(202) 898-0089
http://www.aaf.org/

American Association of Advertising
  Agencies
405 Lexington Ave., 18th Fl.
New York, NY 10174-1801
(212) 682-2500
http://www.aaaa.org/

Distribution Manager

Education and Training
Bachelor's degree plus training minimum; master's degree plus training preferred

Salary
Average—$73,050 per year

Employment Outlook
Good

Definition and Nature of the Work

Distribution managers oversee the transportation of goods from the place where they are made or grown to the location where they are used or consumed. Such managers are employed by almost all large business organizations, including manufacturing firms, wholesale distributors, and retail chains.

The process of moving goods from producer to buyer, called logistics, generally involves several steps. In wholesale distribution, goods arriving from a manufacturer are first inventoried and arrangements are made for shipping goods to a point of sale. In manufacturing distribution, managers are responsible for incoming raw materials as well as inventory control and shipment of finished products.

When making arrangements for shipping, distribution managers must address issues such as how much freight to place on each shipment, what routes the shipments must take, and whether enough truck drivers are available to make the shipments. Once the products ship, they must monitor the progress of the major shipments to ensure they reach their destinations on time. In small companies these tasks are handled by the distribution manager and several assistants. In large companies the distribution manager directs a logistics division with separate departments for receiving, warehousing, and shipping goods.

Supervising the complex operations of a logistics division is usually only part of a distribution manager's work. As a member of the company's top management team, a distribution manager works with marketing executives to ensure that new products reach the right markets at the optimal time. Getting a product to a market on time and at low cost is crucial to its success in competitive retail fields, especially around the holiday season.

A distribution manager in a large company works with a marketing executive to ensure that new products reach the right markets. (© Terry Wild Studio. Reproduced by permission.)

Education and Training Requirements

Distribution managers must have excellent managerial skills and a solid understanding of economics. A college degree in business, accounting, or economics is a prerequisite for the job. Because most logistics departments rely heavily on computers, courses in computer science are very useful. Companies with extremely complex logistics operations (such as multinational corporations) may require candidates to have a master's degree in business administration or distribution management.

Getting the Job

Managers are often hired from within their company's logistics division. Experience as an inventory control analyst, warehouse supervisor, or traffic manager is useful. Distribution managers may also be recruited from other companies. Openings for experienced distribution managers are often listed on Internet job sites and in newspaper want ads.

Advancement Possibilities and Employment Outlook

Experienced and successful distribution managers can advance to top corporate posts. In large companies distribution managers may become vice presidents. Some managers set up their own transportation or logistics consulting firms. According to the U.S. Bureau of Labor Statistics, employment of distribution managers was expected to increase about as fast as the average for all jobs between 2004 and 2014. The demand for goods and the need to distribute them fluctuates with the economy as a whole. As companies continue to put more emphasis on efficient logistics, talented distribution managers will be in demand.

Working Conditions

Working conditions vary, depending on the size of a company's logistics operation. In small companies distribution managers divide their time between the office and the warehouse. Managers working in larger companies may spend all of their time in the office or in meetings with assistants and other managers. Hours also vary according to the volume of goods that need to be handled. Most managers work forty to forty-five hours a week.

Earnings and Benefits

According to the Bureau of Labor Statistics, the average annual salary for distribution managers in 2004 was $73,050. Benefits include paid holidays and vacations, medical insurance, and retirement plans.

Where to Go for More Information

Council of Supply Chain Management
  Professionals
2805 Butterfield Rd., Ste. 200
Oak Brook, IL 60523
(630) 574-0985
http://www.cscmp.org/

National Association of Wholesaler-
  Distributors
1725 K St. NW, Ste. 300
Washington, DC 20006-1419
(202) 872-0885
http://www.naw.org/

E-Commerce Marketing Manager

Definition and Nature of the Work

As the twenty-first century advances many companies are finding new markets and new customers by offering products and services on the World Wide Web. E-commerce marketing managers are responsible for developing and carrying out plans to help companies take advantage of the marketing and sales opportunities available through the Internet.

E-commerce marketing managers help define their companies' objectives for using electronic commerce and decide what computer applications are needed to achieve them. As part of this process marketing managers must develop marketing plans that explain how the e-commerce proposals will increase their companies' business.

E-commerce marketing managers must also monitor their companies' e-commerce strategies as they are being implemented. This includes drawing up a schedule for any projects under way and ensuring that the technical teams meet their deadlines. Developing budgets for projects, monitoring costs, providing status reports to management, and incorporating feedback from the executive level are other responsibilities of e-commerce marketing managers.

Education and Training
Bachelor's degree minimum; master's degree preferred; previous Information Technology (IT) experience necessary

Salary
Median—$84,246 per year

Employment Outlook
Very good

E-commerce marketing managers help companies develop Web sites that will promote their businesses and sell products. (© Anthony Redpath/Corbis.)

Education and Training Requirements

The job of an e-commerce marketing manager combines basic business management skills with a knowledge of Internet-based computer applications. Successful candidates should not only enjoy and be proficient at working in a technical environment, they should have the ability to work effectively with a team in a leadership position.

Employers require at least a bachelor's degree in a business or technical field. For candidates with a business background, courses in computer science or engineering are helpful. For some e-commerce marketing manager positions, a master's degree is required.

In addition to academic training the candidate must have relevant experience in an information technology field. This may include experience developing Internet computer applications, working with e-commerce software programs, or familiarity with computer programming languages such as Java or C++. Previous work involving the design of computer interfaces (the look and feel of a computer program with which a user interacts) is a plus. The position also demands experience in marketing management and a thorough knowledge of the industry for which the e-commerce project is being developed.

Getting the Job

Becoming an e-commerce marketing manager requires years of training and experience. Individuals interested in a position as an e-commerce marketing manager may start out as an e-commerce marketing analyst or a Web designer. Internet job banks list the majority of the openings in these fields but because companies of all types are moving rapidly to provide Internet-based services for their customers, some jobs of this type may be listed in daily newspapers or industry magazines. A person with marketing management experience and a technical background who is working for a company considering an e-commerce initiative should investigate the possibility of creating an e-commerce marketing manager position.

Advancement Possibilities and Employment Outlook

A successful e-commerce marketing manager may advance to a position such as marketing director or chief information officer (CIO; the name given to the person responsible for planning and implementing all of a company's technology initiatives). An e-commerce marketing manager is a type of marketing manager; according to the U.S. Bureau of Labor Statistics, employment of marketing managers was expected to increase faster than the average for all occupations between 2004 and 2014. Employment of e-commerce marketing managers may rise at an even greater rate as many companies continue to expand their e-commerce efforts.

Working Conditions

E-commerce marketing managers are business professionals who work in a modern office setting. The work may entail design and development of computer applications, which may mean long hours at a computer terminal. Because of the need to set and meet deadlines, e-commerce marketing managers often work nighttime and weekend hours to complete projects. Meeting with clients sometimes requires travel at times that are convenient for customers.

Earnings and Benefits

According to Salary.com the median yearly wage for an e-commerce marketing manager was $84,246 in 2006. The top-paid 25 percent made more than $98,127. Salaries depend largely on experience and qualifications. These positions typically include attractive benefits packages that feature paid vacations, exceptional medical benefits, savings and retirement plans, stock options, and profit-sharing plans.

Where to Go for More Information

Internet Society
1775 Wiehle Ave., Ste. 102
Reston, VA 20190-5108
(703) 326-9880
http://www.isoc.org/

Import and Export Worker

Definition and Nature of the Work

Import and export workers handle business transactions that take place between companies in foreign nations and firms in the United States. Import workers deal with transactions that involve bringing raw materials or finished products into the United States. Export workers are involved in sending goods or raw materials from the United States to foreign markets. Some workers handle both import and export agreements.

Foreign trade is carried out under various conditions and terms. The duties of import and export workers vary depending on the situation. Many large companies have foreign trade divisions. Export managers in these firms are responsible for increasing the volume and efficiency of foreign trade. They must also make sure their company deals with dependable customers—legitimate companies from countries that have stable governments and sound economies. Export managers are assisted in this work by foreign representatives who live and work abroad, sometimes traveling from country to country to find new customers and maintain contact with established ones. Foreign representatives are also responsible for monitoring the economic and political situation in their territory. Orders from foreign customers are processed by export sales managers, who draw up contracts and arrange for shipments. Export credit managers review the economic situation of customers needing credit and arrange credit terms.

The import divisions of companies employ support managers to supervise the purchase of goods abroad. The selection of foreign merchandise is often in the hands of buyers who live abroad.

Companies that do not have their own export workers sometimes sell goods abroad through export brokers. These brokers receive commissions (a percentage of the selling price) from the sales they make. Export commission-house brokers are engaged in speculation. They buy domestic goods outright and then sell them in foreign countries. Some companies purchase imports from foreign import merchants for resale in the United States.

Manufacturing operations for U.S. companies in foreign countries are generally maintained by nationals, or natives of those countries. American technical personnel such as engineers and scientists are often sent abroad for short periods to

Education and Training
Bachelor's degree plus training; proficiency in a foreign language necessary

Salary
Varies—see profile

Employment Outlook
Good

Import and export workers handle business transactions that take place between companies in foreign nations and firms in the United States. (© Peter Turnley/ Corbis.)

train nationals. Much of the paperwork involved in foreign trade requires the services of translators, bilingual secretaries, and correspondents.

Education and Training Requirements

Individuals interested in the import and export business need a college degree and knowledge of a foreign language to find a job. Although a liberal arts degree may be acceptable, many employers prefer applicants who have a college degree in law, engineering, or accounting. Some require an advanced degree in business administration.

Most jobs in foreign trade require workers to live in the United States. There is keen competition for positions in which workers live and work abroad. Generally the workers selected to work abroad have years of experience and special skills valued by their employers.

Employers train many of their import and export workers through a combination of classroom courses and on-the-job training under the supervision of an experienced worker. Trainees learn U.S. law governing foreign trade as well as the practices of foreign countries.

Getting the Job

Candidates can apply directly to the companies for which they would like to work. Private employment agencies, newspaper want ads, and job banks on the Internet often carry listings for import and export workers.

Advancement Possibilities and Employment Outlook

Import and export workers advance in a variety of ways. Foreign representatives and buyers can be promoted to managerial and executive positions. They can also go into business for themselves as export brokers or import merchants. Experienced workers can advance to managerial and executive positions in their particular field of expertise. Further education is sometimes required for advancement.

Generally employment in the import and export industry fluctuates with the economy of the United States and the world. A sharp increase in the number of foreign-owned corporations, particularly in India and China, should create new positions for importers and exporters in the future. Workers will also be needed to replace those who leave the field.

Working Conditions

Workers who are employed in the United States work forty hours per week at the minimum. Many foreign representatives and buyers spend a good deal of time traveling. Import and export workers who are stationed overseas encounter a variety of conditions: they must become used to local climates, working habits, and living conditions. Working hours vary with the country. All import and export workers who deal with foreign nationals must be tactful and diplomatic, whether their communications are in person, by letter, or by telephone.

Earnings and Benefits

Earnings vary with education and experience. According to Salary.com the median annual salary for import and export managers in 2006 was $80,024. Import and export clerks, who are typically in charge of checking and filling out paperwork, made a median annual wage of $36,113 in 2006. Some managers and clerks earned much more. Workers stationed overseas receive bonuses in the form of overseas incentive allowances. Benefits generally include paid vacations, health and life insurance, and retirement plans.

Where to Go for More Information

American Association of Exporters and Importers
1050 17th St. NW
Washington, DC 20036
(202) 857-8009
http://www.aaei.org/

National Foreign Trade Council
1625 K St. NW, Ste. 200
Washington, DC 20006
(202) 887-0278
http://www.nftc.org/

United States Chamber of Commerce
1615 H St. NW
Washington, DC 20062-2000
(202) 659-6000
http://www.uschamber.com/

Marketing Director

Definition and Nature of the Work

Marketing directors oversee a company's marketing strategy. For the most part marketing directors concern themselves with market segments, which are large groups of consumers defined by income, ethnicity, age, or a number of other factors. Ultimately marketing directors want to know which market segments will buy their company's products and how best to sell those products to their target market.

The duties of a marketing director vary considerably from company to company. Some marketing directors limit themselves to analyzing the market potential and profitability of various products and to developing strategies to achieve the greatest number of sales of those products in the market. Other directors are responsible not only for analyzing markets and proposing strategies but also for implementing those strategies through market research, product development, advertising, and sales promotion programs. Still other marketing directors have sales managers reporting to them.

Marketing directors use a variety of techniques to determine the potential market for a particular product. For example, the number of babies being born in a

Education and Training
Master's degree in business; extensive experience in other marketing positions required

Salary
Median—$138,470 per year

Employment Outlook
Very good

The duties of a marketing director vary considerably from company to company. Some analyze the market potential and profitability of products, whereas others implement sales strategies or are responsible for the overall sales and profit performance. *(© Earl Dotter. Reproduced by permission.)*

given timeframe determines the size of the potential market for baby foods and diapers. Marketing directors determine the probability and the cost of gaining a certain share of the market. They develop strategies that will counter their competitors' advertising approach and gain their company a larger share of the market at the expense of the competition. Marketing directors study sales figures closely to keep track of how their company's products are selling.

Sometimes marketing directors supervise market research. They use the research data to determine what customers do and do not like about certain products and what improvements and new products consumers want to see in stores. Marketing research may be done by outside research firms or by an inside staff. Regardless of who performs the research, it is usually up to the marketing director to make the final interpretations of the data. Based on what the research reveals, the director must recommend and implement a marketing strategy that is within the budget, resources, and capabilities of the company.

Say a manufacturer wants to enter the lawn mower business. The marketing director must first determine not only how many lawns there are in the United States but also what price and what new features a lawn mower would need to capture a certain share of the market. It would also be necessary to develop an advertising campaign to sell the public on the benefits of the new product. The marketing director would be involved in all of these steps and would determine the methods of sales and distribution to be used.

Education and Training Requirements

Most marketing directors have a master's degree in business. They must be familiar with statistics and math and experienced in marketing and sales. Many years of experience are needed to qualify for the position of marketing director. Some directors start in advertising, sales, or product management. (Product managers are responsible for the marketing and sales of a specific product line or brand of goods.)

Getting the Job

Prospective marketing directors must start at the bottom of the field and work their way up. Students seeking an entry-level position in marketing should consult their school placement office for assistance. Marketing jobs are also listed by career sites on the Internet and in local newspapers; after many years of experience candidates can pursue higher positions in marketing.

Advancement Possibilities and Employment Outlook

Marketing directors already hold a top position in their field. In some cases a director can become executive vice president or president of the company. According to the U.S. Bureau of Labor Statistics, employment of all marketing managers was expected to grow faster than the average for all occupations between 2004 and 2014. However, there are many qualified people competing for marketing director positions. Because this is a top management post, few openings occur each year, and turnover among marketing directors is generally low.

Working Conditions

Marketing directors usually work long, unpredictable hours. Their schedules often vary from day to day as they meet and consult with other executives. Directors are typically under a lot of pressure and must deal with problems stemming from different departments such as sales, product development, and advertising.

Earnings and Benefits

According to Salary.com marketing directors made an annual median salary of $138,470 in 2006. Directors receive standard benefits such as paid vacations, insurance, and retirement plans. Many companies also offer stock options to their marketing directors.

Where to Go for More Information

American Marketing Association
311 S. Wacker Dr., Ste. 5800
Chicago, IL 60606
(800) 262-1150
http://www.marketingpower.com/

Sales and Marketing Executives
    International, Inc.
P.O. Box 1390
Sumas, WA 98295-1390
(312) 893-0751
http://www.smei.org/

Marketing Research Worker

Definition and Nature of the Work

Education and Training
Bachelor's degree minimum

Salary
Varies—see profile

Employment Outlook
Very good

Marketing research workers gather and analyze information about how and why people spend money. This information helps a business make many important decisions, including whether to manufacture a new product, what to call the new product, and which advertising media to use for its promotion. In a competitive marketplace both the public and industries spend billions of dollars each year on goods and services. Businesses understand that it is in their best interest to know what consumers are most likely to buy and why.

Many marketing research workers are employed by independent research firms, advertising agencies, trade associations, and public relations companies; others work for business and industrial firms or for the government. A marketing department may be composed of a marketing research director, junior and senior analysts, survey researchers, field workers, coders, and tabulators. This team of workers carries out various stages of research, including planning, field interviewing, tabulating, and analyzing data.

The marketing research process begins when the marketing research director designs a research project that answers a company's need. For example, a soap company may want to find out why its sales are declining. The director may study the company's past sales records, review the competition, and then decide to do a survey of soap buyers to determine what soap is selling and why.

Before the survey can be conducted, a statistician is usually called in to identify a "sample" group of soap buyers, which is a group that accurately represents the soap-buying public. A senior analyst, project director, or survey researcher then works on developing a questionnaire that asks the sample buyers what soap they currently use, how long they have used it, why they like it, and other related questions. The questionnaire must be carefully worded so that the questions are clear and to the point; otherwise, the results of the survey may be misleading or totally meaningless.

Survey researchers are sent out to present the questionnaire to the sample group of people. Interviews are done in person, over the telephone, or through the mail. Once the questionnaires are completed, editors review them, and then tabulators and coders prepare them for data processing. Analysts study the results of the survey and report their findings to the company's top management. The report might find that soap buyers are choosing soaps that have a special additive. Management must then decide whether to add a special ingredient to the company's product in an effort to increase sales.

Some marketing research workers specialize in advertising. They are called advertising researchers or advertising analysts. Like other marketing research workers, advertising researchers conduct surveys to find out which ads sell which products and why. They also analyze what medium (radio, television, newspapers, magazines, or direct mail) should be used for a certain advertiser. Some advertising researchers pretest commercials before they are shown on television. In addition, they may test-market new products in select cities before making the products available nationwide.

Education and Training Requirements

A bachelor's degree is a minimum requirement for most jobs in marketing research. A strong background in English and courses in marketing, economics, statistics, psychology, sociology, and political science are very useful. Good communications skills are also important. Many graduates start out in trainee jobs as coders or tabulators, then become interviewers or research assistants before moving up to higher-level jobs.

Advanced degrees—especially for those working in the private sector—are becoming increasingly desirable to employers because of the trend toward research in specialized markets. An example of a specialized market is industrial marketing, which focuses on the goods or services that manufacturers sell to other manufacturers. Candidates with a degree in engineering and an advanced degree in marketing are in demand to fill top-level positions in industrial marketing. Those who have other combination backgrounds—for instance, a bachelor's degree in criminology and a master's degree in business administration—are often hired to fill management positions in planning and supervision.

Getting the Job

Individuals interested in becoming marketing researchers may begin with a summer or a part-time job tabulating marketing data or surveying people. This experience is very useful in landing a full-time position. College placement offices usually maintain lists of job openings in marketing research. Want ads in newspapers, Internet job sites, and trade and professional journals may also provide leads on jobs.

Advancement Possibilities and Employment Outlook

Advancement depends on a worker's education, experience, and proven ability. Many workers climb the ladder from research assistant to junior analyst to senior analyst or project director. Some are promoted to top management positions such as marketing research director or vice president of marketing, but these jobs are scarce and require years of experience and outstanding management skills. Sometimes experienced research workers go into business for themselves, conducting local independent marketing surveys.

According to the U.S. Bureau of Labor Statistics, 212,000 people held marketing research worker jobs in 2004. Although this field is very sensitive to the state of the economy, analysts predict that employment of marketing researchers will increase faster than the average for all occupations between 2004 and 2014. Marketing researchers will be needed to accommodate the increasingly varied and complex marketing activities of businesses and organizations such as hospitals that seek to promote their services. As businesses continue to expand globally, more market research workers will also be needed to analyze foreign markets. Openings will result as workers retire or leave the field for other reasons. Opportunities should be particularly good in marketing consulting firms.

Working Conditions

Many independent marketing research firms are located in large cities with diverse populations. Researchers frequently work under pressure, putting in overtime when deadlines must be met. They usually work a minimum of forty hours per week. Although most researchers work in well-lit, ventilated offices, others are expected to do some traveling.

Earnings and Benefits

Field survey workers, coders, and tabulators typically start at about the minimum wage. In 2004 the median annual salary for market research workers varied depending on the position, according to a survey by the Bureau of Labor Statistics. Market research analysts earned a median salary of $56,140 per year with the top-paid 10 percent making more than $105,870. Survey researchers, on the other hand, earned a median annual salary of $26,490 with the top-paid 10 percent making about $56,720. Benefits usually include paid holidays and vacations, health insurance, and retirement plans.

Where to Go for More Information

American Marketing Association
311 S. Wacker Dr., Ste. 5800
Chicago, IL 60606
(800) 262-1150
http://www.marketingpower.com/

Marketing Research Association
110 National Dr., 2nd Fl.
Glastonbury, CT 06033
(860) 682-1000
http://www.mra-net.org/

Media Buyer

Definition and Nature of the Work

Media buyers work for advertising agencies and media-buying agencies. They buy advertising space in magazines or newspapers and purchase advertising time on radio or television. Depending on the kind of media in which they work, they may be called space buyers or time buyers.

Media buyers are specialists who are acquainted with the costs of various media. They collect information about the kinds of audiences that can be reached by the different media and the approximate size of those audiences. In advertising agencies media buyers work with account executives to establish a plan for reaching the greatest number of potential customers at the lowest cost to the client. For example, an advertising account executive and a media buyer might decide to use a combination of radio and newspaper advertising. The agency must gain the approval of the client before the plan is put into action. Media buyers then negotiate agreements with the media sales workers employed by newspapers, magazines, cable services, and radio and television stations.

Media buyers who work for media-buying agencies are responsible for tracking down and buying space in print publications, radio, or television markets. They then package and resell this space to advertising agencies or directly to individual companies. Media-buying agencies save ad agencies and companies the time and trouble involved with having to find and buy ad space themselves.

Media buyers work for advertising agencies and negotiate advertising space in newspapers and magazines and on radio and television stations. *(© Earl Dotter. Reproduced by permission.)*

Education and Training Requirements

Employers generally prefer to hire college graduates who have a degree in advertising, liberal arts, marketing, or business administration. Previous experience in advertising or sales is useful preparation for the job.

Advertising agency and media-buying agency workers generally progress to jobs as media buyers from other positions in a firm. Some begin as clerks or assistants. Many large agencies offer formal training programs that prepare new workers for advancement. At other agencies workers learn through on-the-job experience. Some media buyers start as media sales workers before going to work for an advertising agency or media-buying agency.

Getting the Job

Prospective media buyers should apply directly to the advertising agencies and media-buying agencies for which they would like to work. Newspaper want ads and Internet job sites sometimes list openings in advertising agencies. Private employment agencies can also be helpful in finding a job.

Advancement Possibilities and Employment Outlook

Advancement is based on experience and performance on the job. Media buyers with specialized knowledge may be able to command higher salaries or move into management positions in their firms. Other buyers may transfer to larger agencies and handle higher-budgeted accounts.

According to the U.S. Bureau of Labor Statistics, employment of most non-administrative support workers in the advertising industry was expected to increase faster than the average for all occupations between 2004 and 2014. The increase will be due in large part to the continued expansion of cable television advertising time and Internet advertising space. Despite the positive outlook, applicants for jobs as media buyers are likely to face stiff competition.

Working Conditions

Media buyers work in comfortable offices within an advertising or media-buying agency. They usually work forty hours a week or more, but they may be required to put in extra hours to meet deadlines or arrange contracts. Media buyers generally have a great deal of contact with clients and media sales workers. Like other advertising workers, they work under considerable pressure.

Earnings and Benefits

Earnings for media buyers vary depending on their education, experience, and the location and size of the firm for which they work. According to Salary.com media buyers made a median annual salary of $56,279 in 2006. Benefits generally include paid vacations and holidays, life and health insurance, and retirement plans.

Where to Go for More Information

American Advertising Federation
1101 Vermont Ave. NW, Ste. 500
Washington, DC 20005-6306
(202) 898-0089
http://www.aaf.org/

American Association of Advertising
    Agencies
405 Lexington Ave., 18th Fl.
New York, NY 10174-1801
(212) 682-2500
http://www.aaaa.org/

Product Manager

Definition and Nature of the Work

Product managers are responsible for planning and developing the marketing strategy for a single product or group of products. They work with various company departments, including product development, market research, sales, advertising, and public relations and typically report to a marketing manager or marketing director. Product managers can be found in almost every industry, including computers and data processing services, publishing, retail, and manufacturing.

Because product service has become the key to selling goods and services, product managers play an important role within corporations. They estimate the consumer demand for the product they manage, identify potential customers, stay informed of any competing products on the market, develop pricing strategies, and oversee product development. In addition, they work with advertising and public relations staff to promote the firm's goods and services.

Product managers must be able to supervise large groups of workers, think creatively, focus on the overall objectives of the company, and interact with other corporate areas. The growing complexity of doing business means that managers must be increasingly versatile and keep up to date with technological developments.

Education and Training
Bachelor's degree minimum; typically a master's degree in business administration plus training

Salary
Median—$95,900 per year, including bonuses

Employment Outlook
Very good

Product managers may be responsible for coordinating the activities of various departments while planning marketing efforts for a product or brand. (© Martha Tabor/Working Images Photographs. Reproduced by permission.)

Education and Training Requirements

Although a wide range of educational backgrounds is acceptable for entry into product management, all employers require a bachelor's degree and usually an advanced degree or specialized training. Some employers prefer a broad liberal arts background, while others want managers with a bachelor's or master's degree in business administration. Technical industries such as electronics and computer manufacturing may prefer to hire applicants with a bachelor's degree in engineering or science and a master's degree in business administration.

Recommended courses include marketing, communications, technical writing, economics, statistics, business law, advertising, market research, and management. Knowledge of business software such as Microsoft Excel is essential, and completion of a marketing or product development internship while in school is highly recommended.

Getting the Job

Many companies fill product management positions by promoting experienced staff or by hiring individuals from related professional or technical areas. Therefore, individuals interested in product management should seek an entry-level position as a sales representative, purchasing agent, buyer, market researcher, or product specialist. Entry-level positions in these fields are often listed on Internet job sites and in newspaper want ads. Working in conjunction with local colleges and universities, many firms offer management training programs that can accelerate advancement to a product manager position. Some marketing and related associations also sponsor management training programs.

Advancement Possibilities and Employment Outlook

Product managers have high-profile jobs that put them on the fast track for promotions. Successful managers often become top company executives or start their own businesses.

According to the U.S. Bureau of Labor Statistics, employment of marketing managers (the category into which product managers fall) was expected to grow faster than the average for all occupations between 2004 and 2014. The number of products and services competing for American dollars will likely increase in coming years, fueling the need for more product managers.

Working Conditions

Product managers often work well over forty-hour weeks, including evenings and weekends. There is a great deal of pressure connected with this job due to numerous deadlines, schedule changes, and regular meetings with other managers. Many product managers must travel frequently throughout the United States and abroad to meet with their clients.

Earnings and Benefits

Salaries for product managers vary greatly, depending on education, level of responsibility, experience, and the employer's size, location, and industry. Mercer Human Resources Consulting reported in a 2004 survey that product/brand managers made a median of $95,900 per year in bonuses and wages.

In addition to standard benefits that include health insurance, paid holidays and vacations, and retirement plans, many product managers earn bonuses equal to 10 percent or more of their salaries. Some are given stock options and the use of company cars.

Where to Go for More Information

American Marketing Association
311 S. Wacker Dr., Ste. 5800
Chicago, IL 60606
(800) 262-1150
http://www.marketingpower.com/

Promotion Marketing Association
257 Park Ave. S, Ste. 1102
New York, NY 10010
(212) 420-1100
http://www.pmalink.org/

Purchasing Agent

Definition and Nature of the Work

Purchasing agents are in charge of all buying for their company. Unlike retail or wholesale buyers who purchase products for resale, purchasing agents buy the raw materials, goods, and services their company needs to maintain operations. They also buy supplies and services offered by outside contractors such as office cleaners. Purchasing agents are employed by many types of businesses and by institutions such as schools, hospitals, and government offices.

Purchasing agents, or buyers as they are sometimes called, see that their company has a sufficient supply of the materials it needs to operate. However, agents must avoid tying up too much of the company's money in supplies. Their job is to balance quality with cost to ensure that the best purchases are made. Buying an item, material, or service whose quality is too high for its intended use is a waste of company funds. For instance, buying mahogany crates to ship oranges would be a waste of money. Buying an item of low quality may prove costly as well, because it may break down or otherwise malfunction.

It is vital that purchasers stay up to date on overall market conditions and price trends that affect what they are buying. They use the latest pricing information available on the Internet to compute the price of items, the cost of handling and transportation for those items, and the cost of time spent by workers who unload the stock and fill out shipping paperwork. The timing of purchases must be right as well. If a manufacturer runs out of a part, costly production delays may occur. Timing is also important in getting the best prices: in many industries the cost of supplies varies greatly within a season.

Purchasing agents coordinate their company's production schedule with the schedules of many outside suppliers. Sometimes a supplier may be unable to make a delivery because of a strike or a transportation problem. If agents are able to anticipate such delays, they can arrange to buy important supplies ahead of time or take their business to another company.

Additionally, agents work closely with many of the departments in their own company such as the receiving, traffic, and supply departments. They often employ assistants known as expediters who handle much of the paperwork and other details involved in making purchases, arranging shipping, and settling claims.

Education and Training
Bachelor's degree and on-the-job training; master's degree necessary for positions with some companies

Salary
Median—$47,680 per year

Employment Outlook
Fair

Purchasing agents buy materials for companies so that the company has a sufficient supply of materials to continue operating. They take much of their information from price lists and catalogs. (© Martha Tabor/ Working Images Photographs. Reproduced by permission.)

In a small company one purchasing agent may do all the buying for the firm. Large corporations may employ as many as one hundred purchasing agents, each of whom specialize in one aspect of the job such as purchasing one kind of material or a single part for a certain type of machinery.

Education and Training Requirements

Education requirements in this field vary. In general purchasing agents need a college degree and in some cases a master's degree as well. Most companies prefer applicants who have a degree in business administration. College courses in purchasing, office and traffic management, and marketing are helpful. A good understanding of widely used spreadsheet and word processing software is also valuable. In some companies purchasing agents need a great deal of technical knowledge. Specialty firms such as chemical companies may require their agents to have undergraduate training in science and a master's degree in business.

Some purchasing agents begin as expediters and work their way up to better-paying jobs with more responsibilities. Other beginners are hired as purchasing department trainees. Trainees learn on the job and may receive classroom instruction as well. They may also work for short periods of time in other departments to learn about the company's purchasing needs. Most training periods last one to five years.

Getting the Job

Students can find assistance in their job search at their school placement office. Public and private employment agencies, newspaper want ads, and Internet job sites often list openings for purchasing agents. Interested individuals can also apply directly to the firms for which they would like to work. For a government job candidates need to take the civil service test.

Advancement Possibilities and Employment Outlook

With experience, purchasing agents can advance to the positions of assistant purchasing manager or purchasing department head. They may also be promoted to top posts in the traffic or warehousing department. Workers with a graduate degree in business generally have a better chance for advancement than those without one.

According to the U.S. Bureau of Labor Statistics, purchasing agents held 273,000 jobs in 2004. Employment of purchasing agents was expected to grow more slowly than the average for all occupations between 2004 and 2014. The Internet and computers allow purchasing agents to gain access to vast amounts of information and make deals at the touch of a button. With these innovations agents can do their work much faster, eliminating some of the need for additional agents as business expands.

Aside from technological advances, trends in business show that many more materials—steel and lumber, for instance—are entering the United States from foreign countries. Companies are hiring foreign purchasing agents who speak the language and know the customs of these countries to handle this type of buying. However, there will be a need in the United States to replace purchasing agents who retire or leave their jobs for other reasons.

Working Conditions

Purchasing agents spend most of their time in an office, although they occasionally visit plants and attend conferences. Overtime beyond a standard forty-hour workweek is sometimes necessary, especially in industries in which production is seasonal. Purchasing agents must be problem solvers with an eye for detail and the ability to coordinate many activities.

Earnings and Benefits

Salary varies with the size of the company and the worker's education and experience. Purchasing agents earned a median salary of $47,680 per year in 2004, according to the Bureau of Labor Statistics. The top-paid 10 percent made more than $79,710 a year. Some companies offer bonuses, depending on yearly profits. Benefits include paid holidays and vacations, health insurance, and retirement plans.

Where to Go for More Information

American Purchasing Society
8 E. Galena Blvd., Ste. 203
Aurora, IL 60506
(630) 859-0250
http://www.american-purchasing.com/

Institute for Supply Management
P.O. Box 22160
Tempe, AZ 85285-2160
(800) 888-6276
http://www.ism.ws/

Real Estate Appraiser

Definition and Nature of the Work

Real estate appraisers investigate all aspects of buildings and land to determine their value. This value is used for purchase, sale, investment, mortgage, or loan purposes.

The value of a building is determined by making an appraisal—an estimate of the most probable price for which a property should sell under current market conditions. To make these estimates real estate appraisers begin by visiting a property and talking with people familiar with it. They then measure the property and inspect it for design, construction, and condition.

Having gathered this information, real estate appraisers take a number of other factors into account. They use a variety of standard formulas to assess possible losses in value and reproduction costs. They also consider location and other trends that could influence the future value of the property.

Real estate appraisers search public records for any additional information that may assist them in making an appraisal, including records of previous sales, leases, assessments, and other transactions. The records are usually found in local government offices or computer databases accessible through the Internet.

After all the information on a property has been collected, real estate appraisers make an estimate of the value of the property and prepare a detailed report that includes a legal and physical description of the property, photographs, plans, and an explanation of the estimate. Appraisers must be able to stand behind

Education and Training
At least two years of college, on-the-job training, and a state license

Salary
Median—$43,390 per year

Employment Outlook
Very good

their assessments when questioned by property owners and realtors. Sometimes appraisers are brought in to public hearings to testify on the value of property.

Some real estate appraisers evaluate several different types of real estate; others specialize in appraising commercial, residential, rental, or agricultural property. The work performed may depend on where an appraiser works. Some appraisers choose private practice or partnerships, while others work for private corporations or financial institutions.

Education and Training Requirements

To become a real estate appraiser a candidate has to meet state licensing requirements, which are usually established by a state assessor's board. There are three types of widely accepted licenses: the State Licensed Appraiser license, the Certified General Real Property Appraiser license, and the State Certified Residential Real Property Appraiser license. Candidates working for their licenses are classified as trainees and typically work with licensed, independent appraisers, real estate firms, and financial institutions. Obtaining the basic license—the State Licensed Appraiser—usually requires ninety education hours and thousands of hours of on-the-job training. The other two licenses have much more rigorous requirements; holders of these licenses can appraise property of any value.

General education requirements are a high school diploma and at least two years of college. Many employers, including banks, appraisal firms, and federal agencies, require a bachelor's degree. A degree in real estate or valuation sciences is useful but not required. Valuable college courses include business administration, economics, agriculture, mathematics, architecture, engineering, and writing.

Getting the Job

College placement offices may be helpful in finding entry-level positions for individuals interested in real estate appraising. After gaining the necessary experience and obtaining a license, candidates can apply directly to companies that employ real estate appraisers. Public and private employment agencies, newspaper want ads, and Internet job sites often list openings. Prospective appraisers interested in local, state, or federal government positions should apply to their local civil service agency for further information.

Advancement Possibilities and Employment Outlook

Qualified real estate appraisers with experience may become senior appraisers or senior real estate analysts. Some appraisers may advance by becoming specialists in a particular kind of property, such as industrial or agricultural property. Those with at least a bachelor's degree may move into management positions in commercial banks.

According to the U.S. Bureau of Labor Statistics, employment of real estate appraisers was expected to grow faster than the average for all occupations between 2004 and 2014. As the population grows, real estate activity and the need for appraisers should continue to increase. Although this field is very sensitive to changes in the economy and fluctuating interest rates, jobs should always be available for well-trained appraisers because of a high turnover rate and replacement needs.

Working Conditions

Real estate appraisers often work more than forty hours a week. To contact buyers and sellers, appraisers make many of their appointments outside of office hours. They do a great deal of local traveling to properties to be appraised and to local government offices. Appraisers usually work independently, whether they are in private practice or part of a private corporation. They spend much of their time doing on-site investigations, which may have to be done in bad weather. The rest of their time is usually spent in modern offices, where they complete the paperwork necessary to prepare an appraisal.

Earnings and Benefits

Earnings vary considerably, depending on experience, training, and the nature of the job. Many beginning appraisers work on a freelance basis while they earn their professional qualifications. According to the Bureau of Labor Statistics, in 2004 the median annual salary for real estate appraisers was $43,390. The top-paid 10 percent made more than $81,240 per year.

Benefits usually include paid holidays and vacations and health and retirement plans. Appraisers who own their own businesses or who work on a freelance basis must provide their own benefits.

Where to Go for More Information

American Society of Appraisers
555 Herdon Pkwy., Ste. 125
Herndon, VA 20170
(703) 478-2228
http://www.appraisers.org/

Appraisal Institute
550 W. Buren St., Ste. 1000
Chicago, IL 60607
(312) 335-4100
http://www.appraisalinstitute.org/

National Association of Real Estate
   Appraisers
1224 N. Nokomis NE
Alexandria, MN 56308
(320) 763-7626
http://www.iami.org/

Retail Buyer

Definition and Nature of the Work

Retail buyers work for retail stores, including department and variety stores, specialty shops, and chain stores. They buy the goods that a store sells to its customers. Buyers who work for large department stores usually specialize in one type of merchandise such as home furnishings. Those who work for small stores may buy a variety of merchandise, and those who work for chain stores often purchase goods for a number of the store's outlets.

Buyers must be able to choose items that are appropriate for their store and its clientele. For example, a budget department store will need low-cost goods, whereas a clothing boutique may specialize in relatively expensive clothes for young customers. Buyers usually purchase merchandise about six months before it is shown in the stores. Therefore, they must be able to anticipate trends in fashion and consumer needs.

Retail buyers familiarize themselves with available merchandise through catalogs and by traveling to trade shows that display new consumer goods. Fashion buyers attend seasonal fashion shows held by clothing manufacturers that feature the latest designer styles. In order to choose items that will sell, buyers must know their customers. They do this by examining computerized sales records and by spending time on the selling floors.

Retail buyers also work with the advertising department on sales promotions. Buyers are rewarded for increasing sales in their department. Computers and

Education and Training
Bachelor's degree and training program

Salary
Median—$42,230 per year

Employment Outlook
Fair

A retail buyer and assistant buyer discuss the store's merchandise needs for the upcoming year. (© Terry Wild Studio. Reproduced by permission.)

other business equipment have greatly improved buyers' efficiency by providing instant access to merchandise specifications and inventory records and speeding up the selection and ordering process.

Retail buyers work under merchandise managers. Together they decide how much money is spent on merchandise. The manager determines how much extra the store will charge for an item beyond what the buyer has paid. It is this extra cost that produces the company's profits.

Assistant buyers help buyers with the routine aspects of retailing. They may supervise sales personnel, keep records, verify orders and shipments, and deal with customers who want to return or exchange merchandise.

Education and Training Requirements

Employers generally prefer applicants who have a bachelor's degree from a college or university. Knowledge of the merchandise is essential and some previous experience in retailing is helpful. Companies seek candidates who have good judgment and analytical ability. They also look for creative workers who are willing to take calculated risks.

Some schools offer courses in retailing or buying. Many beginners enter executive training programs directly after graduation. The competition for a spot in these programs is often intense. Some programs place new workers in sales or clerical positions, whereas others offer formal classes. Trainees generally become assistant buyers within a year of being hired. From there they may advance to jobs as buyers. Throughout their careers retail buyers read trade journals and other material to keep abreast of news in the changing marketplace.

Getting the Job

Individuals interested in becoming buyers can apply directly to retail stores. School placement offices may help their students get an interview with prospective employers who visit college campuses. In addition, both public and private employment agencies list jobs in retail sales. Entry-level positions are often included on Internet career sites and in classified ads in newspapers.

Advancement Possibilities and Employment Outlook

Advancement depends mainly on performance. Assistant buyers generally move on to jobs as retail buyers after several years, and from there they may advance to the position of merchandise manager. Managers may go on to become company vice presidents or open their own firms. Advancement to the higher levels of management usually requires a graduate degree in business.

According to the U.S. Bureau of Labor Statistics, retail buyers held 156,000 jobs in 2004. Employment of retail buyers was expected to grow more slowly than the average for all occupations between 2004 and 2014. The Internet and computers allow retail buyers to gain access to vast amounts of information on products and close deals with the touch of a button. With these innovations retail buyers can do their work much faster, eliminating some of the need for additional agents as business expands. Continued mergers of big retail outfits will likely lead to the consolidation and subsequent downsizing of buying departments. Some new openings will result as consumer spending increases and corresponding expansion occurs in retail trade. Jobs will also become available as experienced buyers retire or leave their jobs for other reasons.

Working Conditions

Buyers generally work more than forty hours a week. Most buyers work some evenings, especially during busy seasons. Merchandise managers tend to work more regular hours. Buyers spend about one-third of their working time on buying trips to major cities in the United States, Europe, and East and Southeast Asia. Assistant buyers sometimes accompany them. The work, despite its demanding nature, can be stimulating and glamorous.

Earnings and Benefits

Salaries vary widely, depending on experience and the quantity and type of merchandise purchased. According to the Bureau of Labor Statistics, the median annual income for buyers was $42,230 in 2004. The top-paid 10 percent made more than $79,340 a year. Merchandise managers generally earned higher salaries.

Benefits generally include paid vacations and health and retirement plans. Many stores also provide buyers with cash bonuses and discounts on items purchased in the store.

Where to Go for More Information

American Collegiate Retailing Association
Department of Marketing
Georgia Southern University
P.O. Box 8154
Statesboro, GA 30460
(912) 681-5336
http://www.acraretail.org/

American Marketing Association
311 S. Wacker Dr., Ste. 5800
Chicago, IL 60606
(800) 262-1150
http://www.marketingpower.com/

National Retail Federation
325 Seventh St. NW, Ste. 1100
Washington, DC 20004
(202) 783-7971
http://www.nrf.com/

Sales Engineer

Definition and Nature of the Work

Sales engineers demonstrate and sell highly technical products such as computer networks or manufacturing equipment to large companies and institutions. They also work with their company's engineering and research and development departments to devise new ways of putting their company's products to use.

Most sales engineers work for large manufacturers. Unlike rank-and-file salespeople, sales engineers do not visit potential clients and recite a standard sales pitch. Rather, they are usually brought in after a client has already been in touch with the company. Their job is to listen to potential clients' needs and attempt to explain how their product—be it a turbine or a robot welder—can satisfy those needs. Sales engineers must also demonstrate in extensive, technical detail how their product is better than that of the competition.

Following a sale, sales engineers may supervise the installation of the system and provide training for the employees who will use the product. They also maintain contact with their clients to ensure that the clients' needs have been met and to assist them with any additional problems that may arise well after the purchase.

Sales engineers are in constant contact with customers and have a good idea of the improvements customers would like to see in the products they buy. Together with the research and development departments in their own companies, sales engineers work to bring their products in line with customer expectations.

Education and Training Requirements

Most sales engineers have undergraduate engineering degrees and work for a number of years as engineers before moving to the position of sales engineer. Sometimes employers will hire inexperienced engineers who have just graduated from college and train them further at the company's expense. The training typically involves being paired up with an experienced sales engineer and learning on the job. After training, the new sales engineer will team up with an experienced salesperson in need of engineering knowledge.

Individuals interested in becoming sales engineers must be analytical and detailed oriented. They must be good at solving logic problems. Because they are salespersons, they must also be persuasive, good with people, and impeccably groomed.

Getting the Job

Most sales engineering jobs require prior experience. Students who have earned engineering degrees should visit their college placement office for information on entry-level engineering jobs. After gaining several years of experience, interested individuals can apply directly to companies that employ sales engineers, such as computer systems design companies or makers of manufacturing equipment. Ads for sales engineers may be listed in the classified section of the newspaper or on Internet job sites.

Advancement Possibilities and Employment Outlook

Most sales engineers advance as they receive higher commission rates (a commission is a percentage of the selling price) or larger sales territories. With some additional business training, they can move into top management positions within the companies where they work. Some sales engineers start their own firms and sell equipment for a number of different manufacturers.

According to the U.S. Bureau of Labor Statistics, sales engineers held 74,000 jobs in 2004. Employment of sales engineers was expected to grow as fast as the average for all occupations between 2004 and 2014. As high-tech products become more complex and varied, companies will continue to expand their engineering sales force. Jobs will also become available as sales engineers retire or leave the profession.

Working Conditions

Many sales engineers do a great deal of traveling. Because they work for commissions or bonuses, they usually try to work with customers for as many hours each day as they can. Sales engineers must be friendly and enthusiastic about their work and be able to adjust easily to the personalities of their various customers.

Earnings and Benefits

Earnings for sales engineers vary widely, depending on the industry, the employer, and their degree. According to the Bureau of Labor Statistics, in 2004 sales engineers earned a median annual income of $70,620. The top-paid 10 percent earned more than $117,260 per year.

Benefits usually include health and life insurance, paid holidays and vacations, and retirement plans. Many sales workers are given a company car for business use or are reimbursed for the use of their own car and other travel expenses.

Where to Go for More Information

American Society for Information Science
 and Technology
1320 Fenwick Ln., Ste. 510
Silver Spring, MD 20910
(301) 495-0900
http://www.asis.org

Manufacturing Agents National
 Association
P.O. Box 3467
Laguna Hills, CA 92654
(877) 626-2776
http://www.manaonline.org

Sales Manager

Definition and Nature of the Work

Sales managers train, direct, and supervise their sales staff. They coordinate the operation of their sales department by establishing territories, goals, and quotas for their sales workers. Reviewing market analyses helps them to determine customer needs, sales volume potential, and pricing schedules that will meet company goals.

The specific duties of sales managers vary from company to company. In general sales managers hire, train, and are responsible for the sales workers. In some large companies specialized sales training managers perform these duties. In all companies sales managers assign sales territories, or geographic regions, to selling personnel. They also evaluate the performance of the sales workers. Sales managers represent their companies at trade association conventions and meetings to promote their products. Some monitor customer preferences and direct and supervise product research and development. They may also be in charge of recommending or approving budgets for product research and development.

A company that employs a sales manager usually does so because the firm has many sales workers on its staff. In addition to employing a staff of sales workers, a company may also arrange to have its goods or services marketed by indepen-

Education and Training
Bachelor's degree minimum and prior experience

Salary
Median— $84,220 per year

Employment Outlook
Very good

dent companies such as dealers, distributors, and jobbers. In this situation a sales manager may work closely with the sales staffs of these independent companies. Some sales managers offer direction to the sales personnel of retailers or wholesalers that market their employer's products.

The size of the company dictates the scope and responsibility of the sales manager's job. Small companies may have only one sales manager, while some very large corporations employ managers to direct each level of the sales operation. A large company may employ a general sales manager, home office and overseas sales managers, and regional sales managers.

Education and Training Requirements

Sales managers must be experienced in sales and marketing. They need knowledge of statistics and mathematics. Some employers prefer to hire candidates with a master's degree in business. Sales managers working in highly technical fields such as computer manufacturing may be required to have both a technical degree and a business degree.

Getting the Job

It takes years of accumulated experience to become a sales manager. Many prospective sales managers begin as sales workers or start out in marketing, advertising, or product management. Candidates may apply directly to the firms for which they would like to work or check Internet job banks and the classified ads for entry-level positions.

Advancement Possibilities and Employment Outlook

Sales managers are already at the top of their field. Some sales managers change jobs because they are offered higher salaries or more challenging work. They may advance to the position of company president or vice president.

According to the U.S. Bureau of Labor Statistics, sales managers held 337,000 jobs in 2004. Employment of sales managers was expected to grow faster than the average for all occupations between 2004 and 2014. The number of products and services competing for American dollars will likely increase in coming years. As the marketplace becomes more competitive, more sales managers will be needed to ensure products find their way into the hands of customers.

Working Conditions

Sales managers generally work long, unpredictable hours. Their work revolves around a set number of projects rather than a set number of working hours. The job can be stressful because sales managers are often confronted with problems stemming from other departments such as marketing, product development, and advertising.

Earnings and Benefits

Sales managers in 2004 earned a median annual salary of $84,220, according to the Bureau of Labor Statistics. Those in the high-tech industry made much more. Sales managers for computer systems design companies, for instance, made a median salary of $119,140 per year in 2004.

Benefits usually include paid vacations, health and life insurance, and retirement plans. Many companies also offer stock options to their sales managers.

Where to Go for More Information

American Management Association
1601 Broadway
New York, NY 10019
(212) 586-8100
http://www.amanet.org/

Sales and Marketing Executives
  International
P.O. Box 1390
Sumas, WA 98295-1390
(312) 893-0751
http://www.smei.org/

Sports Management Professional

Definition and Nature of the Work

From high-profile major league and international contests to local professional and amateur events, spectator sports are an increasingly popular source of entertainment. The multibillion-dollar sports industry offers employment opportunities for management, marketing, and supervisory professionals at all levels of competition. Groups employing sports management professionals include academic institutions, major league and minor league professional sports franchises, independent sports confederations (such as the Professional Golfers' Association), sporting goods companies, and independent sports marketing and management consulting firms.

Sports management professionals hold a number of different positions. Promotion and development directors are hired by sports teams and school athletic programs to design and implement promotional campaigns that will increase ticket sales. These directors also negotiate sponsorships in which advertisers and/or sporting goods manufacturers pay a fee to have their ads or products featured at a sporting event.

Sports information directors act as a liaison between teams and athletic departments on the one hand and the news media on the other. They prepare press guides and press releases and organize "media days" at which athletes and coaches make themselves available to reporters, photographers, and the broadcast media. Information directors may also be responsible for creating a club's official publications, including programs, commemorative magazines, and Web sites.

Athletic directors and general managers coordinate the activities of teams and athletic departments. They are responsible for personnel decisions involving coaches, athletes, and support staff; and they often supervise employees who manage sports facilities. Athletic directors and general managers report to team owners (in the case of professional sports) or to university trustees and school boards (in the case of academic sports).

Sports agents or representatives provide a variety of services to athletes and coaches. They negotiate playing or coaching contracts, work out product endorsement fees, and provide financial, investment, and tax advice. Agents may also offer personal and legal advice to clients.

Sports management professionals combine a love for athletics with business and marketing savvy. There is no set career track in the field. Many sports management professionals are former athletes themselves. Some are trained in other professional disciplines, such as law, accounting, or business management, and come to sports management via their original careers.

Sports management is an intensely competitive career field, and individuals wishing to break into it should be prepared to work long hours. It takes years to gain experience and establish contacts in the sports industry. Sports management professionals require sharp negotiating skills, shrewd political instincts, and an overwhelming desire to succeed.

Education and Training Requirements

Sports management and marketing professionals are, as a rule, college educated. Some universities offer programs in sports management; other recommended courses of study include marketing, accounting, business management, and business law. Individuals interested in a career as a sports information director should major in journalism and might consider working in the media before pursuing a career in sports management.

Many top sports supervisors, marketers, and agents are trained as attorneys or have graduate degrees in business management. The educational levels of individuals engaged in the highest levels of negotiations over player contracts, product endorsements, and television rights will continue to increase as the amount of money involved in sports promotion grows.

Getting the Job

Many sports management professionals enter the field with low-level, unglamorous jobs and work their way up. Candidates should pursue internships in team offices or school athletic departments. Volunteering as a coach or official for local athletics is a good way to learn the basics of sports management and show a commitment to athletics and athletes. These jobs may be advertised on career sites on the Internet or in local newspapers.

Advancement Possibilities and Employment Outlook

The sports business is a huge and growing industry. Opportunities in sports management and marketing should grow in the coming years; however, competition for jobs in this "glamour" industry will be intense.

Working Conditions

Work conditions for sports management professionals varies widely depending on the organization or institution for which they work. All sports managers work long hours, especially those involved with professional sports. The work often entails attending sports events at night and on weekends, although for a sports fan that aspect of the job is a tremendous perk. Many sports management jobs require extensive travel with teams or individual athletes.

Where to Go for More Information

American Management Association
1601 Broadway
New York, NY 10019
(212) 586-8100
http://www.amanet.org/

National Association of Sports Officials
2017 Lathrop Ave.
Racine, WI 53405
(262) 632-5448
http://www.naso.org/

Earnings and Benefits

The amount of money to be made in sports management varies widely according to the level of competition and the value of the teams or athletes involved. According to Salary.com, athletic directors at colleges and universities made a median salary of $94,406 in 2006.

Professional league sports agents typically do not earn a set salary. Instead they take home a percentage of a client's pay—usually anywhere from 3 to 10 percent. An agent who represents professional football players could earn millions of dollars per year. Professional team managers who manage major league teams can also make salaries well over $1 million. Those who manage minor league teams make considerably less. Benefits for sports management professionals working in a large organization generally include paid vacations and health and retirement plans.

Store Manager

Definition and Nature of the Work

Store managers are responsible for supervising employees and running their store at a profit. To attract a clientele and move merchandise, managers make sure that their store offers products and services that satisfy the needs and desires of their customers.

Store managers are employed by general merchandise stores, such as department stores and so-called "big box" stores, and by specialty stores, such as supermarkets and sporting goods outlets. The duties of a manager vary with the store's structure and method of operation. Some stores are part of a chain that has a central office and branch outlets. Chain operations require general managers to oversee branch managers, who in turn oversee the managers for each of the outlets. Other stores are independently owned and operated.

The duties of store managers also depend on the size and type of store for which they work. The business aspects of a store can be divided into four categories: merchandising, which includes buying and selling; store operations, which includes hiring personnel and receiving goods; accounting and bookkeeping; and advertising and promotion. In some stores—generally independent ones—store managers are involved in all of these areas. In a small gift shop, for example, the manager may buy the merchandise, sell it to customers, and do the bookkeeping. The same manager may also train sales workers and write advertising copy.

The manager of a large store, on the other hand, is usually involved in setting policy that will be carried out by division heads. Large independent stores often divide management duties among three or four executives. A typical management team featuring division heads might consist of a store manager, an operations manager, a controller, and an advertising manager.

In chain operations managers are usually supervised by area representatives from the central office. Merchandise for all retail store outlets is purchased by a central buying office. Branch managers of outlet stores order only through this central office. Accounting for the whole chain is also handled at a central office. Store managers do their ordering and submit bookkeeping forms or sales reports electronically by computer.

Education and Training Requirements

Educational requirements for store managers vary. Managers reach their positions through years of experience in the retailing business. Positions in large, independent stores are generally the most competitive. For these top jobs in management, candidates may need a bachelor's degree, a master's degree in business administration, years of experience, and a record of success in other jobs.

Chain stores often accept high school graduates into their management training programs. Many, however, prefer applicants who have college train-

The duties of a store manager vary. Some managers oversee all of a store's operations. (© Chuck Savage/ Corbis.)

ing. Trainees generally receive classroom instruction as well as on-the-job training. In many chains trainees start as assistant managers and become store managers in about one to three years.

Getting the Job

Individuals interested in eventually becoming a store manager can apply directly to the stores for which they would like to work. Public and private employment agencies, Internet job banks, and newspaper want ads list jobs for management trainees. Students looking for a job in the field may find help from their school placement office.

Advancement Possibilities and Employment Outlook

Some store managers advance to other management positions. Managers who work for a chain operation may become regional managers or managers of more desirable outlets within the chain. A few find executive positions in the company's headquarters.

According to the U.S. Bureau of Labor Statistics, employment of store managers was expected to grow as fast as the average for all occupations between 2004 and 2014. Growth in the economy should lead to a growth in retailing, which will create more jobs for store managers, but the competition for these openings will be stiff.

Working Conditions

Retailing is highly competitive work. To advance, store managers must increase their stores' sales volume. Management jobs involve great responsibility and a considerable amount of prestige.

Many managers work more than forty hours a week. Management trainees working for a chain operation may be required to move frequently during the first few years of their careers.

Earnings and Benefits

Earnings for store managers vary, depending on their level of responsibility, experience, and sales volume. Specialty apparel and accessory store managers earned a median annual salary of $57,512 in 2004, and managers of general merchandise stores made $48,880 that same year, according to the Bureau of Labor Statistics. Many managers receive bonuses based on their performance or participate in profit-sharing plans that can add substantially to their earnings. Benefits generally include paid holidays and vacations, life and health insurance, and retirement plans.

Where to Go for More Information

National Retail Federation
325 Seventh St. NW, Ste. 1100
Washington, DC 20004
(800) 673-4692
http://www.nrf.com/

Trade Show Manager

Definition and Nature of the Work

Trade show managers are responsible for the overall production of expositions. They may manage public exhibitions, trade shows, or exhibitions sponsored by associations or professional societies. Their work begins with the choice of a site for the show and does not finish until everything has been cleared away.

Advance planning is one of the most important and time-consuming aspects of the job. Trade show managers "package" every aspect of a show before it can be sold. They must decide what type of exhibition will be held and estimate how much it will cost. These factors are vital to the pricing process and the eventual sale of the exhibition space to a buyer.

When a budget has been fixed, the trade show manager selects a location where the exhibition will take place. A number of different factors are taken into account when considering a location. There must be a suitable exhibition facility, overnight accommodations for visitors, and easy access from other areas of the country. Once a location has been chosen, the trade show manager is responsible for negotiating contracts with the city, the facility management, labor unions, and companies that will provide the services required by the exhibitors.

Having made these preparations, the trade show manager must sell the exhibit space that has been reserved. This is done by preparing and sending promotional materials to potential exhibit managers in a given industry. Advertisements are also placed in various trade magazines.

For trade shows, managers also advertise within the industry to attract possible buyers to the exhibition. Consumer exhibitions, however, need more publicity than other trade shows. When organizing consumer shows, trade show managers arrange for advertisements in newspapers and magazines and for radio and television spots.

During trade shows and exhibitions trade show managers talk with exhibitors and deal with any problems that may occur. (© Tom Theobald/ Zuma/Corbis.)

During exhibitions, trade show managers are responsible for making sure that everything runs smoothly. They talk with exhibitors and visitors and deal with any problems that may occur. They also organize additional activities such as meetings and workshops, cocktail parties, and other social functions for exhibitors and buyers.

Not all trade show managers perform all of these functions. In large companies people may specialize in one aspect of trade show management such as advance planning or floor management. Together the specialists work as a team to produce an exposition.

Education and Training Requirements

Employers prefer to hire applicants with a bachelor's degree. Most trade show managers have a bachelor's degree in marketing, advertising, or business management. Some people in the field go on to study for a master's degree. Useful college courses include psychology, sociology, writing, communications, and business. Knowledge of a foreign language may also be helpful.

Many prospective trade show managers gain experience by organizing exhibits for a single company or working for companies that build and design exhibits. Others have experience managing conferences for hotels or other facilities. The Trade Show Exhibitors Association (formerly known as the International Exhibitors Association) also provides a number of training sessions on different aspects of trade show management.

Getting the Job

Individuals interested in becoming trade show managers can apply directly to companies that organize exhibitions. Such companies include industry trade associations and exposition management companies that produce trade and consumer shows. College placement offices may be able to help students find an entry-level position as an assistant to a show manager. Internet job sites and newspapers want ads sometimes list openings in this field.

Advancement Possibilities and Employment Outlook

Trade show managers usually advance by managing increasingly larger and more complex expositions with higher budgets. Many people in this field begin by organizing single exhibits for a particular company as exhibit managers and later advance to managing multiple-company trade shows. Some experienced managers begin their own businesses or act as consultants.

A trade show manager is a type of meeting and convention planner. According to the U.S. Bureau of Labor Statistics, employment of meeting and convention planners was expected to grow faster than the average for all occupations between 2004 and 2014. The number of trade show companies is expected to increase as more small- and medium-sized companies use trade shows to launch new products.

Working Conditions

Most trade show managers do a great deal of traveling to different exhibition locations. Some foreign travel may be required. Before and during a trade show, managers may work long hours, including evenings and weekends. The work is often stressful because of the many details that must be attended to and the numerous deadlines that must be met.

When trade show managers are not at the site of an exhibition, they spend most of their time in modern offices. Much of this time is spent on the telephone selling exhibition space to companies and making arrangements for future shows. Most managers have a staff to assist them with their work.

Earnings and Benefits

According to Salary.com, the median annual salary for trade show managers was $58,748 in 2006. Most companies and associations offer good benefits, which may include company cars and bonuses in addition to paid holidays and vacations and health and retirement plans. Many exhibit managers have the opportunity to travel abroad to work on international trade shows.

Where to Go for More Information

Center for Exhibition Industry Research
8111 LBJ Freeway, Ste. 750
Dallas, TX 75251
(972) 687-9242
http://www.ceir.org/

Trade Show Exhibitors Association
McCormick Place
2301 S. Lake Shore Dr., Ste. 1005
Chicago, IL 60616
(312) 842-8732
http://www.tsea.org/

Books

Exploring the Working World

American Salaries and Wages Survey, 8th ed., Helen S. Fisher. Farmington Hills, MI: Thomson Gale, 2005.

America's Fastest Growing Jobs: Detailed Information on the 140 Fastest Growing Jobs in Our Economy, 8th ed., Michael Farr. Indianapolis, IN: JIST Publishing, 2004.

America's Top 101 Jobs for College Graduates, 6th ed., Michael Farr. Indianapolis, IN: JIST Publishing, 2005.

America's Top 101 Jobs for People without a Four-Year Degree, 7th ed., Michael Farr. Indianapolis, IN: JIST Publishing, 2004.

America's Top 300 Jobs, 9th ed., U.S. Department of Labor. Indianapolis, IN: JIST Publishing, 2004.

Best Career and Education Web Sites: A Quick Guide to Online Job Search, 4th ed., Rachel Singer Gordon and Anne Wolfinger. Indianapolis, IN: JIST Publishing, 2004.

Best Entry-Level Jobs, Ron Lieber and Tom Meltzer. New York: Princeton Review, 2006.

Best Jobs for the 21st Century, 4th ed., Michael Farr and Laurence Shatkin. Indianapolis, IN: JIST Publishing, 2006.

Big Book of Jobs, 2003–2004, U.S. Department of Labor. New York: McGraw-Hill, 2003.

Career Discovery Encyclopedia, 5th ed., 8 vols. Chicago: Ferguson, 2003.

Enhanced Occupational Outlook Handbook, 5th ed., Indianapolis, IN: JIST Publishing, 2005.

Job Hunter's Sourcebook: A Thomson Gale Career Information Guide. Farmington Hills, MI: Thomson Gale, biennial.

Jobs Rated Almanac, 6th ed., Les Krantz. Fort Lee, NJ: Barricade, 2002.

The National JobBank, 2006. Avon, MA: Adams Media, 2006.

Occupational Outlook Handbook series. Washington, DC: United States Government Printing Office, biennial. Briefs, separately published.

Occupational Outlook Quarterly. Washington, DC: United States Government Printing Office. Quarterly publication.

Professional Careers Sourcebook, 7th ed. Farmington Hills, MI: Thomson Gale, 2002.

200 Best Jobs for College Graduates, 3rd ed., Michael Farr and Laurence Shatkin. Indianapolis, IN: JIST Publishing, 2006.

Recommended

Best Jobs for the 21st Century, 4th ed., Michael Farr and Laurence Shatkin. Indianapolis, IN: JIST Publishing, 2006. Lists five hundred jobs and categorizes them into sixty-five "Best Jobs for..." lists. Organizes jobs by category, education required, best growth potential.

Jobs Rated Almanac, 6th ed., Les Krantz. Fort Lee, NJ: Barricade, 2002. Rates 250 jobs and sorts into "best for" and "worst for" rankings. Factors include salary, benefits, and stress level.

300 Best Jobs without a Four-Year Degree, 2nd ed., Michael Farr and Laurence Shatkin. Indianapolis, IN: JIST Publishing, 2006.

VGM's Career Encyclopedia, 5th ed., New York: McGraw-Hill, 2002.

Vocational Careers Sourcebook, 5th ed., Farmington Hills, MI: Thomson Gale, 2002.

Education and Training Opportunities

Acing the College Application: How to Maximize Your Chances for Admission to the College of Your Choice, Michele Hernandez. New York: Ballantine, 2002.

Admission Matters: What Students and Parents Need to Know about Getting Into College, Sally P. Springer and Marion R. Franck. San Francisco: Jossey-Bass, 2005.

Barron's Guide to Graduate Business Schools, Eugene Miller and Neuman F. Pollack. Hauppauge, NY: Barron's Educational Series, revised regularly.

Barron's Guide to Law Schools. Hauppauge, NY: Barron's Educational Series, revised regularly.

Barron's Guide to Medical and Dental Schools, Sol Wischnitzer and Edith Wischnitzer. Hauppauge, NY: Barron's Educational Series, revised regularly.

Barron's Profiles of American Colleges. Hauppauge, NY: Barron's Educational Series, annual.

Bear's Guide to College Degrees by Mail and Internet, 10th ed., John Bear. Berkeley, CA: Ten Speed Press, 2005.

Best 109 Internships, 9th ed., Mark Oldman and Samer Hamadah. New York: Princeton Review, 2003.

The Best 361 Colleges. New York: Princeton Review, annual.

Chronicle Vocational School Manual. Moravia, NY: Chronicle Guidance Publications, annual.

The College Application Essay, Sarah Myers McGinty. New York: The College Board, 2004.

The College Board Book of Majors, 2nd ed. New York: The College Board, 2006.

The College Board Scholarship Handbook. New York: The College Board, annual.

The College Cost and Financial Aid Handbook. New York: The College Board, annual.

College Financial Aid: How to Get Your Fair Share, 6th ed., Peter V. Laurenzo. Albany, NY: Hudson Financial Press, 2002.

The College Handbook. New York: The College Board, annual.

College Majors Handbook with Real Career Paths and Payoffs, 2nd ed., Neeta P. Fogg. Indianapolis, IN: JIST Publishing, 2004.

College Planning for Gifted Students, 3rd ed., Sandra L. Berger. Waco, TX: Prufrock Press, 2006.

College Success Guide: Top 12 Secrets for Student Success, Karine Blackett and Patricia Weiss. Indianapolis, IN: JIST Publishing, 2005.

Complete Book of Colleges. New York: Princeton Review, annual.

Recommended

Acing the College Application: How to Maximize Your Chances for Admission to the College of Your Choice, Michele Hernandez. New York: Ballantine, 2002. Written by former Dartmouth College admissions officer. Frank but reassuring advice on application, essay, and personal interview.

The Insider's Guide to Colleges. New York: St. Martin's Griffin, annual. Surveys students at 320 U.S. and Canadian schools on dorm life, class size, and other campus-related topics.

Vault Guide to Top Internships, Samer Hamadah. New York: Vault, 2005. Provides information on internships offered by 700-plus companies, including Fortune 500 corporations. Nonprofit and government programs also listed.

Fiske Guide to Colleges, Edmund Fiske. Naperville, IL: Sourcebooks, annual.

The Gourman Report: A Rating of Undergraduate Programs in American and International Universities, Jack Gourman. Los Angeles: National Educational Standards, revised regularly.

Guide to College Majors. New York: Princeton Review, 2006.

Guide to the Most Competitive Colleges. Hauppauge, NY: Barron's Educational Series, revised regularly.

How to Choose a College Major, Linda Landis Andrews. New York: McGraw-Hill, 2006.

How to Write Your College Application Essay, Kenneth Nourse. New York: McGraw-Hill, 2001.

The Insider's Guide to Colleges. New York: St. Martin's Griffin, annual.

The Internship Bible, 10th ed. New York: Princeton Review, 2005.

The National Guide to Educational Credit for Training Programs. Washington, DC: American Council on Education, revised regularly.

100 Successful College Application Essays, 2nd ed. New York: New American Library, 2002.

Peterson's Best College Admission Essays, 3rd ed. Princeton, NJ: Thomson Peterson's, 2004.

Peterson's College Money Handbook. Princeton, NJ: Thomson Peterson's, annual.

Peterson's College and University Almanac. Princeton, NJ: Thomson Peterson's, annual.

Peterson's Competitive Colleges. Princeton, NJ: Thomson Peterson's, annual.

Peterson's Financial Aid Answer Book. Princeton, NJ: Thomson Peterson's, annual.

Peterson's Guide to Four-Year Colleges. Princeton, NJ: Thomson Peterson's, annual.

Peterson's Guide to Two-Year Colleges. Princeton, NJ: Thomson Peterson's, annual.

Peterson's Internships. Princeton, NJ: Thomson Peterson's, annual.

Quick Guide to College Majors and Careers, Laurence Shatkin. Indianapolis, IN: JIST Publishing, 2002.

Rugg's Recommendations on the Colleges, Frederick Rugg. Fallbrook, CA: Rugg's Recommendations, annual.

Students' Guide to Colleges: The Definitive Guide to America's Top 100 Schools Written by the Real Experts—the Students Who Attend Them, Jordan Goldman and Colleen Buyers. New York: Penguin, 2005.

The Truth about Getting In: A Top College Advisor Tells You Everything You Need to Know, Katherine Cohen. New York: Hyperion, 2002.

US News Ultimate College Guide. Naperville, IL: Sourcebooks, annual.

Vault Guide to Top Internships, Samer Hamadah. New York, Vault, 2005.

Career Goals

The Career Adventure: Your Guide to Personal Assessment, Career Exploration, and Decision Making, 4th ed., Susan M. Johnston. Upper Saddle, NJ: Prentice-Hall, 2005.

Career Guide to America's Top Industries, 6th ed., U.S. Department of Labor. Indianapolis, IN: JIST Publishing, 2004.

Career Warfare: 10 Rules for Building a Successful Personal Brand and Fighting to Keep It, David F. D'Alessandro and Michele Owens. New York: McGraw-Hill, 2003.

College Majors and Careers: A Resource Guide for Effective Life Planning, 5th ed., Paul Phifer. Chicago: Ferguson, 2003.

Cool Careers for Dummies, Marty Nemko, Paul Edwards, and Sarah Edwards. Foster City, CA: IDG Books, 2001.

Customize Your Career, Roz Usheroff. New York: McGraw-Hill, 2004.

Do What You Are: Discover the Perfect Career for You through the Secrets of Personality Type, 3rd ed., Paul D. Tieger and Barbara Barron-Tieger. New York: Little, Brown, 2001.

50 Best Jobs for Your Personality, Michael Farr and Laurence Shatkin. Indianapolis, IN: JIST Publishing, 2005.

Finding a Career That Works for You: A Step-by-Step Guide to Choosing a Career and Finding a Job, Wilma Fellman. Plantation, FL: Specialty Press, 2000.

Finding Your Perfect Work: The New Career Guide to Making a Living, Creating a Life, 2nd ed., Paul Edwards and Susan Edwards. New York: Penguin, 2003.

The 5 Patterns of Extraordinary Careers: The Guide for Achieving Success and Satisfaction, James M. Citrin and Richard Smith. New York: Crown Business, 2003.

The Global Citizen: A Guide to Creating an International Life and Career, Elizabeth Kruempelmann. Berkeley, CA: Ten Speed Press, 2002.

Guide to Your Career, 5th ed., Alan B. Bernstein. New York: Princeton Review, 2004.

How Hard Are You Knocking? The Job Seeker's Guide to Opening Career Doors, Timothy J. Augustine and Rona Curcio. Winchester, VA: Oakhill Press, 2005.

Job Search and Career Checklists: 101 Proven Time-Saving Checklists to Organize and Plan Your Career Search, Arlene S. Hirsch. Indianapolis, IN: JIST Publishing, 2005.

Monster Careers: How to Land the Job of Your Life, Jeffrey Taylor and Douglas Hardy. New York: Penguin, 2004.

New Guide for Occupational Exploration: Linking Interests, Learning and Careers, 4th ed., Michael Farr and Laurence Shatkin. Indianapolis, IN: JIST Publishing, 2006.

The Play of Your Life: Your Program for Finding the Career of Your Dreams—And a Step-by-Step Guide to Making It a Reality, Colleen A. Sabatino. New York: Rodale, 2004.

What Color Is Your Parachute? A Practical Manual for Job-Hunters and Career-Changers, Richard Nelson Bolles. Berkeley, CA: Ten Speed Press, revised annually.

What Should I Do with My Life? The True Story of People Who Answered the Ultimate Question, Po Brosnan. New York: Random House, 2002.

Where's My Oasis? The Essential Handbook for Everyone Wanting the Perfect Job, Rowan Manahan. New York: Vermillion, 2004.

Recommended

Finding Your Perfect Work: The New Career Guide to Making a Living, Creating a Life, 2nd ed., Paul Edwards and Susan Edwards. New York: Penguin, 2003. Lists types of careers, with emphasis on self-employment opportunities.

What Color Is Your Parachute? A Practical Manual for Job-Hunters and Career-Changers, Richard Nelson Bolles. Berkeley, CA: Ten Speed Press, revised annually. The classic in the genre, and the top-selling career-advice book consistently since the mid-1970s. Updated to reflect twenty-first-century concerns.

Getting the Job and Getting Ahead

Almanac of American Employers, Jack W. Plunkett. Galveston, TX: Plunkett Research Ltd., biennial.

e-Resumes: A Guide to Successful Online Job Hunting, Pat Criscito. Hauppauge, NY: Barron's Educational Series, 2004.

Guide to Internet Job Searching, Margaret Riley Dikel. New York: McGraw-Hill, 2004.

How to Earn What You're Worth: Leveraging Your Goals and Talents to Land Your Dream Job, Sunny Bates. New York: McGraw-Hill, 2004.

How to Get Any Job with Any Major: Career Launch & Re-launch for Everyone Under 30 (or How to Avoid Living in Your Parents' Basement), Donald Asher. Berkeley, CA: Ten Speed Press, 2004.

How to Get Your First Job and Keep It, 2nd ed., Deborah Perlmutter Bloch. New York: McGraw-Hill, 2002.

Insider's Guide to Finding a Job: Expert Advice from America's Top Employers and Recruiters, Wendy S. Enelow and Shelly Goldman. Indianapolis, IN: JIST Publishing, 2004.

International Job Finder: Where the Jobs Are Worldwide, Daniel Lauber and Kraig Rice. River Forest, IL: Planning/Communications, 2002.

International Jobs: Where They Are and How to Get Them, 6th ed., Nina Segal and Eric Kocher. New York: Basic Books, 2003.

Job-Hunting on the Internet, 4th ed., Richard Nelson Bolles and Mark Emery Bolles. Berkeley, CA: Ten Speed Press, 2005.

Job Savvy: How to Be a Success at Work, 3rd ed., LaVerne L. Ludden. Indianapolis, IN: JIST Publishing, 2002.

Job Search Magic: Insider Secrets from America's Career and Life Coach, Susan Britton Whitcomb. Indianapolis, IN: JIST Publishing, 2006.

The Job Search Solution: The Ultimate System for Finding a Great Job Now!, Tony Bashara. New York: AMACOM, 2005.

Job Seeker's Online Goldmine: A Step-by-Step Guidebook to Government and No-Cost Web Tools, Janet E. Wall. Indianapolis, IN: JIST Publishing, 2006.

Knock 'Em Dead 2006: The Ultimate Job Seekers Guide, Martin Yate. Avon, MA: Adams Media, 2006.

National Job Hotline Directory: The Job Finder's Hot List, 3rd ed., Sue Cubbage and Marcia Williams. River Forest, IL: Planning/Communications, 2003.

1000 Best Job Hunting Secrets, Diane Stafford and Moritza Day. Naperville, IL: Sourcebooks, 2004.

Super Job Search: The Complete Manual for Job-Seekers & Career-Changers, 3rd ed., Peter Studner. Los Angeles: Jamenair Ltd., 2003.

10 Insider Secrets to a Winning Job Search: Everything You Need to Get the Job You Want in 24 Hours—Or Less, Todd Bermont. Franklin Lakes, NJ: Career Press, 2004.

Very Quick Job Search: Get a Better Job in Half the Time, 3rd ed., Michael Farr. Indianapolis, IN: JIST Publishing, 2003.

Recommended

How to Get Any Job with Any Major: Career Launch & Re-launch for Everyone Under 30 (or How to Avoid Living in Your Parents' Basement), Donald Asher. Berkeley, CA: Ten Speed Press, 2004. Counsels liberal arts degree-holders on how to package their education and strengths to land a high-paying position.

Knock 'Em Dead 2006: The Ultimate Job Seekers Guide, Martin Yate. Avon, MA: Adams Media, 2006. Offers range of advice for job-hunters at all levels, including resume-building, interview strategies, and salary negotiation tips.

Resumes and Interviews

Adams Job Interview Almanac, 2nd ed., Richard Wallace. Avon, MA: Adams Media Corp., 2005.

Adams Resume Almanac, 2nd ed., Richard Wallace. Avon, MA: Adams Media Corp., 2005.

Amazing Resumes: What Employers Want to See—and How to Say It, Jim Bright and Joanne Earl. Indianapolis, IN: JIST Publishing, 2005.

Competency-Based Resumes: How to Bring Your Resume to the Top of the Pile, Robin Kessler and Linda A. Strasburg. Franklin Lakes, NJ: Career Press, 2004.

Cover Letter Magic, 2nd ed., Wendy S. Enelow and Louise Kursmark. Indianapolis, IN: JIST Publishing, 2004.

Cover Letters That Knock 'Em Dead, 6th ed., Martin Yate. Avon, MA: Adams Media, 2004.

The Elements of Resume Style: Essential Rules and Eye-opening Advice for Writing Resumes and Cover Letters That Work, Scott Bennett. New York: AMACOM, 2005.

Expert Resumes for Career Changers, Wendy S. Enelow and Louise M. Kursmark. Indianapolis, IN: JIST Publishing, 2005.

Fearless Interviewing: How to Win the Job by Communicating with Confidence, Marky Stein. New York: McGraw-Hill, 2002.

Ferguson Guide to Resumes and Job-Hunting Skills, Maurene J. Hinds. Chicago: Ferguson, 2005.

Gallery of Best Resumes: A Collection of Quality Resumes by Professional Resume Writers, 3rd ed., David F. Noble, Ph.D. Indianapolis, IN: JIST Publishing, 2004.

Get the Interview Every Time: Fortune 500 Hiring Professionals' Tips for Writing Winning Resumes and Cover Letters, Brenda Greene. Chicago: Dearborn Trade Publishing, 2004.

How to Interview Like a Top MBA: Job-Winning Strategies from Headhunters, Fortune 100 Recruiters, and Career Counselors, Shel Leanne. New York: McGraw-Hill, 2003.

How to Turn an Interview into a Job, Jeffrey G. Allen. New York: Simon and Schuster, 2004.

McGraw-Hill's Big Red Book of Resumes. New York: McGraw-Hill, 2002.

Monster Careers: Interviewing—Master the Moment That Gets You the Job, Jeffrey Taylor and Doug Hardy. New York: Penguin Books, 2005.

The Resume.com Guide to Writing Unbeatable Resumes, Warren Simons and Rose Curtis. New York: McGraw-Hill, 2004.

The Resume Handbook: How to Write Outstanding Resumes & Cover Letters for Every Situation, 4th ed., Arthur D. Rosenberg and David V. Hizer. Avon, MA: Adams Media, 2003.

Resume Magic: Trade Secrets of a Professional Resume Writer, 2nd ed., Susan Britton Whitcomb. Indianapolis, IN: JIST Publishing, 2003.

Resumes for Dummies, 4th ed., Joyce Lain Kennedy. Indianapolis, IN: Wiley, 2003.

Resumes That Knock 'Em Dead, 6th ed., Martin Yate. Avon, MA: Adams Media, 2004.

301 Smart Answers to Tough Interview Questions, Vicky Oliver. Naperville, IL: Sourcebooks, 2005.

201 Best Questions to Ask on Your Interview, John Kador. New York: McGraw-Hill, 2002.

Winning the Interview Game: Everything You Need to Know to Land the Job, Alan H. Nierenberg. New York: AMACOM, 2005.

Recommended

Resume Magic: Trade Secrets of a Professional Resume Writer, 2nd ed., Susan Britton Whitcomb. Indianapolis, IN: JIST Publishing, 2003. Before and after resume samples provide a how-to on crafting the perfect resume. Includes tips on e-resumes and tricks for scannable-text submissions.

301 Smart Answers to Tough Interview Questions, Vicky Oliver. Naperville, IL: Sourcebooks, 2005. Advice on how to handle the questions designed to unsettle, from explaining gaps in work history to acing arcane trivia volleys.

Mid-Career Options

Change Your Job, Change Your Life: Careering and Re-Careering in the New Boom/Bust Economy, 9th ed., Ron Krannich. Manassas Park, VA: Impact, 2004.

Fearless Career Change, Marky Stein. New York: McGraw-Hill, 2005.

Fire Your Boss, Stephen M. Pollan and Mark Levine. New York: HarperCollins, 2004.

I Don't Know What I Want, But I Know It's Not This: A Step-by-Step Guide to Finding Gratifying Work, Julie Jansen. New York: Penguin Books, 2003.

Over-40 Job Search Guide: 10 Strategies for Making Your Age an Advantage in Your Career, Gail Geary. Indianapolis, IN: JIST Publishing, 2004.

Radical Careering: 100 Truths to Jumpstart Your Job, Your Career, and Your Life, Sally Hogshead. New York: Gotham, 2005.

Second Acts: Creating the Life You Really Want, Building the Career You Truly Desire, Stephen M. Pollan and Mark Levine. New York: HarperCollins, 2003.

Working Identity: Unconventional Strategies for Reinventing Your Career, Hermania Ibarra. Boston: Harvard Business School Press, 2003.

Equality of Opportunity

Dancing on the Glass Ceiling, Nancy Frederick and Candy Deemer. New York: McGraw-Hill, 2004.

Job-Hunting for the So-Called Handicapped or People Who Have Disabilities, 2nd ed., Richard Nelson Bolles and Dale Susan Brown. Berkeley, CA: Ten Speed Press, 2001.

Job Search Handbook for People with Disabilities, 2nd ed., Daniel J. Ryan. Indianapolis, IN: JIST Publishing, 2004.

Lavender Road to Success: The Career Guide for the Gay Community, Kirk Snyder. Berkeley, CA: Ten Speed Press, 2003.

Resources for People with Disabilities, 2nd ed., Shawn Woodyard. Chicago: Ferguson, 2001.

Lists and Indexes of Career and Vocational Information

Encyclopedia of Careers and Vocational Guidance, 13th ed., 5 vols. Chicago: Ferguson, 2006.

O*Net Dictionary of Occupational Titles, 3rd ed. Indianapolis, IN: JIST Publishing, 2004.

Recommended

I Don't Know What I Want, But I Know It's Not This: A Step-by-Step Guide to Finding Gratifying Work, Julie Jansen. New York: Penguin Books, 2003. Experienced career coach identifies the top six reasons people are dissatisfied with their jobs and provides a step-by-step process for finding a career that suits every personality.

Working Identity: Unconventional Strategies for Reinventing Your Career, Hermania Ibarra. Boston: Harvard Business School Press, 2003. Help for those considering a mid-life career change.

Recommended

Dancing on the Glass Ceiling, Nancy Frederick and Candy Deemer. New York: McGraw-Hill, 2004. A former advertising executive teams with a professional executive coach to provide practical as well as inspirational advice for women in the workplace.

Job-Hunting for the So-Called Handicapped or People Who Have Disabilities, 2nd ed., Richard Nelson Bolles and Dale Susan Brown. Berkeley, CA: Ten Speed Press, 2001. From the author of *What Color Is Your Parachute?* Advice for the physically or mentally challenged on finding a career niche.

Internet Sites

Sites with Extensive Links

About.com
http://careerplanning.about.com

Beyond.com
http://www.beyond.com

Jobweb.com
http://www.jobweb.com

JIST Publishing
http://www.jist.com

Job Hunt: Online Job Search Guide and Resource Directory
http://www.job-hunt.org

Vault.com
http://www.vault.com

Vocational Information Center
http://www.khake.com

Career Development Resources

Career Magazine
http://www.careermag.com

Career Resource Homepage
http://www.careerresource.net

Job Hunters Bible
http://www.jobhuntersbible.com

Princeton Review
http://www.princetonreview.com

Quintessential Careers
http://www.quintcareers.com

Online Information and References

AT&T Toll-Free Internet Directory
http://www.tollfree.att.net

The Best Jobs in the USA Today
http://www.bestjobsusa.com

Careers.org
http://www.careers.org

Federal Jobs Digest
http://www.fedworld.gov/jobs/jobsearch.html

Job Finders Online
http://www.planningcommunications.com/jf

Job Safari
http://www.jobsafari.com

Monster Career Center
http://content.monster.com

Occupational Outlook Handbook
http://www.bls.gov/oco

SpherionExchange
http://employee.spherionexchange.com/start.cfm

U.S. Bureau of Labor Statistics Homepage
http://www.bls.gov/home.htm

US News and World Report Career Center
http://www.usnews.com/usnews/biztech/career/career_home.htm

Wall Street Journal Career Journal
http://www.careerjournal.com

Yahoo! Business and Economy
http://dir.yahoo.com/Business_and_Economy

Job Databases and Resume Posting

After College
http://www.aftercollege.com

America's Job Bank
http://www.ajb.org

Career Builder
http://www.careerbuilder.com

Career Mart
http://www.careermart.com

Employment Guide
http://www.employmentguide.com

Yahoo! Hot Jobs
http://hotjobs.yahoo.com

Idealist Nonprofit Career Center
http://www.idealist.org

Job.com
http://www.job.com

JobBank USA
http://www.jobbankusa.com

Job Web
http://www.jobweb.org

Monster Jobs
http://www.monster.com

Monstertrak
http://www.monstertrak.monster.com

NationJob.com
http://www.nationjob.com

Now Hiring
http://www.nowhiring.com

Audiovisual Materials

The following titles include, where possible, the developer's name and location or else the name and location of a distributor. Audiovisual titles may be available through several distributors.

Exploring the Working World

Career Advantage: Strategies for Success series. Video, guide. Princeton, NJ: Films Media Group.

Career Clusters series. Video. Charleston, WV: Cambridge Educational.

Career Exploration series. Video. South Charleston, WV: Meridian Education Corp.

Career Guidance Videos series. Video. South Charleston, WV: Meridian Education Corp.

Career S.E.L.F. Assessment: Finding a Career That Works for You. Video. Charleston, WV: Cambridge Educational.

Careers, Careers, Careers! Video, guide. Princeton, NJ: Films Media Group.

Careers for the 21st Century series. Video, guide. South Charleston, WV: Meridian Education Corp.

Careers without College. Video. Charleston, WV: Cambridge Educational.

The Changing Workplace: Technology and Globalization. Video. Princeton, NJ: Films Media Group.

Choices Today for Career Satisfaction Tomorrow. Video, guide. Charleston, WV: Cambridge Educational.

Complete Job Search System. Video. Charleston, WV: Cambridge Educational.

Connect on the Net: Finding a Job on the Internet. Video. Charleston, WV: Cambridge Educational.

Educational Planning for Your Career. Video. South Charleston, WV: Meridian Education Corp.

The 50 Best Jobs for the 21st Century series. Video. Indianapolis, IN: JIST Publishing.

The JIST Video Guide for Occupational Exploration series. Video. Indianapolis, IN: JIST Publishing.

Internet Careers: College Not Required. Video. Charleston, WV: Cambridge Educational.

Introduction to Career and Educational Exploration. Video. Princeton, NJ: Films Media Group.

JIST TV Series: The Job Search Channel. Video. Indianapolis, IN: JIST Publishing.

Jobs for the 21st Century. Video. Mt. Kisco, NY: Guidance Associates.

Learning for Earning. Video, guide. South Charleston, WV: Meridian Education Corp.

Log On for Success: Using Internet Job Sites. Video, guide. Charleston, WV: Cambridge Educational.

Researching Career Options: New Technologies and Current Techniques. Video. Princeton, NJ: Films Media Group.

School-to-Work Transition. Video. South Charleston, WV: Meridian Education Corp.

Ten Fastest Growing Careers: Jobs for the Future. Video. Mt. Kisco, NY: Guidance Associates.

What Would I Be Good At? Video. Mt. Kisco, NY: Guidance Associates.

What's Out There: How the World of Work is Organized. Video. Princeton, NJ: Films Media Group.

Your Career Search: Taking the First Step. Video. Mt. Kisco, NY: Guidance Associates.

Your Future: Planning Through Career Exploration. Video. South Charleston, WV: Meridian Education Corp.

Getting the Job and Getting Ahead

Career Evaluation. Video. Charleston, WV: Cambridge Educational.

Common Mistakes People Make in Interviews. Video, guide. Charleston, WV: Cambridge Educational.

Exceptional Employee: A Guide to Success on the Job. Video. Charleston, WV: Cambridge Educational.

Exceptional Interviewing Tips: A View from the Inside. Video, workbook. Charleston, WV: Cambridge Educational.

Extraordinary Answers to Common Interview Questions. Video. Charleston, WV: Cambridge Educational.

Finding a Job. Video. Charleston, WV: Cambridge Educational.

First Impressions: Etiquette and Work Habits for New Employees. Video, guide. Charleston, WV: Cambridge Educational.

From Pinkslip to Paycheck: The Road to Reemployment series. Video. Indianapolis, IN: JIST Publishing.

Getting Good Answers to Tough Interview Questions. Video. Indianapolis, IN: JIST Publishing.

Getting the Job You Really Want series. Video, workbook, guide. Indianapolis, IN: JIST Publishing.

How to Find a Job on the Internet. Video. Indianapolis, IN: JIST Publishing.

How to Be a Success at Work series. Video. Indianapolis, IN: JIST Publishing.

The Ideal Resume. Video. Charleston, WV: Cambridge Educational.

If at First: How to Get a Job and Keep It. Video. Mt. Kisco, NY: Guidance Associates.

Interview to Win Your First Job. Video. Indianapolis, IN: JIST Publishing.

Interviewing for a Job. Video. Charleston, WV: Cambridge Educational.

Job Survival Kit. Video. Charleston, WV: Cambridge Educational.

On-the-Job Success series. Video. Indianapolis, IN: JIST Publishing.

Planning Your Career. Video. Charleston, WV: Cambridge Educational.

The Portfolio Resume series. Video. Charleston, WV: Cambridge Educational.

"Quick" Job Search series. Video. Indianapolis, IN: JIST Publishing.

Succeeding on the Job. Video. Charleston, WV: Cambridge Educational.

Success in the Job World series. Video. Indianapolis, IN: JIST Publishing.

Staying on Track in Your Work Search. Video. Princeton, NJ: Films Media Group.

Power Interviewing Skills: Strategies for the Interviewee. Video. Charleston, WV: Cambridge Educational.

Take This Job and Love It: Keys to Surviving Your New Job. Video. Charleston, WV: Cambridge Educational.

Ten Commandments of Resumes. Video. Charleston, WV: Cambridge Educational.

Tough Times Job Strategies. Video, guide. Charleston, WV: Cambridge Educational.

Understanding and Using the O*NET. Video, guide. Charleston, WV: Cambridge Educational.

The Very Quick Job Search Video. Video. Indianapolis, IN: JIST Publishing.

The Video Guide to JIST's Self-Directed Job Search series. Video. Indianapolis, IN: JIST Publishing.

Web Resumes. Video. Charleston, WV: Cambridge Educational.

Computer Software

The following titles include, where possible, the developer's name and location or else the name and location of a distributor. Software titles may be available through several distributors.

Ace the Interview: The Multimedia Job Interview Guide. CD-ROM. Charleston, WV: Cambridge Educational.

Adams Media JobBank FastResume Suite. CD-ROM for Windows. Avon, MA: Adams Media.

Barron's Profiles of American Colleges on CD-ROM. Windows or Macintosh. Hauppauge, NY: Barron's Educational Series.

Cambridge Career Center. CD-ROM. Charleston, WV: Cambridge Educational.

Career Discovery Encyclopedia. CD-ROM. Chicago, IL: Ferguson.

Career Explorer. CD-ROM for Windows. Indianapolis, IN: JIST Publishing.

Career Finder Plus. CD-ROM. Indianapolis, IN: JIST Publishing.

CareerOINKs on the Web. Network. Indianapolis, IN: JIST Publishing.

Careers without College. CD-ROM. Indianapolis, IN: JIST Publishing.

Complete Resume Designer. CD-ROM. Charleston, WV: Cambridge Educational.

Custom Resume Creator. CD-ROM for Windows. Indianapolis, IN: JIST Publishing.

Decisions. CD-ROM. Indianapolis, IN: JIST Publishing.

Electronic Career Planner. CD-ROM for Windows. Indianapolis, IN: JIST Publishing.

Exploring the World of Work. CD-ROM. New York: McGraw-Hill.

JIST Presents Interview Mastery. CD-ROM. Indianapolis, IN: JIST Publishing.

Job Search series. CD-ROM. Indianapolis, IN: JIST Publishing.

Job Survival series. CD-ROM. Indianapolis, IN: JIST Publishing.

The Keys to Interviewing Success: Unlocking Your Professional Future. CD-ROM. Charleston, WV: Cambridge Educational.

Moving on Up: An Interactive Guide to Finding a Great Job. CD-ROM for Windows. Charleston, WV: Cambridge Educational.

Multimedia Career Center. CD-ROM. Charleston, WV: Cambridge Educational.

The Multimedia Career Path. CD-ROM. Charleston, WV: Cambridge Educational.

The Multimedia Guide to Occupational Exploration. CD-ROM. Charleston, WV: Cambridge Educational.

Multimedia Job Search. CD-ROM for Windows. Charleston, WV: Cambridge Educational.

Multimedia Take This Job and Love It. CD-ROM. Charleston, WV: Cambridge Educational.

OOH Career Center. CD-ROM. Charleston, WV: Cambridge Educational.

School-to-Work Career Center. CD-ROM. Charleston, WV: Cambridge Educational.

Success in the World of Work: Succeeding on the Job. CD-ROM. South Charleston, WV: Meridian Education Corp.

Targeting Success. CD-ROM. Indianapolis, IN: JIST Publishing.

General

Books

Careers in Marketing, 3rd ed., Lila B. Stair and Leslie Stair. New York: McGraw-Hill, 2001.

The Complete Idiot's Guide to Marketing, 2nd ed., Sarah White. New York: Alpha Books, 2003.

Medical and Pharmaceutical Sales: How to Land the Job of Your Dreams, 2nd ed., Nikki K. Kerzic. Littleton, CO: Executive Connection, 2002.

Opportunities in Marketing Careers, Margery Steinberg. New York: McGraw-Hill, 2005.

Opportunities in Sales Careers, James Brescoll and Ralph M. Dahm. New York: McGraw-Hill, 2002.

Resumes for Sales and Marketing Careers, 3rd ed., The Editors of McGraw-Hill. New York: McGraw-Hill, 2005.

Sales and Marketing Resumes for $100,000 Careers, 2nd ed., Louise M. Kursmark. Indianapolis, IN: Jist Publishing, 2004.

Ultimate Guide to Direct Marketing, Al Lautenslager. Irvine, CA: Entrepreneur Media, 2005.

Your Successful Sales Career, Brian Azar and Len Foley. New York: AMACOM, 2004.

Internet Sites

AdAge.com Career Center
http://www.crain.com/classified/adage/index.cfm

Adweek
http://www.adweek.com/

American Marketing Association Career Center
http://www.marketingpower.com/

BizOffice.com
http://www.bizoffice.com/

Communicators and Marketers JobLine
http://www.cmjobline.org/

Direct Selling Association
http://www.dsa.org/

MarketingJobs.com Classifieds
http://www.marketingjobs.com/

NationJob Network: Advertising and Media Jobs Page
http://www.nationjob.com/media/

NationJob Network: Marketing Page
http://www.nationjob.com/marketing/

Small Business Administration
http://www.sba.gov/

Real Estate and Insurance

Books

Careers in Real Estate, Mark Rowh. New York: McGraw-Hill, 2002.

The Complete Idiot's Guide to Success as a Real Estate Agent, 2nd ed., Marilyn Sullivan. New York: Alpha Books, 2006.

Opportunities in Real Estate Careers, 2nd ed., Mariwyn Evans. New York: McGraw-Hill, 2002.

Your Successful Real Estate Career, 4th ed., Kenneth W. Edwards. New York: AMACOM, 2003.

Retailing, Wholesaling, and Advertising

Books

Career Opportunities in Advertising and Public Relations, 4th ed., Shelly Field. New York: Facts on File, 2005.

Career Opportunities in the Retail and Wholesale Industry, Shelly Field. New York: Facts on File, 2001.

Careers in Advertising, S. William Pattis. New York: McGraw-Hill, 2004.

How to Get into Advertising, Andrea Neidle and John H. Holmes. Stamford, CT: Thomson Learning, 2003.

Opportunities in Retailing Careers, Roslyn Dolber. New York: McGraw-Hill, 2003.

Pick Me: Breaking into Advertising and Staying There, Nancy Vonk and Janet Kestin. Hoboken, NJ: Wiley, 2005.

Retail Business Kit for Dummies, Rick Segel. Hoboken, NJ: Wiley, 2001.

Start and Run a Profitable Retail Business, Jim Dion and Ted Topping. Bellingham, WA: Self-Counsel Press, 2000.

Successful Franchising: Expert Advice on Buying, Selling, and Creating Winning Franchises, Bradley J. Sugars. New York: McGraw-Hill, 2005.

Directory — Institutions Offering Career Training

The information in this directory was generated from the IPEDS (Integrated Postsecondary Education Data System) database of the U.S. Department of Education. It includes only regionally or nationally accredited institutions offering postsecondary occupational training in marketing and distribution. Because college catalogs and directories of colleges and universities are readily available elsewhere, this directory does not include institutions that offer only bachelor's and advanced degrees.

Advertising Services

CALIFORNIA

Cerritos College
11110 Alondra Blvd.
Norwalk 90650

Fashion Institute of Design &
    Merchandising, Los Angeles
919 South Grand Ave.
Los Angeles 90015

Fashion Institute of Design &
    Merchandising, San Francisco
55 Stockton St.
San Francisco 94108

Southwestern College
900 Otay Lakes Rd.
Chula Vista 91910

FLORIDA

Northwood University, Florida
    Education Center
2600 North Military Trail
West Palm Beach 33409

INDIANA

Vincennes University
1002 North First St.
Vincennes 47591

MASSACHUSETTS

Endicott College
376 Hale St.
Beverly 01915

MICHIGAN

North Central Michigan College
1515 Howard St.
Petoskey 49770

Northwood University
3225 Cook Rd.
Midland 48640

Schoolcraft College
18600 Haggerty Rd.
Livonia 48152

MINNESOTA

Dakota County Technical College
1300 East 145th St.
Rosemount 55068

Saint Cloud Technical College
1540 Northway Dr.
Saint Cloud 56303

MISSOURI

Moberly Area Community College
101 College Ave.
Moberly 65270

Saint Charles County Community
    College
4601 Mid Rivers Mall Dr.
Saint Peter's 63376

NEW YORK

Fashion Institute of Technology
227 West 27th St.
New York 10001

Mohawk Valley Community College,
    Utica Branch
1101 Sherman Dr.
Utica 13501

Rockland Community College
145 College Rd.
Suffern 10901

OKLAHOMA

Metro Area Vocational Technical School
    District 22
1900 Springlake Dr.
Oklahoma City 73111

PENNSYLVANIA

Harcum College
750 Montgomery Ave.
Bryn Mawr 19010

RHODE ISLAND

Johnson and Wales University
8 Abbott Park Place
Providence 02903-3376

TEXAS

Southwest Texas Junior College
2401 Garner Field Rd.
Uvalde 78801

WASHINGTON

Sales Training Institute
1750 112th Ave. Northeast
Ste. E168
Bellevue 98004

WISCONSIN

Blackhawk Technical College
P.O. Box 5009
Janesville 53547

Automotive Sales

ARIZONA

American Express Travel School
3600 East University Dr.
Ste. G1220
Phoenix 85034

FLORIDA

Northwood University, Florida
    Education Center
2600 North Military Trail
West Palm Beach 33409

IOWA

Iowa Western Community College
2700 College Rd.
P.O. Box 4C
Council Bluffs 51502

MICHIGAN

Northwood University
3225 Cook Rd.
Midland 48640

MINNESOTA

Hennepin Technical College
9000 Brooklyn Blvd.
Brooklyn Park 55445

Ridgewater College, A Community and
    Technical College, Willmar
P.O. Box 1097
Willmar 56201

NEBRASKA

Central Community College Area
P.O. Box 4903
Grand Island 68802

NORTH DAKOTA

North Dakota State College of Science
800 North Sixth St.
Wahpeton 58076

TEXAS

Northwood University
1114 West FM 1382
Cedar Hill 75104

WISCONSIN

North Central Technical College
1000 Campus Dr.
Wausau 54401-1899

Floristry

ALABAMA

J F Ingram State Technical College
5375 Ingram Rd.
Deatsville 36022

ARKANSAS

Northwest Technical Institute
709 South Old Missouri Rd.
Springdale 72764

CALIFORNIA

Simi Valley Adult School
3192 Los Angeles Ave.
Simi Valley 93065

Southern California School of Floral
    Design
843 South State College
Anaheim 92806

COLORADO

Trim International Floral School, Ltd.
4800 Dahlia St.
Denver 80216

FLORIDA

Lake County Area Vocational, Technical
    Center
2001 Kurt St.
Eustis 32726

Pasco-Hernando Community College
36727 Blanton Rd.
Dade City 33523-7599

Seminole Community College
100 Weldon Blvd.
Sanford 32773-6199

ILLINOIS

American Floral Art School
529 South Wabash Ave.
Ste. 600
Chicago 60605-1679

IOWA

Eastern Iowa Community College
    District
306 West River Dr.
Davenport 52801-1221

Hawkeye Community College
1501 East Orange Rd.
Waterloo 50704

KANSAS

Kansas City Area Vocational Technical
    School
2220 North 59th St.
Kansas City 66104

Kansas School of Floral Design
826 Iowa St.
Lawrence 66044-1783

MASSACHUSETTS

Cass School of Floral Design
531 Mount Auburn St.
Watertown 02172

New England School of Floral Design
88 West Main St.
Norton 02766

Rittners School of Floral Design
345 Marlborough St.
Boston 02115

MICHIGAN

Grand Rapids Community College
143 Bostwick Ave. NE
Grand Rapids 49503-3295

MINNESOTA

Century Community and Technical
College
3300 Century Ave. N
White Bear Lake 55110

Hennepin Technical College
9000 Brooklyn Blvd.
Brooklyn Park 55445

MISSOURI

Stuppy Mid-America School of Floral
Design
120 East 12th Ave.
North Kansas City 64116

NEW JERSEY

Creative Designs Institute
4530 Hwy. 9 S
Howell 07731

NORTH CAROLINA

Randolph Community College
629 Industrial Park Ave.
Asheboro 27204

OHIO

Alexander's School of Floral Design
25780 Miles Rd.
Bedford Heights 44146

OKLAHOMA

Platt College
3801 South Sheridan
Tulsa 74145

PENNSYLVANIA

Pittsburgh Floral Academy
922 Western Ave.
Pittsburgh 15233

Shaw School of Floral Design
9708 Bustleton Ave.
Philadelphia 19115

WASHINGTON

Lake Washington Technical College
11605 132nd Ave. NE
Kirkland 98034

General Merchandise Distribution

ALABAMA

Shoals Community College
800 George Wallace Blvd.
Muscle Shoals 35662

ALASKA

Mila Administrative Services
3330 Artic Blvd.
Ste. 201
Anchorage 99503

ARIZONA

Arizona Institute of Business and
Technology
925 South Gilbert Rd.
Ste. 201
Mesa 85204

Chaparral Career College
4585 East Speedway Blvd.
Ste. 204
Tucson 85712

Eastern Arizona College
Church St.
Thatcher 85552-0769

Lamson Junior College
1126 North Scottsdale Rd.
Ste. 17
Tempe 85281-1700

Phoenix College
1202 West Thomas Rd.
Phoenix 85013

CALIFORNIA

Brooks College
4825 East Pacific Coast Hwy.
Long Beach 90804

Bryan College of Court Reporting
2511 Beverly Blvd.
Los Angeles 90057

California Academy of Merchandising,
Art & Design
2035 Hurley
Ste. 300
Sacramento 95825

Career Development Center
255 East Bonita Ave.
Pomona 91767

Chabot College
25555 Hesperian Blvd.
Hayward 94545

City College of San Francisco
50 Phelan Ave.
San Francisco 94112

College of Alameda
555 Atlantic Ave.
Alameda 94501

Computer Education Institute
24551 Raymond Way
Ste. 155
Lake Forest 92630

East Los Angeles Skill Center
3921 Selig Place
Los Angeles 90031

Fashion Careers of California
1923 Morena Blvd.
San Diego 92110

Fashion Institute of Design &
Merchandising, Los Angeles
919 South Grand Ave.
Los Angeles 90015

Fashion Institute of Design &
Merchandising, San Diego
1010 Second Ave.
San Diego 92101

Fashion Institute of Design &
Merchandising, San Francisco
55 Stockton St.
San Francisco 94108

Fil-Am Employment and Training
Center
2940 16th St.
Ste. 319
San Francisco 94103

Mount Diablo Vocational Services
490 Golf Club Rd.
Pleasant Hill 94523

Rancho Santiago Community College
District
1530 West 17th St.
Santa Ana 92706

San Diego Mesa College
7250 Mesa College Dr.
San Diego 92111-4998

Santa Barbara Business College
211 South Real Rd.
Bakerfield 93309

Southwestern College
900 Otay Lakes Rd.
Chula Vista 91910

Vallecitos CET, Inc.
597 C St.
Hayward 94541

West Valley College
14000 Fruitvale Ave.
Saratoga 95070

COLORADO

Parks Junior College
9065 Grant St.
Denver 80229

T H Pickens Technical Center
500 Airport Blvd.
Aurora 80011

CONNECTICUT

Huntington Institute, Inc.
193 Broadway
Norwich 06360

Tunxis Community-Technical College
Rtes. 6 and 177
Farmington 06032

University of Bridgeport
380 University Ave.
Bridgeport 06601

DELAWARE

Goldey-Beacom College
4701 Limestone Rd.
Wilmington 19808

FLORIDA

Business Training Institute of Lakeland,
Inc.
4222 South Florida Ave.
Lakeland 33813

International Academy of
Merchandising & Design
5225 Memorial Hwy.
Tampa 33634

Lee County High Technical Center,
Central
3800 Michigan Ave.
Fort Myers 33916

Lindsey Hopkins Technical Education
Center
750 Northwest 20th St.
Miami 33127

Northwood University, Florida
Education Center
2600 North Military Trail
West Palm Beach 33409

Orlando College
5421 Diplomat Cir.
Orlando 32810

Saint Augustine Technical Center
2980 Collins Ave.
Saint Augustine 32095-1919

Suwannee-Hamilton Area Vocational
and Adult Center
415 Southwest Pinewood Dr.
Live Oak 32060

GEORGIA

Albany Technical Institute
1021 Lowe Rd.
Albany 31708

Bauder College
3500 Peachtree Rd. NE
Atlanta 30326

Mable Bailey Fashion College, School of
Fashion and Cosmology
3121 Cross Country Hill
Columbus 31906

Meadows Junior College
1170 Brown Ave.
Columbus 31906

ILLINOIS

College of Du Page
425 22nd St.
Glen Ellyn 60137-6599

The College of Office Technology
1520 West Division St.
Chicago 60622

John A Logan College
700 Logan College Rd.
Carterville 62918

William Rainey Harper College
1200 West Algonquin Rd.
Palatine 60067-7398

INDIANA

Indiana Business College
802 North Meridian St.
Indianapolis 46204

Indiana University, Purdue University,
Fort Wayne
2101 Coliseum Blvd. E
Fort Wayne 46805

Vincennes University
1002 North First St.
Vincennes 47591

IOWA

Iowa Central Community College
330 Ave. M
Fort Dodge 50501

Iowa Western Community College
2700 College Rd.
P.O. Box 4C
Council Bluffs 51502

Kirkwood Community College
P.O. Box 2068
Cedar Rapids 52406

Southwestern Community College
1501 Townline
Creston 50801

KANSAS

Topeka Technical College
1620 Northwest Gage
Topeka 66618

KENTUCKY

Kentucy Tech, Ashland Regional
Technology Center
4818 Roberts Dr.
Ashland 41102

Kentucky Technical, Daviess County
Vocational Technical School
1901 Southeastern Pkwy.
Owensboro 42303

Midway College
512 Stephens St.
Midway 40347-1120

Owensboro Junior College of Business
1515 East 18th St.
P.O. Box 1350
Owensboro 42302

LOUISIANA

Coastal College, Hammond
4304 Yokum Rd.
Hammond 70403

Nicholls State University
University Station
La Hwy. 1
Thibodaux 70310

Remington College
303 Rue Louis XIV
Lafayette 70508

MAINE

Casco Bay College
477 Congress St.
Portland 04101

MASSACHUSETTS

Bay Path College
588 Longmeadow St.
Longmeadow 01106

Bay State College
122 Commonwealth Ave.
Boston 02116

Burdett School
745 Boylston St.
Boston 02116

Dean College
99 Main St.
Franklin 02038

Endicott College
376 Hale St.
Beverly 01915

Fisher College
118 Beacon St.
Boston 02116

Lasell College
1844 Commonwealth Ave.
Newton 02166

Middlesex Community College
Springs Rd.
Bedford 01730

Mount Ida College
777 Dedham St.
Newton Centre 02159

Mount Wachusett Community College
444 Green St.
Gardner 01440

Newbury College, Inc.
129 Fisher Ave.
Brookline 02146

Northern Essex Community College
Elliott Way
Haverhill 01830-2399

MICHIGAN

Davenport College
415 East Fulton
Grand Rapids 49503

Davenport College, Kalamazoo
4123 West Main St.
Kalamazoo 49006-2791

Davenport College, Lansing
220 East Kalamazoo
Lansing 48933

Delta College
University Center 48710

Dorsey Business Schools
30821 Barrington
Madison Heights 48071

Ferris State University
901 South State St.
Big Rapids 49307

Macomb Community College
14500 Twelve Mile Rd.
Warren 48093-3896

Muskegon Community College
221 South Quarterline Rd.
Muskegon 49442

Northwood University
3225 Cook Rd.
Midland 48640

Payne-Pulliam School of Trade and
Commerce, Inc.
2345 Cass Ave.
Detroit 48201-3305

Schoolcraft College
18600 Haggerty Rd.
Livonia 48152

MINNESOTA

Alexandria Technical College
1601 Jefferson St.
Alexandria 56308

Anoka-Ramsey Community College
11200 Mississippi Blvd.
Coon Rapids 55433-3470

Art Institute of Minnesota
825 Second Ave. S
Minneapolis 55402

Century Community and Technical
College
3300 Century Ave. N
White Bear Lake 55110

Dakota County Technical College
1300 East 145th St.
Rosemount 55068

Hennepin Technical College
9000 Brooklyn Blvd.
Brooklyn Park 55445

Lake Superior College
2101 Trinity Rd.
Duluth 55811

Minnesota West Community and
Technical College
1593 11th Ave.
Granite Falls 56241

Normandale Community College
9700 France Ave. S
Bloomington 55431

Northwest Technical College, Detroit
Lakes
900 Hwy. 34 E
Detroit Lakes 56501

Opportunities Industrialization Center,
East Metro
334 Chester St.
Saint Paul 55107

Rochester Community and Technical
College
851 30th Ave. SE
Rochester 55904-4999

University of Minnesota, Crookston
105 Selvig Hall
Crookston 56716

MISSISSIPPI

Coahoma Community College
3240 Friars Point Rd.
Clarksdale 38614

Hinds Community College, Raymond
Campus
Raymond 39154

Meridian Community College
910 Hwy. 19 N
Meridian 39307

Mississippi Gulf Coast Community
College
Central Office
P.O. Box 67
Perkinston 39573

Northwest Mississippi Community
College
510 North Panola Hwy. 51 N
Senatobia 38668

MISSOURI

Moberly Area Community College
101 College Ave.
Moberly 65270

Patricia Stevens College
1415 Olive St.
St. Louis 63103

Penn Valley Community College
3201 Southwest Trafficway
Kansas City 64111

Saint Charles County Community
College
4601 Mid Rivers Mall Dr.
Saint Peter's 63376

Sikeston Area Vocational Technical
School
1002 Virginia St.
Sikeston 63801

Tri County Technical School
Second and Pine
Eldon 65026

NEBRASKA

Lincoln School of Commerce
1821 K St.
Lincoln 68501-2826

Southeast Community College Area
1111 O St.
Ste. 111
Lincoln 68520

NEW HAMPSHIRE

Hesser College
Three Sundial Ave.
Manchester 03103

NEW JERSEY

Berkeley College
44 Rifle Camp Rd.
West Paterson 07424

Brookdale Community College
765 Newman Springs Rd.
Lincroft 07738-1599

Business Training Institute
Four Forest Ave.
Paramus 07652

Ho-Ho-Kus School
50 South Franklin Tpk.
Ramsey 07446

NEW MEXICO

International Business College
650 East Montana
Las Cruces 88001

NEW YORK

Drake Business School
32-03 Steinway St.
Astoria 11103

Fashion Institute of Technology
227 West 27th St.
New York 10001

Genesee Community College
One College Rd.
Batavia 14020

Global Business Institute
1931 Mott Ave.
Far Rockaway 11691

Global Business Institute
209 West 125th St.
New York 10027

Hunter Business School
3601 Hempstead Tpke.
Levittown 11756

Monroe Community College
1000 East Henrietta Rd.
Rochester 14623

Nassau Community College
One Education Dr.
Garden City 11530

Professional Business Institute
125 Canal St.
New York 10002-5049

NORTH CAROLINA

Alamance Community College
P.O. Box 8000
Graham 27253

American Business and Fashion
Institute
1515 Mockingbird Ln.
Ste. 600
Charlotte 28209

Brookstone College
7815 National Service Rd.
Greensboro 27409

NORTH DAKOTA

Minot State University
500 University Ave. W
Minot 58707

Valley City State University
101 Southwest College St.
Valley City 58072

OHIO

Ashtabula County Joint Vocational
School
1565 State Rte. 167
Jefferson 44047

Boheckers Business College
326 East Main St.
Ravenna 44266

Bowling Green State University, Main
Campus
220 McFall Center
Bowling Green 43403

Coshocton County Joint Vocational
School District
23640 County Rd. 202
Coshocton 43812

Ehove Career Center
316 West Mason Rd.
Milan 44846

ITT Technical Institute
1030 North Meridian Rd.
Youngstown 44509

Knox County Career Center
306 Martinsburg Rd.
Mount Vernon 43050

Owens Community College
39335 Oregon Rd.
Toledo 43699-1947

Professional Skills Institute
20 Arco Dr.
Toledo 43607

Stautzenberger College
1637 Tiffin
Findlay 45840

Technology Education College
288 South Hamilton Rd.
Columbus 43213

University of Akron, Main Campus
302 Buchtel Common
Akron 44325-4702

U S Grant Joint Vocational School
3046 Rte. 125
Bethel 45106

Virginia Marti College of Fashion and
Art
11724 Detroit Ave.
P.O. Box 580
Lakewood 44107

Vocational Guidance Services
2239 East 55th St.
Cleveland 44103

Warren County Career Center
3525 North SR 48
Lebanon 45036-1099

Washington State Community College
710 Colegate Dr.
Marietta 45750

OKLAHOMA

Kiamichi AVTS SD #7, Hugo
107 South 15th
Hugo 74743

Metro Area Vocational Technical School
District 22
1900 Springlake Dr.
Oklahoma City 73111

OREGON

Columbia College
8800 Southeast Sunnyside Rd.
Clackamas 97015

PENNSYLVANIA

Allentown Business School
1501 Lehigh St.
Allentown 18103

Baptist Bible College and Seminary
538 Venard Rd.
Clarks Summit 18411

Churchman Business School
355 Spring Garden St.
Easton 18042

Computer Learning Network, Resident
School
1110 Fernwood Ave.
Camp Hill 17011

Consolidated School of Business
2124 Ambassador Cir.
Lancaster 17603

Duffs Business Institute
110 Ninth St.
Pittsburgh 15222

Laurel Business Institute
11-15 Penn St.
Uniontown 15401

Orleans Technical Institute
1330 Rhawn St.
Philadelphia 19111-2899

Philadelphia Elwyn Institute
4040 Market St.
Philadelphia 19104-3003

Westmoreland County Community
College
Youngwood 15697-1895

RHODE ISLAND

Community College of Rhode Island
400 East Ave.
Warwick 02886-1807

Johnson and Wales University
8 Abbott Park Place
Providence 02903-3376

SOUTH DAKOTA

Nettleton Career College
100 South Spring Ave.
Sioux Falls 57104

SOUTH CAROLINA

Florence Darlington Technical College
P.O. Box 100548
Florence 29501-0548

TENNESSEE

Draughons Junior College of Business
Plus Park at Pavilion Blvd.
Nashville 37217

Fugazzi College
5042 Linbar Dr.
Ste. 200
Nashville 37211

Tennesse Technology Center at Athens
1635 Vocational Tech Dr.
P.O. Box 848
Athens 37371-0848

Tennesse Technology Center at
Crossville
P.O. Box 2959
Crossville 38557

Tennesse Technology Center at
Knoxville
1100 Liberty St.
Knoxville 37919

Tennesse Technology Center at
Murfreesboro
1303 Old Fort Pkwy.
Murfreesboro 37129

Tennesse Technology Center at
Nashville
100 White Bridge Rd.
Nashville 37209

Tennesse Technology Center at
Newbern
340 Washington St.
Newbern 38059

Tennesse Technology Center at
Shelbyville
1405 Madison St.
Shelbyville 37160

Tennesse Technology Center at
Whiteville
P.O. Box 489
Whiteville 38075

TEXAS

Alvin Community College
3110 Mustang Rd.
Alvin 77511

Amari Institute, Inc.
4111 Directors Row
Ste. 110
Houston 77092

Austin Community College
5930 Middle Fiskville Rd.
Austin 78752

Cedar Valley College
3030 North Dallas Ave.
Lancaster 75134

Central Texas Commercial College
P.O. Box 1324
Brownwood 76801

Hallmark Institute of Technology
8901 Wetmore Rd.
San Antonio 78216

Lee College
200 Lee Dr.
Baytown 77520-4703

Miss Wade's Fashion Merchandising
P.O. Box 586343
Dallas 75258

South Plains College
1401 College Ave.
Levelland 79336

South Texas Vocational-Technical
Institute, McAllen Branch
2901 North 23rd St.
McAllen 78503

Southern Careers Institute, South Texas
1414 North Jackson Rd.
Pharr 78577

Southwest Institute of Merchandising
and Design
9611 Acer Ave.
El Paso 79925

Southwest Texas Junior College
2401 Garner Field Rd.
Uvalde 78801

Texas State Technical College, Waco
3801 Campus Dr.
Waco 76705

UTAH

Bridgerland Applied Technology Center
1301 North, 600 West
Logan 84321

Latter Day Saints Business College
411 East South Temple
Salt Lake City 84111-1392

Snow College
150 East College Ave.
Ephraim 84627

Utah Valley State College
800 West, 1200 South
Orem 84058

Weber State University
3750 Harrison Blvd.
Ogden 84408

VERMONT

Champlain College
163 South Willard St.
Burlington 05401

VIRGINIA

Commonwealth College, Hampton
1120 West Mercury Blvd.
Hampton 23666

Commonwealth College, Virginia Beach
301 Centre Pointe Dr.
Virginia Beach 23462

ECPI College of Technology
5555 Greenwich Rd.
Ste 300
Virginia Beach 23462

ECPI Technical College
800 Moorefield Park Dr.
Richmond 23230

ECPI Technical College
5234 Airport Rd.
Roanoke 24012

National Business College
1813 East Main St.
Salem 24153

WASHINGTON

Bates Technical College
1101 South Yakima Ave.
Tacoma 98405

Bellingham Technical College
3028 Lindbergh Ave.
Bellingham 98225

Clark College
1800 East McLoughlin Blvd.
Vancouver 98663-3598

Columbia Basin College
2600 North 20th Ave.
Pasco 99301

Highline Community College
P.O. Box 98000
Des Moines 98198-9800

Lake Washington Technical College
11605 132nd Ave. NE
Kirkland 98034

Olympic College
1600 Chester Ave.
Bremerton 98337-1699

Sales Training Institute
1750 112th Ave. Northeast
Ste. E168
Bellevue 98004

Spokane Falls Community College
West 3410 Fort George Wright Dr.
Spokane 99224

WEST VIRGINIA

Huntington Junior College
900 Fifth Ave.
Huntington 25701

Mercer County Technical Education
Center
1397 Stafford Dr.
Princeton 24740

Shepherd College
King St. Ikenberry Hall
Shepherdstown 25443

WISCONSIN

Blackhawk Technical College
P.O. Box 5009
Janesville 53547

Chippewa Valley Technical College
620 West Clairemont Ave.
Eau Claire 54701

Fox Valley Technical College
1825 North Bluemound Dr.
Appleton 54913-2277

Lakeshore Technical College
1290 North Ave.
Cleveland 53015

Madison Area Technical College
3550 Anderson St.
Madison 53704

Milwaukee Area Technical College
700 West State St.
Milwaukee 53233-1443

Northeast Wisconsin Technical College
2740 West Mason St.
P.O. Box 19042
Green Bay 54307-9042

Waukesha County Technical College
800 Main St.
Pewaukee 53072

Western Wisconsin Technical College
304 North Sixth St.
P.O. Box 908
La Crosse 54602-0908

WYOMING

Central Wyoming College
2660 Peck Ave.
Riverton 82501

Hardware and Building Materials Distribution

ALASKA

Alaska Vocational Technical Center
809 Second Ave.
Seward 99664

FLORIDA

Saint Augustine Technical Center
2980 Collins Ave.
Saint Augustine 32095-1919

MASSACHUSETTS

Dean College
99 Main St.
Franklin 02038

OREGON

Umpqua Community College
P.O. Box 967
Roseburg 97470

UTAH

Odgen-Weber Applied Technology
Center
559 East Avc Ln.
Ogden 84404-6704

Salt Lake Community College, Skills
Center, South City Campus
1575 South State St.
Salt Lake City 84115

WASHINGTON

Columbia Basin College
2600 North 20th Ave.
Pasco 99301

WISCONSIN

Chippewa Valley Technical College
620 West Clairemont Ave.
Eau Claire 54701

Insurance Managing and Selling

CALIFORNIA

Latin American College of Business
4534 Whittier Blvd.
Los Angeles 90022

FLORIDA

Daytona Beach Community College
1200 Volusia Ave.
Daytona Beach 32114

Florida Community College at
Jacksonville
501 West State St.
Jacksonville 32202

Pasco-Hernando Community College
36727 Blanton Rd.
Dade City 33523-7599

Seminole Community College
100 Weldon Blvd.
Sanford 32773-6199

KANSAS

Norris Training Systems
400 North Woodlawn
Ste. 113
Wichita 67208

MICHIGAN

Ross Business Institute
37065 South Gratiot
Clinton Township 48036

Ross Business Institute
22293 Eureka
Taylor 48180

NEW JERSEY

ARC School of Insurance
255 Rte. 46 E
Denville 07834

Financial Supermarkets
100 North Sixth St.
Paterson 07522

South Jersey Professional School of
Business
Rte. 70 and Cropwell Rd.
Marlton Square Shopping Center
Marlton 08053

NEW YORK

Hill School of Insurance
139 Fulton St.
Manhattan 10038

The Sobelsohn School
370 Seventh Ave.
New York 10001

OHIO

Hondros College
4807 Evanswood Dr.
Columbus 43229

OREGON

Center for Professional Studies
755 Northeast Third
Ste. C
Bend 97701

Oregon Business College
2300 Oakmont Way
Ste. 106
Eugene 97401

PENNSYLVANIA

Community College of Allegheny
County
800 Allegheny Ave.
Pittsburgh 15233-1895

UTAH

O'Brien Schools
575 East, 4500 South
Salt Lake City 84107

WASHINGTON

Real Estate School of Washington
12004C Northeast Fourth Plain Blvd.
Vancouver 98662

WISCONSIN

Madison Area Technical College
3550 Anderson St.
Madison 53704

Marketing, Distribution, and Purchasing

ALABAMA

Community College of the Air Force
130 West Maxwell Blvd.
Montgomery 36112-6613

James H. Faulkner State Community
College
1900 U.S. Hwy. 31 S
Bay Minette 36507

Jefferson State Community College
2601 Carson Rd.
Birmingham 35215-3098

ALASKA

People Count, Inc.
P.O. Box 1310
Kenai 99611

ARIZONA

Mesa Community College
1833 West Southern Ave.
Mesa 85202

Mundus Institute
4745 North Seventh St.
Ste. 100
Phoenix 85014

ARKANSAS

Rich Mountain Community College
1100 Bush St.
Mena 71953

University of Arkansas Community
College, Batesville
P.O. Box 3350
Batesville 72503

Westark College
P.O. Box 3649
Fort Smith 72913

CALIFORNIA

Career Management Institute
1855 West Katella Ave.
Orange 92687

City College of San Francisco
50 Phelan Ave.
San Francisco 94112

Coastline Community College
11460 Warner Ave.
Fountain Valley 92708

De Anza College
21250 Stevens Creek Blvd.
Cupertino 95014

Fashion Institute of Design &
Merchandising, Los Angeles
919 South Grand Ave.
Los Angeles 90015

Fashion Institute of Design &
Merchandising, San Francisco
55 Stockton St.
San Francisco 94108

Fresno City College
1101 East University Ave.
Fresno 93741

Fullerton College
321 East Chapman Ave.
Fullerton 92832-2095

Gemological Institute of America
5345 Armada Dr.
Carlsbad 92008

Goodwill Industries of Santa Cruz
350 Encinal St.
Santa Cruz 95060

Los Angeles Trade Technical College
400 West Washington Blvd.
Los Angeles 90015-4181

Marin Regional Occupational Program
P.O. Box 4925
San Rafael 94913

Mira Costa College
One Barnard Dr.
Oceanside 92056-3899

Moorpark College
7075 Campus Rd.
Moorpark 93021

Orange Coast College
2701 Fairview Rd.
Costa Mesa 92626

Palomar College
1140 West Mission
San Marcos 92069-1487

San Diego City College
1313 12th Ave.
San Diego 92101

Santa Rosa Junior College
1501 Mendocino Ave.
Santa Rosa 95401-4395

Sierra College
5000 Rocklin Rd.
Rocklin 95677

Solano County Community College
District
4000 Suisun Valley Rd.
Suisun 94585-3197

Southwestern College
900 Otay Lakes Rd.
Chula Vista 91910

COLORADO

Aims Community College
Box 69
Greeley 80632

Arapahoe Community College
2500 West College Dr.
Littleton 80160-9002

Colorado Mountain College
P.O. Box 10001
Glenwood Springs 81602

Community College of Denver
P.O. Box 173363
Denver 80217

Denver Institute of Technology
7350 North Broadway
Denver 80221

Front Range Community College
3645 West 112th Ave.
Westminster 80030

Northeastern Junior College
100 College Dr.
Sterling 80751

Pikes Peak Community College
5675 South Academy Blvd.
Colorado Springs 80906-5498

CONNECTICUT

Manchester Community Technical
College
60 Bidwell St.
Manchester 06040-1046

Middlesex Community-Technical
College
100 Training Hill Rd.
Middletown 06457

Naugatuck Valley Community-
Technical College
750 Chase Pkwy.
Waterbury 06708

Norwalk Community-Technical College
188 Richards Ave.
Norwalk 06854

Ridley Lowell Business and Technical
Institute
470 Bank St.
New London 06320

Tunxis Community-Technical College
Rtes. 6 and 177
Farmington 06032

DELAWARE

Delaware Technical and Community
College, Terry
1832 North Dupont Pkwy.
Dover 19901

Delaware Technical Community
College, Stanton-Wilmington
400 Stanton-Christiana Rd.
Newark 19702

DISTRICT OF COLUMBIA

University of the District of Columbia
4200 Connecticut Ave. NW
Washington 20008

FLORIDA

Brevard Community College
1519 Clearlake Rd.
Cocoa 32922

Broward Community College
225 East Las Olas Blvd.
Fort Lauderdale 33301

Daytona Beach Community College
1200 Volusia Ave.
Daytona Beach 32114

Florida Auction School
5305 South Pine Ave.
Ocala 34480

Florida Community College at
Jacksonville
501 West State St.
Jacksonville 32202

Indian River Community College
3209 Virginia Ave.
Fort Pierce 34981

Lindsey Hopkins Technical Education
Center
750 Northwest 20th St.
Miami 33127

Manatee Community College
5840 26th St. W
Bradenton 34207

Miami-Dade Community College
300 Northeast Second Ave.
Miami 33132

Orlando College
5421 Diplomat Cir.
Orlando 32810

Polk Community College
999 Ave. H NE
Winter Haven 33881

Saint Petersburg Junior College
8580 66 St. N
Pinellas Park 34665

Santa Fe Community College
3000 Northwest 83rd St.
Gainesville 32606

Seminole Community College
100 Weldon Blvd.
Sanford 32773-6199

Southeastern Academy
233 Academy Dr.
P.O. Box 421768
Kissimmee 34742-1768

Washington-Holmes Technical Center
757 Hoyt St.
Chipley 32428

GEORGIA

Albany Technical Institute
1021 Lowe Rd.
Albany 31708

Atlanta Area Technical School
1560 Stewart Ave. SW
Atlanta 30310

Augusta Technical Institute
3116 Deans Bridge Rd.
Augusta 30906

Carroll Technical Institute
997 South Hwy. 16
Carrollton 30117

Coosa Valley Technical Institute
785 Cedar Ave.
Rome 30161

Dekalb Technical Institute
495 North Indian Creek Dr.
Clarkston 30021

Moultrie Area Technical Institute
361 Industrial Dr.
Moultrie 31768

National Business Institute
243 West Ponce De Leon Ave.
Decatur 30030

North Metro Technical Institute
5198 Ross Rd.
Acworth 30102-3012

Valdosta Technical Institute
4089 Valtech Rd.
Valdosta 31602-9796

Walker Technical Institute
265 Bicentennial Trail
Rock Spring 30739

HAWAII

Heald College School of Business and
Technology
1500 Kapiolani Blvd.
Honolulu 96816

Kapiolani Community College
4303 Diamond Head Rd.
Honolulu 96816

IDAHO

Boise State University
1910 University Dr.
Boise 83725

Eastern Idaho Technical College
1600 South, 2500 East
Idaho Falls 83404

Idaho State University
741 South Seventh Ave.
Pocatello 83209

ILLINOIS

Belleville Area College
2500 Carlyle Rd.
Belleville 62221

Black Hawk College
6600 34th Ave.
Moline 61265

City Colleges of Chicago, Harold
Washington College
30 East Lake St.
Chicago 60601

City Colleges of Chicago, Harry S
Truman College
1145 Wilson Ave.
Chicago 60640

City Colleges of Chicago, Wilbur Wright
College
4300 North Narragansett
Chicago 60634

College of Du Page
425 22nd St.
Glen Ellyn 60137-6599

College of Lake County
19351 West Washington St.
Grayslake 60030-1198

Danville Area Community College
2000 East Main St.
Danville 61832

Elgin Community College
1700 Spartan Dr.
Elgin 60123

Illinois Central College
One College Dr.
East Peoria 61635-0001

Illinois Eastern Community Colleges,
Olney Central College
305 North West St.
Olney 62450

Illinois Valley Community College
815 North Orlando Smith Ave.
Oglesby 61348-9692

International Academy of
Merchandising & Design
One North State St.
Ste. 400
Chicago 60602

John A Logan College
700 Logan College Rd.
Carterville 62918

Joliet Junior College
1215 Houbolt Rd.
Joliet 60431

Kankakee Community College
P.O. Box 888
Kankakee 60901

Kishwaukee College
21193 Malta Rd.
Malta 60150

Lake Land College
5001 Lake Land Blvd.
Mattoon 61938

Midstate College
244 Southwest Jefferson
Peoria 61602

Moraine Valley Community College
10900 South 88th Ave.
Palos Hills 60465-0937

Oakton Community College
1600 East Golf Rd.
Des Plaines 60016

Parkland College
2400 West Bradley Ave.
Champaign 61821

Robert Morris College
180 North Lasalle St.
Chicago 60601

Rock Valley College
3301 North Mulford Rd.
Rockford 61114

South Suburban College
15800 South State St.
South Holland 60473

Waubonsee Community College
Rte. 47 at Harter Rd.
Sugar Grove 60554-0901

William Rainey Harper College
1200 West Algonquin Rd.
Palatine 60067-7398

INDIANA

International Business College
3811 Illinois Rd.
Fort Wayne 46804

International Business College,
Indianapolis
7205 Shadeland Station
Indianapolis 46256

Ivy Tech State College, Central Indiana
One West 26th St.
Indianapolis 46206-1763

Ivy Tech State College, Lafayette
3101 South Creasy Ln.
P.O. Box 6299
Lafayette 47903

Ivy Tech State College, Northeast
3800 North Anthony Blvd.
Fort Wayne 46805

Ivy Tech State College, Northwest
1440 East 35th Ave.
Gary 46409

Ivy Tech State College, Wabash Valley
7999 U.S. Hwy. 41
Terre Haute 47802-4898

Vincennes University
1002 North First St.
Vincennes 47591

IOWA

American Institute of Commerce
2302 West First St.
Cedar Falls 50613

American Institute of Commerce
1801 East Kimberly Rd.
Davenport 52807

Des Moines Community College
2006 Ankeny Blvd.
Ankeny 50021

Hamilton College, Main Campus
1924 D St. SW
Cedar Rapids 52404

Hawkeye Community College
1501 East Orange Rd.
Waterloo 50704

Iowa Central Community College
330 Ave. M
Fort Dodge 50501

Iowa Lakes Community College
19 South Seventh St.
Estherville 51334

Kirkwood Community College
P.O. Box 2068
Cedar Rapids 52406

North Iowa Area Community College
500 College Dr.
Mason City 50401

Northeast Iowa Community College
Hwy. 150 S
P.O. Box 400
Calmar 52132-0400

Northwest Iowa Community College
603 West Park St.
Sheldon 51201

Western Iowa Tech Community College
4647 Stone Ave.
P.O. Box 5199
Sioux City 51102-5199

KANSAS

The Brown Mackie College
126 South Santa Fe St.
Salina 67402-1787

Butler County Community College
901 South Haverhill Rd.
El Dorado 67042

Flint Hills Technical College
3301 West 18th St.
Emporia 66801

Hutchinson Community College
1300 North Plum St.
Hutchinson 67501

Johnson County Community College
12345 College Blvd.
Overland Park 66210-1299

Kansas City Area Vocational Technical
School
2220 North 59th St.
Kansas City 66104

Kansas City Kansas Community College
7250 State Ave.
Kansas City 66112

KAW Area Technical School
5724 Huntoon
Topeka 66604

Manhattan Area Technical College
3136 Dickens Ave.
Manhattan 66503

Salina Area Vocational Technical
School
2562 Scanlan Ave.
Salina 67401

Seward County Community College
Box 1137
Liberal 67905-1137

Washburn University of Topeka
1700 College Ave.
Topeka 66621

Wichita Area Technical College
201 North Water
Wichita 67202-1292

LOUISIANA

Delta School of Business and
Technology
517 Broad St.
Lake Charles 70601

Louisiana Technical College, Lafayette
Campus
1101 Bertrand Dr.
Lafayette 70502-4909

Louisiana Technical College, Sullivan
Campus
1710 Sullivan Dr.
Bogalusa 70427

MARYLAND

Allegany College of Maryland
12401 Willowbrook Rd. SE
Cumberland 21502

Catonsville Community College
800 South Rolling Rd.
Catonsville 21228

Fleet Business School
2530 Riva Rd.
Ste. 201
Annapolis 21401

Harford Community College
401 Thomas Run Rd.
Bel Air 21015

Prince Georges Community College
301 Largo Rd.
Largo 20774-2199

MASSACHUSETTS

Bay Path College
588 Longmeadow St.
Longmeadow 01106

Bay State College
122 Commonwealth Ave.
Boston 02116

Dean College
99 Main St.
Franklin 02038

Greenfield Community College
One College Dr.
Greenfield 01301-9739

Holyoke Community College
303 Homestead Ave.
Holyoke 01040

International Auction School
Rte. 5
South Deerfield 01373

Mount Ida College
777 Dedham St.
Newton Centre 02159

Newbury College, Inc.
129 Fisher Ave.
Brookline 02146

North Shore Community College
One Ferncroft Rd.
Danvers 01923

Northeastern University
360 Huntington Ave.
Boston 02115

Northern Essex Community College
Elliott Way
Haverhill 01830-2399

Springfield Technical Community
College
One Armory Square
Springfield 01105

MICHIGAN

Baker College of Flint
G1050 West Bristol Rd.
Flint 48507

Baker College of Muskegon
1903 Marquette Ave.
Muskegon 49442

Davenport College
415 East Fulton
Grand Rapids 49503

Davenport College, Kalamazoo
4123 West Main St.
Kalamazoo 49006-2791

Davenport College, Lansing
220 East Kalamazoo
Lansing 48933

Delta College
University Ctr.
University Center 48710

Grand Rapids Community College
143 Bostwick Ave. NE
Grand Rapids 49503-3295

Jackson Community College
2111 Emmons Rd.
Jackson 49201-8399

Lansing Community College
419 North Capitol Ave.
Lansing 48901-7210

Macomb Community College
14500 Twelve Mile Rd.
Warren 48093-3896

Monroe County Community College
1555 South Raisinville Rd.
Monroe 48161

Mott Community College
1401 East Court St.
Flint 48503

Schoolcraft College
18600 Haggerty Rd.
Livonia 48152

Washtenaw Community College
P.O. Drawer 1
Ann Arbor 48106-1610

West Shore Community College
3000 North Stiles Rd.
Scottville 49454

MINNESOTA

Alexandria Technical College
1601 Jefferson St.
Alexandria 56308

Century Community and Technical
College
3300 Century Ave. N
White Bear Lake 55110

Continental Auctioneers School
30 Sandy Ct.
North Manakota 56003

Dakota County Technical College
1300 East 145th St.
Rosemount 55068

Duluth Business University, Inc.
412 West Superior St.
Duluth 55802

Globe College of Business
175 Fifth St. E
P.O. Box 60
Saint Paul 55101-2901

Hennepin Technical College
9000 Brooklyn Blvd.
Brooklyn Park 55445

Hibbing Community College
1515 East 25th St.
Hibbing 55746

Itasca Community College
1851 Hwy. 169 E
Grand Rapids 55744

Lake Superior College
2101 Trinity Rd.
Duluth 55811

Minnesota School of Business
1401 West 76th St.
Richfield 55423

Normandale Community College
9700 France Ave. S
Bloomington 55431

North Hennepin Community College
7411 85th Ave. N
Brooklyn Park 55445

Northwest Technical College, East
Grand Forks
Hwy. 220 N
East Grand Forks 56721

Northwest Technical College, Moorhead
1900 28th Ave. S
Moorhead 56560

Rasmussen College, Eagan
3500 Federal Dr.
Eagan 55122

Red Wing-Winona Technical College,
Winona
1250 Homer Rd.
P.O. Box 409
Winona 55987

Ridgewater College, A Community and
Technical College
Two Century Ave. SE
Hutchinson 55350

Ridgewater College, A Community and
Technical College, Willmar
P.O. Box 1097
Willmar 56201

Saint Cloud Technical College
1540 Northway Dr.
Saint Cloud 56303

South Central Technical College,
Mankato
1920 Lee Blvd.
North Mankato 56003

University of Minnesota, Crookston
105 Selvig Hall
Crookston 56716

MISSISSIPPI

Itawamba Community College
602 West Hill St.
Fulton 38843

Mississippi Gulf Coast Community
College
Central Office
P.O. Box 67
Perkinston 39573

Northeast Mississippi Community
College
Cunningham Blvd.
Booneville 38829

Southwest Mississippi Community
College
College Dr.
Summit 39666

MISSOURI

East Central College
P.O. Box 529
Union 63084

Longview Community College
500 Longview Rd.
Lees Summit 64081

Maple Woods Community College
2601 Northeast Barry Rd.
Kansas City 64156

Missouri Auction School
213 South Fifth St.
St Joseph 64501

Moberly Area Community College
101 College Ave.
Moberly 65270

Saint Charles County Community
College
4601 Mid Rivers Mall Dr.
Saint Peter's 63376

State Fair Community College
3201 West 16th
Sedalia 65301-2199

Three Rivers Community College
Three Rivers Blvd.
Poplar Bluff 63901

MONTANA

Billings Business College
2520 Fifth Ave. S
Billings 59101

Western College of Auctioneering
P.O. Box 50310
Billings 59105

NEBRASKA

Metropolitan Community College Area
5300 North 30th St.
Omaha 68111

Northeast Community College
801 East Benjamin
P.O. Box 469
Norfolk 68702-0469

Southeast Community College Area
1111 O St.
Ste. 111
Lincoln 68520

NEVADA

Morrison College
140 Washington St.
Reno 89503

NEW HAMPSHIRE

Franklin Pierce College
College Rd.
Rindge 03461

Hesser College
Three Sundial Ave.
Manchester 03103

NEW JERSEY

Bergen Community College
400 Paramus Rd.
Paramus 07652

Brookdale Community College
765 Newman Springs Rd.
Lincroft 07738-1599

Camden County College
P.O. Box 200
Blackwood 08012

Cumberland County College
College Dr.
P.O. Box 517
Vineland 08360

Gloucester County College
1400 Tanyard Rd.
Sewell 08080

Middlesex County College
155 Mill Rd.
Edison 08818-3050

Passaic County Community College
One College Blvd.
Paterson 07505-1179

Raritan Valley Community College
P.O. Box 3300
Lamington Rd.
Somerville 08876

NEW MEXICO

Albuquerque Technical Vocational
Institute
525 Buena Vista SE
Albuquerque 87106

New Mexico State University, Dona Ana
Box 30001
Dept. 3DA
3400 South Espina
Las Cruces 88003-0105

Southwestern Indian Polytechnic
Institute
9169 Coors Rd. NW
Albuquerque 87120

NEW YORK

Adirondack Community College
Bay Rd.
Queensbury 12804

Broome Community College
P.O. Box 1017
Binghamton 13902

Cayuga County Community College
Franklin St.
Auburn 13021

Dutchess Community College
53 Pendell Rd.
Poughkeepsie 12601

Genesee Community College
One College Rd.
Batavia 14020

Herkimer County Community College
Reservoir Rd.
Herkimer 13350-1598

Hudson Valley Community College
80 Vandenburgh Ave.
Troy 12180

Mohawk Valley Community College,
Utica Branch
1101 Sherman Dr.
Utica 13501

Monroe Community College
1000 East Henrietta Rd.
Rochester 14623

Nassau Community College
One Education Dr.
Garden City 11530

Orange County Community College
115 South St.
Middletown 10940

Rockland Community College
145 College Rd.
Suffern 10901

Suffolk County Community College,
Ammerman Campus
533 College Rd.
Selden 11784

Suffolk County Community College,
Western Campus
Crooked Hill Rd.
Brentwood 11717

Sullivan County Community College
1000 Leroy Rd.
Loch Sheldrake 12759-4002

SUNY College of Technology at Alfred
Alfred 14802

SUNY College of Technology at Canton
Cornell Drive
Canton 13617

SUNY College of Technology at Delhi
Delhi 13753

SUNY Ulster County Community
College
Cottekill Rd.
Stone Ridge 12484

SUNY Westchester Commmunity
College
75 Grasslands Rd.
Valhalla 10595

NORTH CAROLINA

American Business and Fashion
Institute
1515 Mockingbird Ln.
Ste. 600
Charlotte 28209

Asheville Buncombe Technical
Community College
340 Victoria Rd.
Asheville 28801

Central Piedmont Community College
P.O. Box 35009
Charlotte 28235-5009

Coastal Carolina Community College
444 Western Blvd.
Jacksonville 28546-6877

Fayetteville Technical Community
College
2201 Hull Rd.
Fayetteville 28303-0236

Forsyth Technical Community College
2100 Silas Creek Pkwy.
Winston Salem 27103

Guilford Technical Community College
Box 309
Jamestown 27282

Kings College
322 Lamar Ave.
Charlotte 28204

Mendenhall School of Auctioneering
6729 Auction Rd.
Archdale 27263

Wayne Community College
3000 Wayne Memorial Dr.
Goldsboro 27533-8002

NORTH DAKOTA

Bismarck State College
P.O. Box 5587
Bismarck 58506-5587

North Dakota State College of Science
800 North Sixth St.
Wahpeton 58076

OHIO

Bradford School
6170 Busch Blvd.
Columbus 43229

Bryant and Stratton Business Institute
691 Richmond Rd.
Richmond Height 44143

Cincinnati State Technical and
Community College
3520 Central Pkwy.
Cincinnati 45223

Columbus State Community College
550 East Spring St.
P.O. Box 1609
Columbus 43216

Cuyahoga Community College District
700 Carnegie Ave.
Cleveland 44115-2878

Lima Technical College
4240 Campus Dr.
Lima 45804

Muskingum Area Technical College
1555 Newark Rd.
Zanesville 43701

Northwestern College
1441 North Cable Rd.
Lima 45805

Owens Community College
39335 Oregon Rd.
Toledo 43699-1947

Owens Community College, Findlay
Campus
300 Davis St.
Findlay 45840

Sinclair Community College
444 West Third St.
Dayton 45402

Technology Education College
288 South Hamilton Rd.
Columbus 43213

Terra State Community College
2830 Napoleon Rd.
Fremont 43420

Trumbull County Joint Vocational
School District
528 Educational Hwy.
Warren 44483

University of Akron, Main Campus
302 Buchtel Common
Akron 44325-4702

University of Cincinnati, Main Campus
P.O. Box 210127
Cincinnati 45221-0127

University of Cincinnati, Raymond
Walters College
9555 Plainfield Rd.
Blue Ash 45236

University of Toledo
2801 West Bancroft
Toledo 43606

Youngstown State University
One University Plz.
Youngstown 44555

OKLAHOMA

Central Oklahoma Area Vocational
Technical School
Three Court Circle
Drumright 74030

De Marge College
3608 Northwest 58
Oklahoma City 73112

Francis Tuttle Area Vocational
Technical Center
12777 North Rockwell Ave.
Oklahoma City 73142-2789

Great Plains Area Vocational Technical
School
4500 West Lee Blvd.
Lawton 73505

Metro Area Vocational Technical School
District 22
1900 Springlake Dr.
Oklahoma City 73111

Northeastern Oklahoma Agricultural
and Mechanical College
200 I St. NE
Miami 74354

Oklahoma State University, Okmulgee
1801 East Fourth St.
Okmulgee 74447-3901

Tulsa Community College
6111 East Skelly Dr.
Tulsa 74135

OREGON

Bassist College
2000 Southwest Fifth Ave.
Portland 97201

Franklin Institute of Sales
1058 Hemlock
Lake Oswego 97034

PENNSYLVANIA

Butler County Community College
College Dr.
Oak Hills
Butler 16003-1203

Central Pennsylvania Business School
College Hill Rd.
Summerdale 17093-0309

Community College of Allegheny
County
800 Allegheny Ave.
Pittsburgh 15233-1895

Community College of Philadelphia
1700 Spring Garden St.
Philadelphia 19130

Harcum College
750 Montgomery Ave.
Bryn Mawr 19010

Harrisburg Area Community College,
Harrisburg
One Hacc Dr.
Harrisburg 17110

ICM School of Business
10-14 Wood St.
Pittsburgh 15222

ICS Center for Degree Studies
925 Oak St.
Scranton 18508

Keystone College
P.O. Box 50
La Plume 18440-0200

Pennsylvania College of Technology
One College Ave.
Williamsport 17701

Saint Joseph's University
5600 City Ave.
Philadelphia 19131

Sales Development Institute
2510 Township Line Rd.
Upper Darby 19083

South Hills School of Business and
Technology
480 Waupelani Dr.
State College 16801

University of Pittsburgh, Central Office
4200 Fifth Ave.
Pittsburgh 15260

Wilma Boyd Career Schools, Inc.
1412 Beers School Rd.
Moon Township 15108-2549

Yorktowne Business Institute
West Seventh Ave.
York 17404

RHODE ISLAND

Johnson and Wales University
8 Abbott Park Place
Providence 02903-3376

Sawyer School
101 Main St.
Pawtucket 02860

SOUTH CAROLINA

Central Carolina Technical College
506 North Guignard Dr.
Sumter 29150

Greenville Technical College
Station B
P.O. Box 5616
Greenville 29606-5616

Midlands Technical College
P.O. Box 2408
Columbia 29202

Piedmont Technical College
P.O. Drawer 1467
Greenwood 29648

Tri-County Technical College
P.O. Box 587
Pendleton 29670

Trident Technical College
P.O. Box 118067
Charleston 29423-8067

SOUTH DAKOTA

Western Dakota Technical Institute
800 Mickelson Dr.
Rapid City 57701

TENNESSEE

Nashville Auction School
2407B Pulaski Pk
Columbia 38402

Pellissippi State Technical Community
College
P.O. Box 22990
Knoxville 37933-0990

TEXAS

Austin Institute of Real Estate
7801 North Lamar
Ste. F35
Austin 78752

Central Texas College
P.O. Box 1800
Killeen 76540-1800

Laredo Community College
West End Washington St.
Laredo 78040

Midland College
3600 North Garfield
Midland 79705

North Harris Montgomery Community
College District
250 North Sam Houston Pkwy. E
Ste. 300
Houston 77060

South Plains College
1401 College Ave.
Levelland 79336

Southwest Texas Junior College
2401 Garner Field Rd.
Uvalde 78801

Tarrant County Junior College
1500 Houston St.
Fort Worth 76102

Texas State Technical College, Waco
3801 Campus Dr.
Waco 76705

UTAH

Dixie College
225 South, 700 East
Saint George 84770

Latter Day Saints Business College
411 East South Temple
Salt Lake City 84111-1392

Salt Lake Community College
P.O. Box 30808
Salt Lake City 84130

Utah Career College
1144 West, 3300 South
Salt Lake City 84119-3330

Weber State University
3750 Harrison Blvd.
Ogden 84408

VERMONT

Champlain College
163 South Willard St.
Burlington 05401

VIRGINIA

National Business College
1813 East Main St.
Salem 24153

WASHINGTON

Bates Technical College
1101 South Yakima Ave.
Tacoma 98405

Bellingham Technical College
3028 Lindbergh Ave.
Bellingham 98225

Centralia College
600 West Locust St.
Centralia 98531

Clark College
1800 East McLoughlin Blvd.
Vancouver 98663-3598

Columbia Basin College
2600 North 20th Ave.
Pasco 99301

Green River Community College
12401 Southeast 320th St.
Auburn 98092

Sales Training Institute
1750 112th Ave. Northeast
Ste. E168
Bellevue 98004

Shoreline Community College
16101 Greenwood Ave. N
Seattle 98133

Skagit Valley College
2405 College Way
Mount Vernon 98273

South Puget Sound Community College
2011 Mottman Rd. SW
Olympia 98512

Spokane Community College
North 1810 Greene Ave.
Spokane 99207

Spokane Falls Community College
West 3410 Fort George Wright Dr.
Spokane 99224

Walla Walla Community College
500 Tausick Way
Walla Walla 99362

Yakima Valley Community College
P.O. Box 1647
Yakima 98907

WISCONSIN

Blackhawk Technical College
P.O. Box 5009
Janesville 53547

Chippewa Valley Technical College
620 West Clairemont Ave.
Eau Claire 54701

Fox Valley Technical College
1825 North Bluemound Dr.
Appleton 54913-2277

Gateway Technical College
3520 30th Ave.
Kenosha 53144-1690

Lakeshore Technical College
1290 North Ave.
Cleveland 53015

Madison Area Technical College
3550 Anderson St.
Madison 53704

Madison Junior College of Business
31 South Henry St.
Madison 53703-3110

Mid-State Technical College
500 32nd St. N
Wisconsin Rapids 54494

Milwaukee Area Technical College
700 West State St.
Milwaukee 53233-1443

Moraine Park Technical College
235 North National Ave.
Fond Du Lac 54936-1940

North Central Technical College
1000 Campus Dr.
Wausau 54401-1899

Northeast Wisconsin Technical College
2740 West Mason St.
P.O. Box 19042
Green Bay 54307-9042

Southwest Wisconsin Technical College
1800 Bronson Blvd.
Fennimore 53809

Waukesha County Technical College
800 Main St.
Pewaukee 53072

Western Wisconsin Technical College
304 North Sixth St.
P.O. Box 908
La Crosse 54602-0908

Wisconsin Indianhead Technical
College
505 Pine Ridge Dr.
Shell Lake 54871

WYOMING

Casper College
125 College Dr.
Casper 82601

Real Estate Services

ALABAMA

American Real Estate Institute, Inc.
2426 Spruce
Montgomery 36107

Ben Porter Real Estate School
3409 South Memorial Pkwy.
Huntsville 35801

ALASKA

Commonwealth School of Real Estate
4105 Turnagain Blvd.
Anchorage 99517

ARIZONA

Arizona Institute of Real Estate
2310 North Fourth St.
Flagstaff 86004

Brodsky School of Real Estate
720 South Craycroft
Tucson 85711

Bud Crawley Real Estate School
5251 North 16th St.
Ste. 250
Phoenix 85016

Ford Schools, Inc.
4425 Olive Ave.
Ste. 128
Glendale 85302

Professional Institute of Real Estate
10207 North Scottsdale Rd.
Scottsdale 85253

ARKANSAS

Arkansas-Oklahoma School of Real
Estate, Fort Smith
2201 Dodson
Fort Smith 72901

National Real Estate School
5323 John F Kennedy Blvd.
North Little Rock 72116

CALIFORNIA

American River College
4700 College Oak Dr.
Sacramento 95841

American School
P.O. Box 2948
Torrance 90509

Anthony Schools, Foster City
1065 East Hillsdale Blvd.
Ste. 112
Foster City 94404-1614

California School of Real Estate
7700 Edgewater Dr.
Ste. 745
Oakland 94621

Cerritos College
11110 Alondra Blvd.
Norwalk 90650

Chabot College
25555 Hesperian Blvd.
Hayward 94545

Chaffey Community College
5885 Haven Ave.
Rancho Cucamonga 91737-3002

City College of San Francisco
50 Phelan Ave.
San Francisco 94112

College of San Mateo
1700 West Hillsdale Blvd.
San Mateo 94402

College of the Canyons
26455 Rockwell Canyon Rd.
Santa Clarita 91355

Cuyamaca College
900 Rancho San Diego Pkwy.
El Cajon 92019

El Camino College
16007 Crenshaw Blvd.
Torrance 90506

Exacta Schools
22691 Lambert St.
Ste. 504
Lake Forest 92630

Fullerton College
321 East Chapman Ave.
Fullerton 92832-2095

Glendale Community College
1500 North Verdugo Rd.
Glendale 91208-2894

Los Angeles Southwest College
1600 West Imperial Hwy.
Los Angeles 90047

Manna Institute
18832 Norwalk Blvd.
Artesia 90701

Mercury Real Estate Schools
1775 East Lincoln Ave.
Ste. 203
Anaheim 92805

Mission College
3000 Mission College Blvd.
Santa Clara 95054-1897

Moorpark College
7075 Campus Rd.
Moorpark 93021

Mulhearn Licensing School
16911 Bellflower Blvd.
Bellflower 90706

Rainbow Real Estate School
8342 Garden Grove Blvd.
Ste. 6
Garden Grove 92644

Rancho Santiago Community College
District
1530 West 17th St.
Santa Ana 92706

Realty Institute
2086 South East St.
San Bernardino 92408

Riverside Community College
4800 Magnolia Ave.
Riverside 92506-1299

San Diego Mesa College
7250 Mesa College Dr.
San Diego 92111-4998

San Joaquin Delta College
5151 Pacific Ave.
Stockton 95207

Santa Rosa Junior College
1501 Mendocino Ave.
Santa Rosa 95401-4395

Sierra College
5000 Rocklin Rd.
Rocklin 95677

West Coast Schools
5385 El Camino Real
Atascadero 93422

West Los Angeles College
4800 Freshman Dr.
Culver City 90230

COLORADO

A J Educational Services, Inc.
2930 West 72nd Ave.
Westminster 80030

Century 21 Academy Real Estate School
3520 Galley Rd.
Ste. 200
Colorado Springs 80909

Colorado Association of Realtors Real
Estate School
309 Inverness Way S
Englewood 80112

Colorado Real Estate Institute
1780 South Bellaire St.
Ste. 222
Denver 80222

Jones Real Estate Colleges, Inc.
1919 North Union Blvd.
Colorado Springs 80909

Jones Real Estate Colleges, Inc.
2150 South Cherry
Denver 80222

Jones Real Estate Colleges, Inc.
172 Riverview Dr.
Durango 81301

CONNECTICUT

Connecticut Association of Realtors
111 Founders Plz.
11th Fl.
East Hartford 06108

DELAWARE

Delaware School of Real Estate
7234 Lancaster Pike
Ste. 200
Hockessin 19707

FLORIDA

Florida Community College at
Jacksonville
501 West State St.
Jacksonville 32202

GEORGIA

Barney Fletcher School, Atlanta
  Institute of Real Estate
3200 Cobb Galleria Pkwy.
Ste. 275
Atlanta 30339

Georgia Institute of Real Estate
5784 Lake Forest Dr.
Atlanta 30328

HAWAII

Fahrni School of Real Estate
98-277 Kamehameha Hwy.
Aiea 96701

Hawaii Institute of Real Estate
841 Bishop St.
Room B11
Honolulu 96813

Vitousek Real Estate School
560 North Nimitz Hwy.
Honolulu 96813

ILLINOIS

Coldwell Banker School of Real Estate
1211 West 22nd St.
Ste. 700
Oak Brook 60523

Illinois Academy of Real Estate
316 North Lake St.
Aurora 60506

Illinois Academy of Real Estate, Tom
  Brinkoetter Co.
1698 East Pershing Rd.
Decatur 62526

Institute for Development of Sales
  Potential, Inc.
1645 Hicks
Ste. L
Rolling Meadows 60008

Jmars School of Real Estate Education
4363 North Harlem Ave.
Norridge 60634

National Real Estate Schools
6321 North Avondale Ave.
Ste. 218
Chicago 60631

Real Estate Institute of America
343 Torrence
Calumet City 60409

Real Estate Training, Inc.
16 North Wolf Rd.
Northlake 60164

Ronald D Ladley & Co. National
  Academy of Real Estate
1999 Wabash
Ste. 205
Springfield 62704

Zittel School of Real Estate
4950 North Harlem Ave.
Harwood Heights 60656

IOWA

Iowa Real Estate School
3501 West Town Pkwy.
West Des Moines 50266

Iowa Real Estate School of Cedar Rapids
770 Seventh Ave.
Marion 52302

Key Real Estate School
501 South Main
Council Bluffs 51503

KANSAS

Real Estate School of Lawrence
P.O. Box 3271
Lawrence 66046

Topeka Institute of Real Estate
5120 West 28th
Topeka 66614-2399

KENTUCKY

Family Style School of Professional
  Licensing
7711 Beulah Church Rd.
Louisville 40228

Jefferson Community College
109 East Broadway
Louisville 40202

Realtors Institute
161 Prosperous Pl.
Lexington 40509

LOUISIANA

Bob Brooks School of Real Estate &
  Insurance, Inc.
6721 Pecue Ln.
Baton Rouge 70817

Louisiana Realtors Institute
P.O. Box 14780
Baton Rouge 70898

MAINE

Casco Bay College
477 Congress St.
Portland 04101

MARYLAND

Century 21 Real Estate School
P.O. Box 2048
Glen Burnie 21060

Champion Institute of Real Estate
541B Baltimore Annapolis Blvd.
Severna Park 21146

The Columbia Academy of Real Estate,
  Inc.
9186 Carriage House Ln.
Columbia 21045

Diplomat Real Estate Center
5505 Sargent Rd.
Hyattsville 20782

Farrall Institute
P.O. Box 40
Waldorf 20604

H T Brown Real Estate Institute
201 Washington Blvd.
Laurel 20707

Long & Foster Institute of Real Estate
200 Orchard Ridge Rd.
Gaithersburg 20878

Maryland School of Real Estate
Seven Park Ave.
Gaithersburg 20877

O'Brien Institute of Real Estate, Inc.
Rte. 5
P.O. Box 584
Charlotte Hall 20622

O'Connor, Piper, and Flynn School of
  Real Estate
22 West Padonia Road Training Center
Timonium 21093

Pro Real Estate Academy
9300 Livingston Rd.
Fort Washington 20744

Weichert Real Estate School
6610 Rockledge Dr.
Ste. 100
Bethesda 20817

MASSACHUSETTS

American Real Estate Academy
771 Main St.
Waltham 02154

Greater Springfield Association of
  Realtors School
221 Industry St.
Springfield 01104

Lee Institute
310 Harvard St.
Brookline 02146

Real Estate Salesman School
1847 Memorial Dr.
Chicopee 01020

MICHIGAN

Currey Management Institute
6875 Rochester Rd.
Ste. B
Rochester 48306

Ferris State University
901 South State St.
Big Rapids 49307

Lansing Community College
419 North Capitol Ave.
Lansing 48901-7210

NCI Associates, Ltd.
27637 John Rd.
Madison Heights 48071

The Real Estate School
755 West Big Beaver
Ste. 1390
Troy 48084

U.S. Brokers Institute, Inc.
300 East Beltline NE
Grand Rapids 49506

MINNESOTA

Dearborn Financial Institute
2051 Killebrew Dr.
Ste. 110
Bloomington 55425-1870

Minnesota Multi Housing Association
8030 Old Cedar Ave.
Ste. 202
Bloomington 55425

MISSOURI

Career Education System
8600 Ward Pkwy.
Ste. 1130
Kansas City 64114

Professional School of Real Estate,
  Insurance & Appraisal
400 North Bush
Mountain Grove 65711

Real Estate Prep School of Kansas City
5210 Northeast Chouteau Traffic Way
Kansas City 64119-2509

Real Estate School of Springfield
306 East Pershing
Springfield 65806

Saint Louis Community College, Forest
  Park
5600 Oakland Ave.
Saint Louis 63110

Thrust International School of Real
  Estate
198 Historic 66 E
Waynesville 65583

NEBRASKA

Nebraska School of Real Estate
225 North Cotner
Ste. 106
Lincoln 68505

Professional School of Real Estate
4645 Normal Blvd.
Ste. 105
Lincoln 68510

Randall School of Real Estate
11224 Elm St.
Omaha 68144

NEVADA

Northern Nevada Real Estate School
3951 South McCarren Blvd.
Reno 89502

Real Estate School of Nevada, Inc.
4180 South Sandhill Rd.
Unit 10B
Las Vegas 89121

Silver State Schools
4480 West Spring Mountain Rd.
Ste. 700
Las Vegas 89102

Southern Nevada School of Real Estate
3441 West Sahara
Ste. C5
Las Vegas 89102

NEW JERSEY

Kovats Real Estate and Insurance School
230 West Passaic St.
Maywood 07607

M W Funk Sales Institute
22 Springdale Rd.
Cherry Hill 08003

Ocean School of Real Estate
586 Rte. 70
Brick 08723

Princeton School of Real Estate
238 West Delaware Ave.
Pennington 08534

South Jersey Professional School of
  Business
Marlton Square Shopping Ctr.
Rte. 70 and Cropwell Rd.
Marlton 08053

Weichert Real Estate School
1625 Rte. 10 E
Morris Plains 07950

Zacharie School of Real Estate
675 Rte. 72
Village Harbour Exec Camp
Ste. 1006A
Manahawkin 08050

NEW MEXICO

New Mexico Real Estate Institute
8205 Spain NE
Ste. 109
Albuquerque 87109

NEW YORK

The Sobelsohn School
370 Seventh Ave.
New York 10001

NORTH CAROLINA

Brunswick Community College
P.O. Box 30
Supply 28462

OHIO

Cuyahoga Community College District
700 Carnegie Ave.
Cleveland 44115-2878

Hondros Centers
4807 Evanswood Dr.
Columbus 43229

Sinclair Community College
444 West Third St.
Dayton 45402

University of Akron, Main Campus
302 Buchtel Common
Akron 44325-4702

OREGON

Abdill Career Schools
843 East Main
Ste. 203
Medford 97504

Center for Professional Studies
755 NE 3rd
Ste. C
Bend 97701

Century 21 Penisula School of Real
   Estate
8040 North Lombard
Portland 97203

Norman F Webb Real Estate Courses
1112 12th St. SE
Salem 97302

Oregon Business College
2300 Oakmont Way
Ste. 106
Eugene 97401

Real Estate School of Eugene
1142 Willagillespie Rd.
Ste. 34
Eugene 97401

PENNSYLVANIA

Greater Philadelphia Realty Board Real
   Estate School
2010 Rhawn St.
Philadelphia 19152

Pennsylvania State University, Main
   Campus
201 Old Main
University Park 16802

SOUTH CAROLINA

Fortune School of Real Estate
P.O. Box 3845
Myrtle Beach 29578

South Carolina Institute of Real Estate
Ten Diamond Ln.
Columbia 29210

Wyatt Institute of Real Estate
710 East North St.
Greenville 29601

TEXAS

American Inspectors Institute
13614 Midway Rd.
Ste. 111
Dallas 75244

Austin Institute of Real Estate
7801 North Lamar
Ste. F35
Austin 78752

Champions School of Real Estate
3724 Fm 1960 W
Ste. 116
Houston 77068

Houston Community College System
22 Waugh Dr.
Houston 77270-7849

McLennan Community College
1400 College Dr.
Waco 76708

North Lake College
5001 North MacArthur Blvd.
Irving 75038-3899

Richland College
12800 Abrams Rd.
Dallas 75243-2199

San Antonio College
1300 San Pedro Ave.
San Antonio 78284

Spencer School of Real Estate
1200 Post Oak Blvd.
Ste. 330
Houston 77056

Spencer School of Real Estate
17000 El Camino Real
Houston 77058

UTAH

O'Brien Schools
575 East, 4500 South
Salt Lake City 84107

VIRGINIA

Alpha College of Real Estate
11861 Canon Blvd.
Ste. A
Newport News 23606

Alpha College of Real Estate
2697 International Pkwy.
Ste. 180
Virginia Beach 23452

Coldwell Banker Institute of Real Estate
465 Maple Ave. W
Ste. B
Vienna 22180

Moseley-Flint School of Real Estate
8543 Mayland Dr.
Bldg. B
Richmond 23294

WASHINGTON

Clark County Association of Realtors
4420E Northeast Saint John's Rd.
Vancouver 98661

Lake Washington Technical College
11605 132nd Ave. NE
Kirkland 98034

Real Estate School of Washington
12004C Northeast Fourth Plain Blvd.
Vancouver 98662

Seattle Community College, North
   Campus
9600 College Way N
Seattle 98103

WEST VIRGINIA

Brenda White School of Real Estate
603 Morgantown Ave.
Fairmont 26554

Charleston College
1034 Bridge Rd.
Charleston 25314

Jack Kelley's Northeastern College of
   Real Estate
Rte. 2
Box 184T
Martinsburg 25401

Real Estate Career Center
120 Eastern Hts.
523 11th St.
Huntington 25701

Teays Valley School of Real Estate
4350 Teays Valley Rd.
Scott Depot 25560-0230

WISCONSIN

Chippewa Valley Technical College
620 West Clairemont Ave.
Eau Claire 54701

Madison Area Technical College
3550 Anderson St.
Madison 53704

Robbins and Lloyd School of Real Estate
5309 North 118th Ct.
Milwaukee 53225

Wauwatosa Real Estate Institute, Inc.
11622 West North Ave.
Wauwatosa 53226

Index

All jobs mentioned in this volume are listed and cross-referenced in the index. Entries that appear in all capital letters have occupational profiles. For example, ADVERTISING MANAGER, AUCTIONEER, CASHIER and so on are profiles in this volume. Entries that are not capitalized refer to jobs that do not have a separate profile but for which information is given.

Under some capitalized entries there is a section titled "Profile includes." This lists jobs that are mentioned in the profile. For example, in the case of SPORTS MANAGEMENT PROFESSIONAL, jobs that are described in the profile are Athletic director, General manager, Promotion/development director, Sports agent, and Sports information director.

Some entries are followed by a job title in parentheses after the page number on which it can be found. This job title is the occupational profile in which the entry is discussed. For instance, the Bakery clerk entry is followed by the profile title (Supermarket worker).